This is the first book that I have seen that gives a comprehensive and comprehensible explanation of, and a game plan for, creating a business plan for independent films. Jeremy demystifies the very difficult subject matter of film finance. I highly recommend this book to independent filmmakers and investors alike!

> — Hillary Bibicoff, Partner, Entertainment Attorney, Greenberg
> Glusker Fields Claman & Machtinger LLP

An amazing reference for anyone even thinking about writing business plans for films. Clear, concise, understandable — and a great overview of the nuts and bolts behind how an indie film makes money.

> — Arie Posin, Director, *The Chumscrubber*, starring Carrie-Anne
> Moss, Rita Wilson, and Oscar nominees Glenn Close and
> Ralph Fiennes

For the new filmmaker, you should consider this to be the definitive handbook to getting your movie financed. If you follow Jeremy's guidance, by the time you're finished, you will understand your movie from every financial angle necessary and your investors will love you for it. Then onward to the creative process.

> — Matthew Rhodes, Executive Producer, *An Unfinished Life,*
> starring Robert Redford and Morgan Freeman; Producer,
> *Passengers*, starring Oscar nominee Anne Hathaway

Through the use of copious examples and a thorough, disciplined approach, Juuso has created a tremendous template for Producers to utilize as they create their business plan. I regret not having this at my disposal in my early attempts…

> — Wrye Martin, Producer, *The Life of Reilly* (SXSW feature film
> selection); Producer/Director, *Aswang* (Sundance feature film
> selection)

Raising money for independent films is one of the most daunting and confusing parts of working in entertainment. But Jeremy Juuso not only makes it seem possible, he gives you a practical, doable, and step-by-step approach for putting together a business plan. If you can't get money using this book, your film probably doesn't deserve to get made.

> — Chad Gervich, TV Writer/Producer (*Reality Binge, Speeders,*
> *Foody Call*) and author (*Small Screen, Big Picture: A Writer's*
> *Guide to the TV Business*)

This book tells you everything you need to know to get that business plan in place. Extremely detailed but liberally sprinkled with a sense of humor, this book is both enjoyable AND helpful.

— Matthew Terry, screenwriter, teacher, and filmmaker; *www.hollywoodlitsales.com*

It's an often-missed fact that the movie business *is* a business and the independent filmmaker needs to inspire trust and confidence in any would-be investor. What Jeremy Juuso has done is provide the most comprehensive template available for building a professional business plan that will get your movie financed. With clear, easy-to-understand examples, Juuso has written the definitive reference work for both independent filmmakers and their investors — an indispensable addition to any filmmaker's library.

— Robert Grant, SCI-FI-LONDON

Required reading for any indie filmmaker (and investor!). In 30 steps that you can't afford to ignore, Jeremy Juuso explains how to put together a business plan that will attract the capital you need for your film. Easy to read and down to earth — don't miss it!

— Rob Goald, Film Department, University of Nevada, Las Vegas

GETTING THE MONEY

a step-by-step guide
for writing business plans for film

jeremy juuso

Published by Michael Wiese Productions
3940 Laurel Canyon Blvd. # 1111
Studio City, CA 91604
tel. 818.379.8799
fax 818.986.3408
mw@mwp.com
www.mwp.com

Cover Design: MWP
Interior Book Design: Gina Mansfield Design
Editor: Linda Norlen

Printed by McNaughton & Gunn, Inc., Saline, Michigan
Manufactured in the United States of America

Grateful acknowledgment is made for permission to reprint data from reports
from Baseline StudioSystems. Copyright 2003–2004 by Baseline StudioSystems.
The data is owned and reprinted by permission of Baseline StudioSystems.

Library of Congress Cataloging-in-Publication Data

Juuso, Jeremy, 1976–
Getting the money: a step-by-step guide for writing business plans for film / by
Jeremy Juuso.
     p. cm.
ISBN 978-1-932907-64-3
1. Motion pictures--Production and direction. 2. Motion picture industry--
Finance. I. Title.
PN1995.9.P7J88 2009
384'.83--dc22
                                         2009010828

TABLE OF CONTENTS

ACKNOWLEDGMENTS... ix

INTRODUCTION.. xi

CHAPTER 1: **FINANCIAL PROJECTIONS**... 1

Step 1. Compare your film to other great films (Comparable Films Table)... 1

Step 2. Predict your fame and glory (Income Projections Table)................. 9

Step 3. Forecast when everyone gets a Ferrari (Cash Flow Projections Table).... 14

Step 4. Sum it all up (Investor Projections Table)....................................... 24

Sample Financial Projections Sections.. 31

CHAPTER 2: **MARKET ANALYSIS & MARKETING STRATEGY**........................... 49

Step 5. Describe how independent films are doing (... be honest).............. 49

Step 6. Preach the importance of word-of-mouth....................................... 51

Step 7. Talk about how independent films are marketed............................. 52

Step 8. What's your target audience and how will you reach them?.............. 53

Sample Market Analysis & Marketing Strategy Sections.............................. 55

CHAPTER 3: **MOTION PICTURE DISTRIBUTION**... 67

Step 9. Tell them how your movie makes it to Grandma's iPod.................... 68

Step 10. Break the news gently: you pay the charges,
distributors make the decisions... 68

Step 11. Describe independent film distributors (nicely)............................. 70

Step 12. What do they look for in a film?.. 71

Step 13. What's your strategy for snagging a distributor? — No begging........ 72

Sample Motion Picture Distribution Section... 73

CHAPTER 4: **COMPANY DESCRIPTION**.. 81

Step 14. Identify yourself!
(Or at least your film's business entity.)....................... 81

Step 15. Who's on your team?.. 82

Sample Company Description Section............................... 83

CHAPTER 5: **PRODUCT DESCRIPTION**... 87

Step 16. Write a story synopsis for your film...................... 87

Step 17. Describe the project's other important details............ 88

Sample Product Description Section................................ 90

CHAPTER 6: **FINANCING**.. 93

Step 18. Briefly scare the crap out of the investor
(a.k.a. the mini-risk statement).......................... 93

Step 19. Explain how you intend to fund this gamble/film........... 94

Step 20. Explain how you intend to distribute the winnings......... 94

Step 21. Depict the ugly truth about residuals.................... 95

Sample Financing Section... 97

CHAPTER 7: **INDUSTRY OVERVIEW**... 99

Step 22. Portray the wonderful process of moviemaking
(without the blood & sweat)............................... 99

Step 23. Studio Films vs. Independent Films.......................100

Step 24. Describe the current and future state of the movie industry.........100

Sample Industry Overview Section.................................104

CHAPTER 8: **EXECUTIVE SUMMARY**..109

Step 25. Restate the whole plan... in one page....................109

Sample Executive Summaries......................................111

CHAPTER 9: **INFORMATION AND RISK STATEMENT**.................................... 117

Step 26. Legal junk (a.k.a. keeping you out of jail).................................... 117

Step 27. Scare the crap out of the investor
(a.k.a. the full risk statement).. 120

Sample Information and Risk Statement.. 122

CHAPTER 10: **COMPLETED PLAN**... 125

Step 28. Put it in the right order... 125

Step 29. Get a good lawyer.. 126

Step 30. Make a great film!... 126

APPENDIX A: SAMPLE PLAN IN ITS ENTIRETY.. 127

APPENDIX B: NITTY GRITTY DETAILS... 165

APPENDIX C: RECOMMENDED READING... 205

INDEX.. 211

ABOUT THE AUTHOR.. 221

ACKNOWLEDGMENTS

Drum roll, please....

I'd first like to thank my mother, Dr. Ilona Linnoila, and my late father, Dr. Markku Linnoila, for raising me and teaching me the work habits necessary to sit down and get a job done. Their love and support have made everything in my life possible.

As you could probably imagine, a book like this is not the most fun in the world to write. There was plenty of prodding and pushing from my wife, Christina Mauro, to sit down and get it done. And for her everlasting love and support I am grateful. My friend, Arleigh Hays, helped hatch the idea for even doing a book in the first place. I owe her many thanks as well.

For their assistance as I was researching this book, I want to thank Sandra Archer and the rest of the staff at the Margaret Herrick Library in Los Angeles. I can't tell you how invaluable it is to have a library staff that actually knows what it is talking about and cares about helping patrons. Thanks!

I also want to thank Jody O'Riordan at Baseline StudioSystems during the time of this writing for her patience and attention to detail in answering all of my picky questions about the company's data.

Last, and certainly not least, I want to thank my publisher Michael Wiese for giving me the opportunity to get this book out into the world. And another thanks to his right-hand man, Ken Lee, for helping guide me through all the steps to making it a reality, not the least of which was introducing me to my copy editor, Linda Norlen, and my designer, Gina Mansfield, to both of whom fell the unenviable task of wrestling this behemoth to the ground. Thanks, team!

INTRODUCTION

Welcome to what will be an incredibly rewarding process: the writing of a business plan for your film. Once complete, you will have a supreme command over all aspects of your film project, including its financing, marketing, and distribution. This command will give you the best shot at making a film that will not be forgotten. Writing a thorough business plan, of course, is painstaking work. The job of this book is to greatly reduce that pain.

WHAT IS A BUSINESS PLAN?

Quite simply, it is a plan for how you intend to successfully run your business, or in your case, make a successful feature film. It is often used, either in conjunction with other legal documents or by itself, to demonstrate to potential investors that you know what you are doing and can be trusted with money.

When I wrote my first business plan, there were no books that took you through a step-by-step approach to writing one. That is what this book attempts to do, especially with regard to the numbers. You will be told exactly where to go and exactly what to do. It's also written in such a way that you can make your own assumptions about how to do things and insert these assumptions freely into your own plan.

WHO IS THIS BOOK FOR?

This book will be most useful to you if you are an independent filmmaker interested in producing a low-budget independent film. "Independent" can mean various things, but in this book it refers to a film with no funding from a U.S. studio (Warner Brothers, Universal, Sony, Fox, Disney, or Paramount). In particular, there can be no studio funding of a film's development, preproduction, principal photography, or postproduction costs prior to initial release, though initial release can be at a festival. An independent film can be distributed by a studio or its subsidiaries, just not financed by them. This does lead to the imperfect situation of films made by companies such as Lionsgate or Overture being grouped into the same category as films made by my cousin who lives in a garage. However, for the purposes of writing a film business plan, this definition will suffice.

As for my definition of "low budget," I am referring to films with budgets of $5–$10 million and below, though closer to $5 million and below. Beyond $10 million, some of book's strategies do not fully hold. Notice also that the book is meant only for the writing of a single-film business plan. This book does not describe how to do a multi-film plan, because no fully informed investor would invest in many films at once, unless *perhaps* the investment covered some 30+ films (see the mention of portfolios in Appendix B, Step 27). Often investors who think they are fully informed make simultaneous investments in far fewer films, with the end result of many investors getting burned.

The book is tailored to writing a business plan suited to approaching angel investors for 100% of the monies needed to make your film. "Angel investors" are those wealthy individuals willing to look at you and say, "Here, I trust you with this money. Now go and make your movie." However, the guidelines and principles in the book can be adapted to other financing scenarios where equity (that is, cash from an individual or a company — not a loan) is less than 100% of the deal.

WHAT RESOURCES WILL YOU NEED?

Doing research, either in the library or online, will be essential to completing your business plan. Several online resources will be essential. They are *IMDb.com* and online subscriptions to *The Hollywood Reporter* and *Variety*. *IMDb.com* is free and the subscriptions to *Reporter* and *Variety* are in the $15–$20 range per month. *IMDb.com* also has a very useful upscale version for about $13 per month called *IMDbPro.com*. One quick tip, when using the search engines on *The Hollywood Reporter* and *Variety* websites (which, I warn you, can sometimes be a bit inefficient), use quotes around the phrases you are researching. For instance, if typing in "assumption agreements," use quotes around the entire phrase, or else you will end up with all the articles containing the word "assumption" or "agreements," even if they are separated by other words.

If you are in Los Angeles, an outstanding resource is the Margaret Herrick Library. It is run by The Academy of Motion Picture Arts and Sciences and contains virtually anything you could ever desire to know about films. Recent articles are categorized into files called "clipping files" that you pick up and physically thumb through. They seriously reduce the amount of searching you have to do.

I must warn you that writing a business plan will not only cost you time, but also money, the bulk of which will go to ordering data for your financial projections. You will need data for approximately 8 to 15 films and will order the data from Baseline StudioSystems at about $50 per film. Baseline StudioSystems ("BLSS") is the leading provider of financial data and projections for films. (Nobody paid me to say that — I wish.) I've taken steps within the book to keep down your number of films ordered, but the 8-15 range still comes to roughly $400 to $750 total. If you can find a cheaper, more efficient way of getting the data you need, by all means do so. My treatment and analysis of the BLSS data can be applied to film data from any reliable source.

Finally, you will need access to Microsoft Excel or someone who has it and can perform all the necessary Excel tasks for you. Without it, there will be some items you cannot complete and others that will seem that way because of the time it will take to complete them. To save time and headache you can visit *mwp.com* (the publisher's website) where you will find free, preformatted Excel spreadsheets available to you.

I know it sucks to hear that you'll be spending money to write your business plan. But if you don't, you may be sitting there five years from now wishing you had.

HOW'S THE BOOK WRITTEN?

I based the book on three business plans written in 2004. They are a science fiction romance (entitled *Sci-Fi Rom* and budgeted at $0.5 million), halfamil a mass appeal horror-comedy (entitled *Mass H-Com* and budgeted at $1.2 million), and a psychological thriller (*Psych Thrill*, $1.5 million) — obviously, the original names have been changed. They are presented throughout the text in the form of sample plans modified from their original 2004 formats. Small parts of them have been XXX'd out to protect the original material. In the sample plans, I've also changed the names of the movies for which I ordered data from Baseline StudioSystems. This was done to protect the original data.

The plans themselves are presented throughout the book as examples, but have not been updated except where noted. One reason for this is to make sure the plans I am currently writing don't show up competing against me. The other is because only by doing the research and updating the plans yourself (don't worry, I give you advice on which sections need which kinds of updates) will you be able to answer investor questions about what is in your plan. Ultimately, updating the plans needn't be a source of stress, because the core concepts presented in the sample plans remain largely unchanged today, and the items most in need of update are facts and figures used in the plans to illustrate those concepts.

The book is written in the order that I recommend *writing* your business plan, not *presenting* it. At the end of the book (Appendix A) I have assembled the sample plan of one film (*Psych Thrill*) in the order that I recommend presenting a business plan. As for each chapter, each one reflects a section of a business plan and is presented in numbered steps. Sometimes, I will refer you to more detailed steps, or just to more details in general, in Appendix B. You can skip going to Appendix B and still get through each chapter. Appendix B is just there to provide more details and reasoning behind what is going on in each chapter or step. After the steps in each chapter are examples from the sample plans.

TWO DIRTY SECRETS OF BUSINESS PLANS!

Remember, a business plan is a plan for how you intend to successfully run your business.

Dirty Secret #1: In most cases it is *against the law* to use a business plan by itself to raise money for your film. If you are approaching investors who are expert in making films and will be actively involved in all phases of making your film, then using a business plan alone is okay. However, if you are using a business plan to raise funds from people who will not be involved in the making of your film, then using a business plan alone is *against the law*. Despite this fact, hundreds of filmmakers every year break the law. Most of them do so unknowingly.

To make sure your are on the right side of the law, after writing your business proposal, I would recommend hiring an entertainment attorney with expertise in the financing of independent films. Some are willing to work for deferred fees and/or a stake in your film's profits. Have the attorney guide you on how to properly approach potential investors with whom you have a pre-existing relationship and how to hand those investors a copy of your business plan. Once this is done, any investors that express interest in investing in your film can be sent a Private Placement Memorandum (PPM) as part of a private placement offering. The PPM is a complex legal document that will include essential elements of your business plan and basically ensure that you cannot be legitimately sued or prosecuted for breaking laws regarding the raising of money. A "private placement offering" is the technical term used to describe the raising of money from people you know. PPMs are expensive (upwards of $10,000–$20,000), so don't forget to include one in the budget of your film. Don't worry, some attorneys will not charge you the full price until your budget has been raised, in which case the money comes out of your budget.

Dirty Secret #2: The forecasts that occur in a business plan (or any-where, for that matter) for how much money a film might make are a crock of baloney. That's right — straight out of your grandma's mouth, a crock of baloney! The box office success of a single film is entirely unpredictable, and it is box office success that drives the performance of a film in other formats (DVD, pay TV, etc.). Appendix B, Step 27, has some great information on the matter.

So what's the point then of even writing a business plan? The business plan for your film signals to an investor that (1) you are passionate about it (why else would you put the effort into doing a plan); (2) you have integrity (your plan is well researched and forthright); and (3) you have knowledge (at the very least you know what is in the plan — which is a lot — even if you have limited industry experience). Additionally, of the successful films in your plan to which you will be comparing your own film, some will have made money that is out of this world. Such an enticement is precisely why some investors disregard the unpredictability of films and invest anyway.

Okay… that's great, you say, but how do I proceed to make a plan that is meant to forecast an event (the performance of a film) that is entire-ly unpredictable? You proceed as if it were predictable. Think about this: If you were an investor about to take a huge gamble by investing in a film, would you rather give your money to a group of filmmakers whose plan had no numbers because numbers "don't matter anyway," or to a group that logically spells out why its film will be successful, even though you realize (and the filmmakers' business plan states) that such logic statistically has no bearing on the film's performance? I would give to the latter. At least that group is passionate and has integrity and knowledge.

TWO LAST PIECES OF ADVICE...

The underlying assumption to make when writing a business plan is that your film will be successful (though the vast majority are not). That is to say, it will be sought after by distributors, it will be distributed, and it will earn considerable money above and beyond what was invested in it. By making this assumption, you greatly simplify the details you have to explain to investors and cut out the many complicated scenarios faced by not-so-successful or not-so-sought-after films. Notice, I am in no way saying to sugarcoat the harsh realities facing any movie investment. I am merely saying to focus on the realities facing a successful picture. Do not fear: As Chapter 9 will illustrate, the harsh realities facing any picture, successful or not, will also be highlighted for investors.

Finally, please do not construe any of the information in this book as legal advice. For that you need an attorney, specifically an entertainment attorney, with expertise in the financing of independent films. In fact, you will need access to one who can review your plan once it is done. NEVER start sending out business plans without such an attorney who has reviewed your plan and advised you on how to approach investors with it.

AND OFF WE GO!

Well… this is it. Good luck. And as with anything you pursue in the entertainment industry, stick to it. The first step to success is persistence.

My film is sought after by distributors, it is being distributed, and it will earn considerable money above and beyond what was invested in it.

¹FINANCIAL PROJECTIONS

The overall goal in the Financial Projections section is to make predictions for how your film will do financially, if it is successful. Of course, everyone familiar with films knows that predicting how a film is going to do is about as impossible as predicting the exact time and size of an earthquake. However, that is no excuse to take this section lightly. The more logical and thorough you can be here, the more interest in you an investor will take. You will be demonstrating your thinking ability and discipline. See Appendix B for a primer on some of the finer details of this section, or you can wait and check it out later.

STEP 1. COMPARE YOUR FILM TO OTHER GREAT FILMS.
(COMPARABLE FILMS TABLE)

In this step you create a table that you can point to and say, "Here. See this? These films show that you can make money with a movie like mine." For films that don't appeal to a mass audience, such as a science-fiction romance or a lesbian-serial-killer drama, make a table with films that are similar in theme to yours (you can use foreign films if you want). For films that have mass appeal, like a comedy or a horror, stick to finding the most profitable films you can, *regardless of subject matter* — that's right, I said regardless of subject matter. Because your film is of mass appeal, it is geared toward an audience that is at least as big as the audiences of the most profitable films. Then, when you point to your table, you can say, "See how much money those films made? My film targets at least as many people as they did." Of course we will keep the most obscenely profitable films off the table — obscenity is bad, especially in a business plan. Appendix B has some more tips.

STEP 1A. Go to *http://www.blssresearch.com/contact.aspx* and contact Baseline StudioSystems ("BLSS") through their website or call 310-482-3444. Request a list of all of BLSS's films that meet these requirements:

1) released in the past five years;
2) released domestically (Canada + U.S.);
3) budgeted at a certain level or less (see below);
4) had a max screen count domestically of 1000 or less.

Make clear in your request that you intend to order FRCE reports and other data but that you would like to start by whittling down your choices from this list. A list request like this costs nothing, but subsequent requests are priced at $25–$100.

Let me expand on requirements 3 and 4:

3) The idea here is to keep your comparable films within a certain budget range so that all the films roughly resemble one another in terms of production value. If your film's budget is $2.5 million or under, request films with budgets at $5 million and below. My experience forecasting on behalf of films is centered on budgets around $2.5 million and below. However, if your budget goes beyond that, I would recommend ordering films with budgets no more than $2.5 million above yours. For example, if your film is budgeted at $5 million, stick to comparable films at $7.5 million and below.

4) A screen is simply a movie screen where a movie plays; a movie theater often has more than one (think of your nearest mall's multiplex), in which case, the theater is often called a "venue," "site," or "engagement." With rare exception, even very popular low-budget independent films do not exceed 800 screens in domestic release and most do not exceed 600. In having the 1000–screen restriction, you are covering yourself if for some reason you end up needing to use one of those rare exceptions for your table. It also keeps your table from being ridiculously biased (as opposed to just biased) by blocking out films that earned upwards of $100 million and $200 million in box office. See Appendix B for an important note about how people track screen count.

- Request from BCSS movie requirements
- Once you recieve it, go on Imdb to whittle down choices
FINANCIAL PROJECTIONS   3
- Check the independent status and get rid of any that aren't
- Contact Baseline for FRCE reports for remaining movies
-- fill out excell spreatsheet after the FRCE repts come in

STEP 1B. For each movie Baseline StudioSystems sends you (and they will send you a ton!), use *IMDb.com* to record some more information about the movie. You will record the film's domestic gross, the number of screens it opened on, and the date of its release. You might also want to check the film's description and record its rating (NC-17, R, PG-13, etc.).

To find these pieces of data examine the main IMDb page of a film. Check the menu down the left hand side of the page and under the section entitled "Other Info," click on the "box office/business" link. This will take you to a page with the information you need. Keep in mind that the largest dollar amount with a "(USA)" next to it actually represents the domestic gross — how much box office a film earned in the U.S. *and* Canada.

Keep going until you have a group of about 8-15 films you would feel comfortable putting on your Comparable Films Table. Try to stick to films with high domestic grosses, but know that films with grosses of only $1 million might also work. Also try to keep the opening screen count as low as possible (see Appendix B).

STEP 1C. Check the independent status of each film in your final group. Remember, it only counts as "independent" if none of the development, preproduction, principal photography, and postproduction costs were paid for by a studio or its subsidiaries (distribution is okay).

First, go to the IMDb page for each film. On the left hand menu again, under the heading "Overview," click on "Company Credits." At the top of the new page will be the list "Production Companies." Check that none of the following appear as production companies (this list is constantly changing):

Sony	Buena Vista (a.k.a. Disney)	Twentieth Century-Fox
Screen Gems	Hollywood Pictures	Fox 2000
Sony Pictures Classics	Miramax	Fox Atomic**
TriStar	Touchstone	Fox Searchlight
MGM (part owner of)	Walt Disney Pictures	
Universal	Paramount	Warner Brothers
Focus Features	DreamWorks*	New Line
Rogue*	MTV Films	Picturehouse**
	Nickelodeon Movies	Warner Independent**
	Paramount Vantage	

*No longer a studio subsidiary
**Defunct

Sometimes an independent film still ends up having a studio subdivision listed. In such cases the listing may or may not include "(presents)" after the subdivision's name. Unfortunately, there's no rule for when the film in such a case is independent and when it is not. (Sorry, not very helpful, I know.)

Next, do a more thorough check. Search for articles about the film and its production companies on the web. IMDb may have some articles in a link off of the movie's main page. If you live in Los Angeles, a movie's "production clipping file" at the Margaret Herrick Library will hold all sorts of information — the file is literally a tiny folder with cutout magazine and newspaper articles in it. In general, the earlier the article's date, the better the independent-status information it will have (see Appendix B).

Take out any films from your final group that end up not being independent.

STEP 1D. Contact Baseline StudioSystems ("BLSS") again and order an FRCE report (Film Revenue and Cost Estimates) for each film in your final group. The report costs $19.95 per film. Be prepared that some of these films will have to be discarded once you crunch the FRCE numbers. At the end of all this, you will want at least four films, and ideally will get many more, for your comparable films table.

STEP 1E. This next step is a doozy — it's very long. But hang in there. Find a friend who is good at Excel to make a blank comparable films table, formatted like the one in the sample plans (see the end of the chapter). Or you can find one at *mwp.com* — the website for the publisher of this book. Then fill in the data using your FRCE report and crunch the numbers. Put the newest films on the left of the table and the oldest on the right. Follow this table to show you how:

Table 1.1: How to Fill in Your Comparable Films Table and What It Means

	FRCE figure to use / Calculation To Do	Estimate/Actual?	U.S./Canadian?	Special Notes
DOMESTIC (U.S.)[1]				
Box Office Gross	DOM_GROSS	Actual	U.S. and Canadian	Will match your IMDb box office in nearly all cases.
Less Exhibitor Share[2]	DOM_GROSS minus DOM_RENTALS	Estimate	U.S. and Canadian	Money the movie theaters keep.
Gross Film Rentals	DOM_RENTALS	Estimate	U.S. and Canadian	Money left over after theaters take their share of box office.
Home Video Revenue	DOM_VIDEO_GROSS plus DOM_DVD_GROSS	Estimate	U.S. only	Based on first shipments to retailers for rental and sell-through.
Pay TV Revenue	Ordered Later (Step 1G)	Estimate	U.S. only	Money from cable/satellite, pay-per-view, and video-on-demand.
Gross Ancillary Revenue	Add up 'Home Video' plus 'Pay TV'	Estimate	-	None
Domestic Gross[3]	Add up 'Gross Film Rentals' and 'Gross Ancillary'	Estimate	-	None
Less Distribution Fee (35%)	Multiply 'Domestic Gross' by 0.35	Estimate	-	What distributors charge for their services.
Less Prints & Advertising[4]	DOM_PRINT_ADVERT_COSTS	Estimate	-	Cost of advertising and making prints for the box office release.
Less Other Distributor Costs[5]	Multiply 'Domestic Gross' by 20%	Estimate	U.S. and Canadian	See the footnotes.
Net Domestic Receipts	'Domestic Gross' minus the three items above	Estimate	-	None
FOREIGN				
Foreign Gross[6]	Use The Hollywood Reporter's "The Going Rate"	Estimate		This is explained in the text.
Less Sales Agent Fee & Expenses (35%)[7]	Multiply 'Foreign Gross' by 0.35	Estimate		What the foreign sales agent charges for his/her/its work.
Net Foreign Receipts	'Foreign Gross' minus the 'Sales Agent' figure	Estimate	-	None
TOTAL				
TOTAL PRODUCER'S REP GROSS[8]	'Net Domestic Receipts' plus 'Net Foreign'	Estimate	-	See the footnotes.
Less Producer's Rep Fee (15%)	Multiply 'Producer's Rep Gross' by 0.15	Estimate	-	None
TOTAL PRODUCER'S GROSS	'Producer's Rep Gross' minus 'Producer's Rep Fee'	Estimate	-	None
Less Negative Cost[9]	NEGATIVE_COSTS	Both	-	See the footnotes.
NET INVESTOR/PRODUCER PROFIT	'Total Producer's Gross' minus 'Negative Cost'	Estimate	-	None

FOOTNOTES:

1: DOMESTIC - For 'Box Office Gross' and 'Prints & Advertising,' domestic refers to U.S. & Canada, for all other data points it refers only to U.S.

2: Exhibitor Share - Theater owners' share of the box office revenue.

3: Domestic Gross - Sum of 'Gross Film Rentals' and 'Gross Ancillary Revenue.'

4: Prints & Advertising (P&A) - Cost of the marketing campaign and copies made of the original negative ('prints') for the theatrical release.

5: Other Distributor Costs - Expenses outside of P&A for which the distributor is reimbursed such as residuals and DVD manufacturing, marketing, and distribution costs.

6: Foreign Gross - Canada excluded; money received from advances by foreign distributors for the right to distribute in all formats; per territory data available.

7: Sales Agent - Markets to and collects advances from foreign distributors. Residuals are included as part of expenses.

8: Producer's Rep - Seeks out and negotiates domestic distribution and sales agent agreements.

9: Negative Cost - Costs incurred to shoot the film and create the negative off of which all copies of the film are made; also known as the 'budget' of the film.

Notice anything weird? How about how many times the word "Estimate" appears on the table? The reason for this is that the actual money a movie makes or costs to distribute is privately held information almost never given out to anyone, not even to a place like Baseline StudioSystems. Fortunately, Baseline has vast expertise in estimating those numbers it provides that are estimates.

As promised on the table, let me explain how to do the "Foreign Gross" (also, see Appendix B for more detailed notes about the table). Get a hold of the latest article from *The Hollywood Reporter* entitled "The Going Rate." It's usually published twice a year and shows a table with prices films might fetch when they are sold for distribution in countries outside the U.S. and Canada.

For each film on your comparable films table, look at "The Going Rate" and find out which budget range it falls into. If it is on the border of two budget ranges, for instance — a $1 million film could go into either the $750K–$1M or the $1M–$3M category — pick the smaller range. Then look down the column of that budget range and add up all the money that the film could make from all the territories. Use each country's highest dollar amount. For instance, if a film falls in the $750–$1M budget range and France shows a dollar range of $25K–$50K, use $50K. Then, once you've added everything up, multiply your total by 0.75 if you do not have any significantly name actors in your cast; leave the total alone if you do. The result is your film's "Foreign Gross."

By the way, if your film has a very low budget that falls below the lowest budget range, that's okay. Use the numbers from the lowest budget range available.

Now, I know what you're thinking, "But the article is from 2009, and the film was released in 2005!" What we are saying with the foreign part of the comparable films table is, "See these successful films from the past? This is how they might have done in today's foreign marketplace." After all, it is today's foreign marketplace you will be using when you make your foreign projections. For more details on the foreign marketplace… You guessed it, Appendix B.

STEP 1F. After crunching the numbers, examine your "NET INVESTOR/ PRODUCER PROFIT." Don't fret yet if some of the films show a negative number here. When you order your pay TV data from Baseline Studio-Systems it will likely push profit up by about 10%–15% of your domestic box office. So if your box office was $10 million, your "Pay TV Revenue" will push Net Inv./Prod. Profit up by about $1.0–$1.5 million. If this range of amount won't help a particular film get out of the negative, I would remove that film from the table. Of course, it is possible that the pay TV figure you will end up ordering has a different impact from what I am saying because of changing market conditions. If you badly need a film that's in the red to stay on your table, it might be best to wait to remove it until you order the pay TV numbers.

STEP 1G. For the remaining films on the table, you will need domestic "Pay TV" figures. Contact Baseline StudioSystems ("BLSS") again and request "Domestic Pay TV figures" for each of the remaining films; such a request costs $30. You will notice that, along with these figures, BLSS will send you domestic TV (otherwise known as domestic "free TV" figures) and international TV and pay TV figures; ignore all of them. Domestic free TV revenues do not really apply to low-budget independents (see Appendix B) and our foreign gross calculations use different international data.

STEP 1H. If a lot of time has passed (i.e., months) since you began your comparable films table, check with BLSS if any of its estimated data for films released in the past year has changed. P&A figures and home video revenues are especially subject to change if a film receives awards, nominations, or considerations for them. BLSS revises its figures accordingly. Generally speaking, if the date you obtained the data was one or more years after a film's release, do not expect any estimates to have changed significantly.

STEP 1I. The time has come, no more beating around the bush, no more hoping beyond hope. Remove any films showing a negative profit. And then… replace each remaining film's negative cost with the budget of your film. Next, see what the result is and remove those films that now show a negative profit. Finally, for the films that are left (those that have survived the cut), put back in their negative costs. Check this chart out to see what I mean:

Table 1.2: Putting the final hatchet to your Comparable Films ($ millions)	Pic 1	Pic 2	Pic 3	Pic 4	Pic 5	Avg
TOTAL PRODUCER'S GROSS	$1.9	$3.6	$5.7	$6.6	$8.1	$5.2
Less Negative Cost	$1.0	$1.8	$2.0	$2.0	$4.5	$2.3
NET INVESTOR/PRODUCER PROFIT	$0.9	$1.8	$3.7	$4.6	$3.6	$2.9
TOTAL PRODUCER'S GROSS	$1.9	$3.6	$5.7	$6.6	$8.1	$5.2
Less **YOUR FILM's** Negative Cost	$2.2	$2.2	$2.2	$2.2	$2.2	$2.2
NET INVESTOR/PRODUCER PROFIT	-$0.3	$1.4	$3.5	$4.4	$5.9	$3.0

Gone!

The top half of the table shows how five movies show a positive profit. The bottom half shows how the movie called "Pic 1" (what an original name) shows a negative profit, with the rest staying positive. The difference between the two halves is that I substituted my film's negative cost ($2.2 million in this example) with each comparable film's negative cost on the bottom half. As much as I hate to do it, in this example I would throw Pic 1 off my table.

The logic behind this move is that the comparable films table demonstrates what could happen with revenue on your film. Well, if the revenue of one of the comparable films does not end up covering your negative cost, then you would not want to compare your film to it.

STEP 1J. Take a deep breath. Congratulations! Now the numeric part of your comparable films table is done. Next, add notes to the bottom of it. Feel free to copy the ones off the sample tables at the end of the chapter; they are self-explanatory and/or summarize what we have discussed in depth above.

STEP 1K. Finally, discuss the comparable films table in the text of your plan. See the sample plans for examples. You are saying to the investor: "See these films? They show the same kind of audience size as my film, and look at how they did." (Or, in the case of foreign revenue, I should say, "might have done.") Additionally, see Appendix B for a quick discussion of the text appearing in the sample plans about distributor advances.

STEP 2. PREDICT YOUR FAME AND GLORY.
(INCOME PROJECTIONS TABLE)

Here you predict how much money your movie *might* make, NOT how much it *will* make! Remember, movies are some of the hardest things in the world to predict. (I'm not exaggerating.) Telling your potential investors anything that even resembles a promise can land you in some hot water, or even worse, doing business plans for fellow inmates. Don't forget, these predictions are under the assumption that your film will be a success. In fact, before we go any further, add the warning that appears in bold at the top of the Financial Projections sample pages to your own page.

Did you do it? Good. On with the show!

STEP 2A. Make a table formatted just like the sample Income Projections Tables (*mwp.com* also carries a copy).

STEP 2B. For the "Medium Success" column, plug in your average domestic box office and home video numbers from the Comparable Films Table. Don't worry about throwing away high and low numbers that might have affected your averages (see Appendix B). If you feel like the averages are too high, cut them in half, take 25% off, or reduce them by some other such amount. As you can see with *Sci-Fi Rom*, I cut the box office and home video averages in half. This is basically because the film is so weird — admittedly great, but weird. All the films on its Comparable Films Table were in more established genres. Also, whatever you do to one, do the same to the other; if you cut box office in half, cut home video in half as well.

The "Medium Success" projections are what you will focus on most with you investor. What exactly is a "Medium Success" prediction? I would describe it as a medium level of success or a middle-of-the-road great outcome — sounds insane, I know. Keep in mind, 70%–80% of all major films do not make money (and the success rate for minor films is worse); so what you are predicting is based on numbers from films (your comparable films) that performed exceptionally well.[1] This being said, because of the cap on maximum screen count, you probably left even better films off your Comparable Films Table; so, as exceptional as your table might have been, it could have been even more exceptional.

---

[1] 70%-80% figure drawn from Harold L. Vogel, *Entertainment Industry Economics: A Guide for Financial Analysis*, 7th ed. (Cambridge and New York: Cambridge University Press, 2007), 65, 133.

STEP 2C. Still in the "Medium Success" column, establish your Exhibitor Share. To do so, you will need to do a little bit of maneuvering. Look back at your comparable films, and for each comparable film, calculate what its Exhibitor Share percentage was. Here's an example:

Table 1.3: Estimating an Exhibitor Share % for *Sci-Fi Rom* ($ millions)								
	Pic A	Pic B	Pic C	Pic D	Pic E	Pic F	Pic G	Avg
Exhibitor Share*	$1.105	$2.668	$1.934	$1.389	$3.265	$2.068	$4.100	NA
Box Office Gross**	$2.376	$5.739	$4.160	$2.872	$7.022	$4.447	$9.180	NA
Exhibitor Share %	46.5%	46.5%	46.5%	48.4%	46.5%	46.5%	44.7%	46.5%

*Source: Derived from Baseline StudioSystems domestic rentals figures.
**Source: Baseline StudioSystems

I divided each film's "Exhibitor Share" by its "Box Office Gross" to get "Exhibitor Share %." Then I took the average of the Exhibitor Share %'s to get 46.5%. In fact, this 46.5% appears in parentheses as a rounded 47% on the Projected Income Table.

Finally, multiply your Medium box office forecast by the average exhibitor share percentage to get your Medium "Exhibitor Share." In the case of *Sci-Fi Rom*, this comes to:

($2.557 million) x (46.5%) = $1.189 million

Appendix B has a warning on how not to do this step.

STEP 2D. Establish your pay TV number. This is pretty much the same as Step 2C except with pay TV numbers. Look back at your comparable films, and for each comparable film, calculate for it a pay TV licensing percentage. Here's an example:

Table 1.4: Estimating a Pay TV Licensing % for *Psych Thrill* ($ millions)						
	Pic L	Pic M	Pic J	Pic N	Pic K	Avg
Pay TV Revenue*	$0.531	$2.204	$2.280	$6.507	$0.916	NA
Box Office Gross*	$1.221	$8.821	$5.384	$25.530	$3.609	NA
Pay TV Licensing % (estimated)	43.5%	25.0%	42.3%	25.5%	25.4%	32.3%

*Source: Baseline StudioSystems

I divided each film's "Pay TV Revenue" by its "Box Office Gross" to get "Pay TV Licensing %." Then I averaged all the pay TV licensing percentages together to get 32.3%.

Finally, multiply your "Medium Success" box office forecast by the average pay TV percentage to get your Medium "Pay TV Revenue." In the case of *Psych Thrill*, this comes to:

($8.913 million) x (32.3%) = $2.879 million

STEP 2E. The only two "Medium Success" numbers left to forecast are "Prints & Advertising" (P&A) and "Foreign Gross." P&A will be much like the previous two steps. Take each comparable film's P&A, see what percentage of box office it is, and take an average. Here's a demonstration:

Table 1.5: Estimating a P&A % for *Mass H-Com* ($ millions)										
	Pic B	Pic S	Pic Q	Pic E	Pic M	Pic R	Pic N	Pic G	Pic K	Avg
Prints & Advertising*	$1.341	$1.409	$1.706	$1.196	$5.618	$2.273	$12.796	$1.800	$2.000	NA
Box Office Gross*	$5.739	$3.799	$21.244	$7.022	$8.821	$5.309	$25.530	$9.180	$3.609	NA
P&A %	23.4%	37.1%	8.0%	17.0%	63.7%	42.8%	50.1%	19.6%	55.4%	35.2%

*Source: Baseline StudioSystems

Next, multiply it by your Medium box office projection to get your P&A. For *Mass H-Com*:

$$(\$10.028 \text{ million}) \times (35.2\%) = \$3.530 \text{ million}$$

STEP 2F. For your Foreign Gross, just like with the Comparable Films Table, get the latest "The Going Rate" article and find what budget range your film fits into. If it falls into more than one, pick the lower one. Then for each country/region listed, calculate the number that is halfway between the numbers listed. For instance, if France lists 50K–100K, you will take 75K. Then, add up all the halfway numbers of the countries/regions... You're right, it sucks, it's a lot of work, but hang in there — just think of yourself on the Oscar podium thanking the publishers of *The Hollywood Reporter* for "The Going Rate"! (Or not.)

Next, multiply your total by 0.75 if your film does not have at least one significantly name actor; leave it alone otherwise. The result becomes your projected "Medium Success" Foreign Gross. Don't forget, if you cut your Medium box office and home video figures in half or reduced them at all, do the same to your Foreign Gross result. For instance, with *Sci-Fi Rom* I cut my Foreign Gross in half (for all my scenarios, Low, Medium, and High) because I had done the same to its Medium box office and home video.

While you're at it, you also might as well do all of Step 2F using each country/region's high and low numbers from "The Going Rate" article because... You guessed it, they'll serve as your "High Success" and "Low Success" Foreign Gross projections.

STEP 2G. Admire your "Medium Success" projections. The rest of your Medium projections should have flown off of the numbers already established, just like the Comparable Films Table. You subtract "Exhibitor Share" from "Box Office Gross" for "Gross Film Rentals," add up "Home Video Revenue" and "Pay TV Revenue" for "Gross Ancillary Revenue," and so on all the way down the table until you arrive at "Net Investor/ Producer Profit." Use 20% as the rate for "Other Distributor Costs" (see the Comparables Table for a reminder) and, of course, insert your project's negative cost at the bottom. See Appendix B for a note on deferrals.

STEP 2H. Now for the hardest part, the "Low Success" projections. For reasons that will become apparent later, take the budget of your film and multiply it by 20%. See the number you get? That's what you want for your Low forecast's Net Investor/Producer Profit. For instance, with *Sci-Fi Rom*:

20% x $0.5 million = $0.1 million

So my goal for *Sci-Fi Rom*'s Net Investor/Producer Profit in the "Low Success" column is $0.1 million. I input box office, home video, and pay TV numbers that will get me there. As you can see, this means box office of $0.470 million (rounded on the table to $0.5 million), home video of $0.942 million, and pay TV of $0.177 million. In fact, keep box office and home video in the same ratio as they were in the "Medium Success" projections. With *Sci-Fi Rom* this ratio comes to:

Medium Home Video / Medium Box Office = $5.127 million / $2.557 million
= 2.0 ratio

Low Home Video / Low Box Office = $0.942 million / $0.470 million
= 2.0 ratio

(The "/" means "divided by.")

Adjust only the pay TV up or down to get your Net Investor/Producer Profit exactly correct. Your Foreign Gross should already have been done and need not be adjusted. Remember, it is created just the same way as your "Medium Success" foreign gross, except that you use the lowest end of each country's money range from "The Going Rate" (see Step 2F).

And the rest of your numbers (Exhibitor Share, P&A, etc.) should use the same percentages from the Medium scenario, except this time multiplied against your "Low Success" results (see Steps 2C, 2E, and 2G).

If you have trouble with this step, Appendix B suggests a detailed step-by-step approach (sound familiar?) to getting your "Low Success" projections. The approach is a bit complex, but keep in mind the end goal: getting your Net Investor/Producer Profit to be 20% of your negative cost.

STEP 2I. Take another deep breath. Next are the "High Success" projections and they are practically done at this point. To do them, subtract your "Low Success" box office gross from your "Medium Success" box office gross. For *Psych Thrill*, this goes:

Medium Box Office Gross - Low Box Office Gross = $8.913 million - $1.300 million
= $7.613 million

Add the result to your Medium box office gross and the total becomes your High box office gross. Again for *Psych Thrill*:

Medium Box Office + Medium/Low Difference = $8.913 million + $7.613 million
= $16.526 million

Check that the result is not higher than your highest box office gross from your Comparable Films Table. If it is, type in that highest number as your "High Success" box office projection. We don't want any box office projections higher than our highest Comparable Films numbers.

After you have done this for the box office, do the same thing for home video. My result for *Psych Thrill* is $34.553 million. But then I look and see what the highest Comparable Films Home Video Revenue is: $26.847 million. So I drop the $34.553 and use the $26.847 million as my High forecast.

For the pay TV revenue, multiply Step 2D's average pay TV percentage against your box office High projection (don't worry if the result ends up higher than the highest Comparable Films pay TV), and for Foreign Gross, repeat Step 2F using the highest end of each country/region's money range from "The Going Rate." Once again, as for the rest of your numbers (Exhibitor Share, P&A, etc.), use the same percentages from the "Medium Success" scenario, except this time multiply them against your "High Success" results (see Steps 2C, 2E, and 2G).

STEP 2J. Write the text discussing your projections. Use the sample plans as guidance and don't forget, never make any promises. Regarding tone, keep the writing simple, dry, and to the point. This is not a place to scream, "Rah! Rah! Rah!" While it is okay to emphasize the positive, the facts should, on the whole, speak for themselves. Appendix B has several other tips.

STEP 2K. I need to take this step to congratulate you. Look at what you've done so far — and really look at it, because it's a lot — you've just made comparisons and predictions for your movie! Pat yourself on the back, take a break if you need to, and then go on to the next step.

STEP 3. FORECAST WHEN EVERYONE GETS A FERRARI.
(CASH FLOW PROJECTIONS TABLE)

Now you will predict when everything from your Income Projections Table happens. When the budget money will be spent, when money will be made, and when the various fees and P&A and other expenses will have to be paid for. Unfortunately, what your cash flow will look like is greatly determined by the kind of distribution deal you will get, and since distribution deals vary so widely, cash flows can vary widely as well. However, it is a good idea to provide potential investors with at least a very rough idea as to how money might flow in, and in the same breath, to tell them that the cash flow they are seeing is just that, a very rough idea.

If you are unclear about what cash flow projections are, go on back to Appendix B for a brief lesson — it's actually entertaining, I promise.

STEP 3A. Make a table formatted just like the sample Cash Flow Projections Tables (see *mwp.com* for a free one). Even though you have a "Low Success," "Medium Success," and "High Success" scenario on your Income Projections Table, you will only show investors a projected cash flow for your Medium scenario. Cash flows for the other two must be made, but should be left out of your plan in order to keep things simple. Of course, be prepared to provide them if an investor wants a copy. All of the following steps will apply to cash flow projections for any scenario, "Low Success," "Medium Success," or "High Success."

STEP 3B. Spread out your income from the Medium column of your Income Projections Table according to the following cash flow schedule:

Table 1.6: Percentages to Use for Your Cash Flow Projections

	YEAR 1				YEAR 2				YEAR 3			
	Quarter 1	Quarter 2	Quarter 3	Quarter 4	Quarter 1	Quarter 2	Quarter 3	Quarter 4	Quarter 1	Quarter 2	Quarter 3	Quarter 4
Movie												
Negative Cost	70.0%	10.0%	10.0%	10.0%								
Gross Film Rentals									45.0%	53.0%	2.0%	
Home Video Revenue											72.0%	5.5%
Pay TV Revenue									NA	NA	NA	NA
Distribution Fee												
Prints & Advertising									45.0%	53.0%	2.0%	
Other Distributor Costs									NA	NA	NA	NA
Dom Subtotal									*NA*	*NA*	*NA*	*NA*
Foreign Gross										30.0%	30.0%	30.0%
Sales Agent Fee & Costs									NA	NA	NA	NA
Frgn Subtotal									*NA*	*NA*	*NA*	*NA*
Producer's Rep Fee									*NA*	*NA*	*NA*	*NA*
TOTAL	$ -	$ -	$ -	$ -	$ -	$ -	$ -	$ -	$ -	$ -	$ -	$ -
RUNNING TOTAL	$ -	$ -	$ -	$ -	$ -	$ -	$ -	$ -	$ -	$ -	$ -	$ -
RETURNED TO INVESTORS	$ -	$ -	$ -	$ -	$ -	$ -	$ -	$ -	$ -	$ -	$ -	$ -
CUMULATIVE RETURNED	$ -	$ -	$ -	$ -	$ -	$ -	$ -	$ -	$ -	$ -	$ -	$ -

Table 1.6 (cont'd): Percentages to Use for Your Cash Flow Projections

| | YEAR 4 | | | | YEAR 5 | | | | YEAR 6 |
	Quarter 1	Quarter 2	Quarter 3	Quarter 4	Quarter 1	Quarter 2	Quarter 3	Quarter 4	Quarter 1
Movie									
Negative Cost									
Gross Film Rentals	2.75%	2.75%	2.75%	2.75%	2.75%	2.20%	2.20%	2.20%	2.15%
Home Video Revenue		100.0%							
Pay TV Revenue	NA	NA	NA	NA	NA	NA	NA	NA	NA
Distribution Fee	NA	NA	NA	NA	NA	NA	NA	NA	NA
Prints & Advertising									
Other Distributor Costs	NA	NA	NA	NA	NA	NA	NA	NA	NA
Dom Subtotal	*NA*	*NA*	*NA*	*NA*	*NA*	*NA*	*NA*	*NA*	*NA*
Foreign Gross	15.0%	15.0%		10.0%					
Sales Agent Fee & Costs	NA	NA	NA	NA					
Frgn Subtotal	*NA*	*NA*	*NA*	*NA*	*NA*	*NA*	*NA*	*NA*	*NA*
Producer's Rep Fee	*NA*	*NA*	*NA*	*NA*	*NA*	*NA*	*NA*	*NA*	*NA*
TOTAL	$ -	$ -	$ -	$ -	$ -	$ -	$ -	$ -	$ -
RUNNING TOTAL	$ -	$ -	$ -	$ -	$ -	$ -	$ -	$ -	$ -
RETURNED TO INVESTORS	$ -	$ -	$ -	$ -	$ -	$ -	$ -	$ -	$ -
CUMULATIVE RETURNED	$ -	$ -	$ -	$ -	$ -	$ -	$ -	$ -	$ -

As an example of how the table works, Gross Film Rentals are spread out 45.0% in Year 3, Quarter 1; 53.0% in Year 3, Quarter 2; and 2.0% in Year 3, Quarter 3. If I had a film with $1.0 million in gross film rentals on the Income Projections Table, I would have $0.450 million in film rentals in Year 3, Quarter 1; $0.530 million in Year 3, Quarter 2; and $0.020 million in Year 3, Quarter 3. You can check this with the sample plans.

Remember, any instances where money is spent or fees or expenses are charged mean the numbers have to be negative (in parentheses). Also, you will have to work out with your producers how you want your Negative Cost spread out. They may suggest you use different percentages or even suggest that the budget be spent over only two quarters instead of four. *Sci-Fi Rom*'s negative cost percentages had to be altered because it was being shot in one day. See Appendix B for more notes.

STEP 3C. Estimate when distribution for your film will begin. After post is complete and sometimes during post, your film will hopefully find a distributor. Then that distributor will decide when to release your film and begin distribution. For the purposes of the cash flow table, we need to estimate when that distribution begins because that is when your film starts to generate money.

Generally speaking, successful American independent films, such as the ones you will find on your comparables table, and the one for which you are actually drawing up your business plan, will be released within one year after postproduction. As a result, I assume *Mass H-Com* and *Psych Thrill* will be released one year after postproduction is over. For both these movies you can see one full year (four empty quarters) with no numbers on the cash flow table before release begins. See Appendix B for the different assumptions I made for *Sci-Fi Rom*.

After checking out the appendix, adjust your cash flow accordingly. Most times you won't need to.

STEP 3D. Calculate your "Distribution Fee" for each quarter. In every quarter where you have a number in one or more of the boxes for "Gross Film Rentals," "Home Video Revenue," or "Pay TV Revenue," add up all those numbers. For *Mass H-Com* in Year 3, Quarter 3, this means:

Gross Film Rentals + Home Video Revenue = $0.108 million + $10.368 million
= $10.476 million

The "Pay TV Revenue" box for that quarter is empty. Then, multiply your total by the distribution fee of 35%. Continuing with the *Mass H-Com* example:

35% x $10.476 million = $3.666 million

$3.666 million is what you would input into your "Distribution Fee" box for that quarter.

STEP 3E. Do the exact same thing you just did in Step 3D. Except, you will use a rate of 20% and you will be calculating the "Other Distributor Costs" for each quarter that needs it.

STEP 3F. Find your "Dom Subtotal" for each quarter (the "Dom" stands for "Domestic"). It represents how much money the domestic distributor owes you for that quarter. The number can be the source of a lot of headache. To explain, I'm going to take it very slowly and spread this step out over two steps.

In any quarter where you computed a Distribution Fee or an Other Distributor Costs, add up all the domestic items for that quarter. Looking at Year 4, Quarter 1 in *Sci-Fi Rom*'s cash flow:

Dom Subtotal = Gross Film Rentals + Home Video Revenue + Pay TV Revenue
              + Distribution Fee + Prints & Advertising + Other Distributor Costs

         = $0.027 mill. + $3.691 mill. + ($1.302 mill.) + ($0.009 mill.) + ($0.744 mill.)

         = $1.663 million

         (on the table it is $1.664 because of Excel's rounding – see the beginning of Appendix B for a reminder)

Go ahead and do this for all your quarters and then move on to the next step.

STEP 3G. Welcome back. Now examine your table. If there are no negative Domestic Subtotals, you are finished with Domestic Subtotals and can move on to "Sales Agent Fee & Costs" in the next step.

If you have negative subtotals, check if your Domestic Subtotals look like those of *Mass H-Com* and *Psych Thrill*. That is, see if you first have two negative subtotals followed by the rest positive. If not, go on back to

Appendix B. If so, leave the two negatives alone, but also add them into the first positive subtotal. Looking at Year 3, Quarter 3 of *Mass H-Com*:

Dom Subtotal = Gross Film Rentals + Home Video Revenue + Pay TV Revenue
                    + Distribution Fee + Prints & Advertising + Other Distributor Costs

= $0.108 mill. + $10.368 mill. + ($3.666 mill.) + ($0.071 mill.) + ($2.095 mill.)

(Remember, parentheses around a number mean it is negative.)

= $4.644 million

You will notice that $4.644 million is not what appears on *Mass H-Com*'s table. This is because I still have to include the two previous quarters' negative Domestic Subtotals. Doing this I get:

$4.644 million + ($0.500 million) + ($0.589 million) = $3.555 million

And this is what appears in *Mass H-Com*'s Year 3, Quarter 3 Domestic Subtotal (actually, $3.554 appears because of rounding, again).

Go ahead and do what I just did for *Mass H-Com* for your film. If the result is positive, go ahead to the next step, though you might want to check Appendix B for some of the reasoning behind what we are doing. If adding the two negatives to the first positive subtotal results in a negative number, go on back to Appendix B.

STEP 3H. Compute each quarter's Sales Agent Fee & Costs. For each quarter with a Foreign Gross amount, multiply the amount by 35% and this becomes the quarter's Sales Agent Fee & Costs. I'll spare you the demonstration.

STEP 3I. For each quarter with a Foreign Gross, add the Foreign Gross to the Sales Agent Fee & Costs (a negative number) to arrive at the quarter's "Foreign Subtotal." This result will always be a positive number.

STEP 3J. Now you are going to calculate each quarter's Producer's Rep Fee. This will depend on how your Domestic Subtotals were treated in Step 3G. Hang with me here. If all of your Domestic Subtotals were positive, simply add together each quarter's Domestic Subtotal and Foreign Subtotal. Then multiply the total by 15%, and your result is the quarter's Producer's Rep Fee.

If your Domestic Subtotals looked like *Mass H-Com*'s and *Psych Thrill*'s, and I did not send you back to the appendix, do the same thing. Except, do not use any of the negative Domestic Subtotals when calculating your fee. For instance, you'll notice no Producer's Rep Fee in Year 3, Quarters 1 & 2 of *Mass H-Com* and *Psych Thrill* — both quarters had negative Domestic Subtotals and no Foreign Subtotals.

If you were sent back to the appendix when computing your Domestic Subtotals, unfortunately, back you go. The details on how to handle the Producer's Rep Fee will be covered there as well.

STEP 3K. If you haven't already done so, for any quarter with a Domestic Subtotal that is negative (or zero) and a Foreign Subtotal that is positive, calculate the quarter's Producer's Rep Fee. Simply multiply the Foreign Subtotal by 15% and ignore the Domestic Subtotal.

STEP 3L. Calculate the "TOTAL" for each quarter. Fortunately, most of the legwork for this step has already been done. For all the quarters in which there is a Negative Cost number, bring that number down as your total. There will be no other revenues or charges during those quarters because all that will be happening is the making of the movie, no distribution for quite some time.

For all the quarters in which there is a Producer's Rep Fee, check if the Fee was calculated using the Domestic Subtotal, the Foreign Subtotal, or both. If it was calculated using both, add together the quarter's Domestic Subtotal, Foreign Subtotal, and Producer's Rep Fee for your "TOTAL." If the fee was only calculated using one Subtotal, take that Subtotal and add it to the Producer's Rep Fee.

For all other quarters, type in a zero dollar amount, $0.000, for the quarter.

STEP 3M. Compute the "RUNNING TOTAL" for all quarters. The Running Total is just that, the running total of how much cash the picture has generated (or lost). Starting with the first quarter, you simply enter the first quarter's Total into this row. For the second quarter Running Total, you add the second quarter's Total to the first quarter's Running Total. For the third quarter Running Total, you add the third quarter's Total to the second quarter's Running Total. For the fourth quarter... You get the picture. Follow along with the sample plan tables to help.

STEP 3N. For each quarter, input the amount returned to investors. This step is actually going to be spread out among the next few steps (I've marked them with *s). Hang in there! This is the final push to the cash flow finish line.

Take your budget and multiply it by 1.2. For example, with *Sci-Fi Rom* this goes:

$$1.2 \text{ x Budget} = 1.2 \text{ x } \$0.500 \text{ million}$$
$$= \$0.600 \text{ million}$$

Now, for the rest of the cash flow steps, remember this number! Let's call it your "Running Priority Total" or RPT for short… What are we calling it? That's right, your "Running Priority Total" or RPT for short.

This is the amount that you must return to investors before you yourself can start collecting money — the amount may change if you choose to pay back your investors differently than I recommend (see the appendix, Step 4D). Appendix B, Steps 3N–3R, have a little more info on the logic of these steps.

STEP 3O. For any quarters where your "TOTAL" is zero or negative, obviously no money is returned to investors. Enter \$0.000 million into "RETURNED TO INVESTORS."

STEP 3P. To help us along with the next several steps, let's refer to this table:

Table 1.7: *Sci-Fi Rom* cash returned to investors ($ millions)								
	YEAR 3			YEAR 4				YEAR 5
	Quarter 2	Quarter 3	Quarter 4	Quarter 1	Quarter 2	Quarter 3	Quarter 4	Quarter 1
TOTAL	$ -	$ 0.057	$ 0.068	$ 1.485	$ 0.178	$ 0.089	$ 0.471	$ 0.054
RUNNING TOTAL	$ (0.500)	$ (0.443)	$ (0.375)	$ 1.110	$ 1.289	$ 1.378	$ 1.849	$ 1.903
RPT	$ 0.600	$ 0.600	$ 0.543	$ 0.475	$ -	$ -	$ -	$ -
RETURNED TO INV.	$ -	$ 0.057	$ 0.068	$ 0.980	$ 0.089	$ 0.045	$ 0.236	$ 0.027
CUMULATIVE RET.	$ -	$ 0.057	$ 0.125	$ 1.105	$ 1.194	$ 1.239	$ 1.474	$ 1.501

Ugly, isn't it? It shows a bottom portion of *Sci-Fi Rom*'s cash flow table with an added row for the Running Priority Total (RPT). I've also crossed out the items not to pay attention to and cut the table short by a bunch of quarters (six to be exact).

If a quarter's "TOTAL" is positive, subtract it from your Running Priority Total (RPT) and check the result. If the result is positive or zero, make the result your new Running Priority Total and go ahead to Step 3Q. This applies to Year 3, Quarters 3 & 4 of the table.

If the result is negative, take the quarter's "TOTAL" and subtract *from it* your RPT. In Year 4, Quarter 1 of our table this comes to:

[Year 4, Quarter 1 "TOTAL"] - RPT = $1.485 million - $0.475 million
= $1.010 million

Next, multiply the result by 0.5. This brings our result to:

0.5 x $1.010 million = $0.505 million

Finally, add it to your RPT:

$0.505 million + RPT = $0.505 million + $0.475 million
= $0.980 million

And this is the amount you enter for the quarter in "RETURNED TO INVESTORS." Wait! Don't go anywhere yet. Here's a summary of what we just did:

Amount Returned = Running Priority Total + 0.5 x (TOTAL - Running Priority Total)

Skip ahead to Step 3R.

STEP 3Q. Okay. You're in the midst of doing each quarter's "RETURNED TO INVESTORS." If you've come here, to Step 3Q, it means that: (1) a quarter's "TOTAL" is positive; AND (2) when you subtracted it from your Running Priority Total (RPT), the result was positive or zero.

So now, enter the quarter's "TOTAL" into your "RETURNED TO INVESTORS" and look at the next quarter, starting all over again with Step 3O. This step applies to Year 3, Quarters 3 & 4 of Step 3P's sample.

STEP 3R. For the rest of the quarters showing a positive "TOTAL," multiply the "TOTAL" by 0.5 and enter the result into "RETURNED TO INVESTORS." This applies to our table's Year 4, Quarters 2 and on (including the rest of the quarters not shown).

STEP 3S. For each quarter calculate a running total of the cash returned to investors (otherwise known on the table as "CUMULATIVE RETURNED"). You do this the exact same way you did "RUNNING TOTAL."

Specifically, in Year 1, Quarter 1 enter the quarter's "RETURNED TO INVESTORS" number into the quarter's "CUMULATIVE RETURNED" number; there should be no cash being returned, because the budget is just beginning to be spent in this quarter. For the next quarter's "CUMULATIVE RETURNED" total, you add Year 1, Quarter 2's "RETURNED TO INVESTORS" to Year 1, Quarter 1's "CUMULATIVE RETURNED" total. Again, there should be no cash returned. For the Year 1, Quarter 3 "CUMULATIVE RETURNED" total, you add Year 1, Quarter 3's "RETURNED TO INVESTORS" number to Year 1, Quarter 2's "CUMULATIVE RETURNED" total.

Keep going for all the quarters and don't worry, eventually the process will become slightly more exciting as you run into quarters where you are not just adding zero amounts to zero amounts. Follow along with the sample tables to help.

STEP 3T. Crap! I'm running out of letters. But that doesn't matter so much because we are… ALMOST DONE! For this step, check your table.

Add up all the numbers across each row and see if the totals match the Income Projections Table. For instance, if you add together the numbers across all the quarters of the "Home Video Revenue" row, the result should match your "Medium Success" "Home Video Revenue" projection from the Income Projections Table. If you add together the numbers across all the quarters of your "Distribution Fee" row, the total should equal the "Distribution Fee" projection from your You-Know-What Table (no, not Pain-in-the-!*#@ Table). You get the picture. Don't bother adding up your Domestic Subtotal and Foreign Subtotal rows; errors in these two rows will be caught via the other checks we do.

Another check to do is to add up the quarters of the "TOTAL" row and make sure the result matches the final quarter's "RUNNING TOTAL." Do the same for the "RETURNED TO INVESTORS" row and match the result to the final quarter's "CUMULATIVE RETURNED" row. Finally, check your final quarter's "RUNNING TOTAL" and see that it matches the Income Projections Table's "NET INVESTOR/PRODUCER PROFIT."

If any of these checks do not match, go back and find the problem so that they do. I wish I had better news, but one of the royal pains in the neck about putting together these financial tables is finding and correcting your errors. Don't feel bad if you spend considerable time doing this; it's all part of the process. If you want to be super-positive about it, just think of it as the magic of moviemaking — isn't it exciting!

STEP 3U. Write the text for this portion of the plan. This is not a section for pumping up how great your film is gonna' do. All you should be doing is describing is how it might play out over time. In fact, the cash flow is pretty much the least certain aspect of the entire plan. Make the text dry, straightforward, and to the point, emphasizing how the actual cash flow (i.e., the actual result in the future) depends on the contracts received. Because you will only be printing the "Medium Success" cash flow scenario, don't forget to mention that the other two scenarios are available on request. Apart from this, not much more to say. The table and its footnotes should do most of the talking. Use the text in the sample plans as a guideline.

STEP 3V. Party!!!

STEP 4. SUM IT ALL UP.
(INVESTOR PROJECTIONS TABLE)

This is where you bring it all together into the bottom line: how much money might be made, if the picture is successful. You will measure this in several different ways and put it together onto a table. The steps here are pretty straight forward, although some of the concepts behind them are not. Good ol' Appendix B will be especially useful here. I'll refer to it as we go. The steps below refer to all three projection scenarios (Low, Medium, and High).

STEP 4A. You know the drill by now. Make a table like table 4 of the sample plans. We'll fill it in as we go.

STEP 4B. Type in the "Total Cash Returned to Investors/Producer." If you look back at your cash flow table and add up all the positive numbers from the TOTAL row, the result will be what you want. It is all the cash returned to the investors and producer before being divvied up between the two.

STEP 4C. Put the budget of the film into "Less Negative Cost."

STEP 4D. Input the investor priority return into "Less Investor Priority Return." "What is the 'investor priority return'?" you ask. Well, it is the amount of money you are going to give back to the investors before splitting any profits and after already paying them back the amount of the budget. For a more in-depth discussion, see Appendix B, but for now, know that it is 20% of the budget of your film (unless you choose another percentage).

STEP 4E. Calculate "Adjusted Investor/Producer Profit." To do so, subtract the negative cost and priority return from the "Total Cash Returned to Investors/Producer." What we are doing is coming up with the total that you are going to split 50/50 with the investors.

STEP 4F. Calculate "Investor 50% Share of Adjusted." Multiply "Adjusted Investor/Producer Profit" by 50%. The result is the investor's share of left-over profit after being paid back the cost of the film and their 20% priority return.

STEP 4G. Next, you will work your way up to the total amount of money paid back to investors. Following along with the table, in the next two rows, type in again the investor priority return and the negative cost. Then, add these amounts to your "Investor 50% Share of Adjusted," and type the result into "TOTAL CASH RETURNED TO INVESTORS." This is how much total cash the investors can expect to receive under your particular scenario during the first three-and-a-quarter years (3.25 years) of release.

What we are doing seems repetitive, but it lays out clearly for the investor how we arrive at the money they are projected to receive. Starting at the top of the table, we take the total cash received and subtract out monies so the 50/50 split can be calculated. Then we take the 50/50 split and add back the same monies in order to show how much money the investor can expect to receive under our scenario. Better to be repetitive and clear than brief and confusing.

STEP 4H. Input "Amount Invested by Investors." This corresponds to the budget of the film (yes, we are typing it into the table a third time). Now, since we have the total cash the investors earned from their investment and the size of their initial investment, we can move on and calculate how much the investors earned from their movie investment.

STEP 4I. The first calculation of what the investors earned will be "NET INVESTOR RETURN." This is just a simple case of subtraction. Subtract

"Amount Invested by Investors" from "TOTAL CASH RETURNED TO INVESTORS." The result is the total amount of money that investors earned from their investment, after getting paid back the cost of the film. Basically, it is the investors' profit.

STEP 4J. This step depends on the type of company you will be setting up for raising, spending, and finally returning the money from your project. In the case of the sample films, an LLC (Limited Liability Company) is assumed — see Appendix B for an introduction to LLCs.

With an LLC, a certain number of equally priced units are up for investment. The total price of all the units can equal the budget of the film. What we will do now is see how much profit each unit would return under our forecast scenario.

The process is very straightforward. Take your "NET INVESTOR RETURN" and divide it by the number of LLC units you have available. In the case of Mass H-Com LLC's "Medium," this comes to:

NET INVESTOR RETURN / Number of LLC units = $2.972 million / 24 units
= $0.124 million

(Remember, "/" means "divided by.")

Then, take it a step further and multiply your answer by 1,000,000. This brings *Mass H-Com*'s amount to $123,817 (the $0.124 million does not end up as $124,000 because the $2.972 million and $0.124 million are rounded numbers). By doing this an investor can see, "Aha. A $50,000 unit would give me back a net return of $123,817."

Finally, input the amount into "NET RETURN PER $50,000 UNIT." The dollar amount of the units ($50,000 in this case) will depend on the size of your LLC.

STEP 4K. Another way of measuring what investors might earn is called "return on investment," or ROI for short. It is very easy to calculate. Simply take the "NET INVESTOR RETURN" and divide it by the "Amount Invested by Investors." For *Mass H-Com* "Medium" this comes to:

NET INVESTOR RETURN / Amount Invested by Investors = $2.972 million / $1.200 million
= 248%

The return on investment (ROI) is a bit like measuring the interest rate on your savings account. If I started the year with $100 in my savings account and ended the year with $110 in the account, I would know that I earned $10, or 10% in interest over the course of the year.

On the table we call the ROI the "*NON-ANNUALIZED* ROI" because unlike the interest in our bank account example, the amount earned here is measured over the course of many years (non–annualized), not just one year (annualized).

STEP 4L. Calculate your film's "ANNUALIZED IRR." IRR means "internal rate of return." I will spread this process out over several steps, but before I do so, check Appendix B for a discussion of what IRR is. Then, prepare yourself, these next several steps have the highest level of math you will need in the whole book, not the most math, but the highest level. Let's go slowly. Remember, you are almost DONE with the Financial Projections chapter. Hang in there!

Examine the portion of your cash flow that says "RETURNED TO INVESTORS." This row of numbers, in addition to the negative cost of your film, will determine the internal rate of return (IRR).

Using Excel, on a separate spreadsheet row, hidden from investors' view, enter your negative cost followed by each of the numbers from the "RETURNED TO INVESTORS" row. Use one box (or "cell") for each number. With *Psych Thrill*'s Medium scenario the new row looks like the following:

Table 1.8: Sample Excel excerpt with columns and row labeled (*Psych Thrill*; $ millions)

	C	D	E	F	G … K	L	M	N	O	P	Q	R	S	T	U	V	W	X
14	-1.500	0.000	0.000	0.000	0.000	0.000	0.000	2.714	0.387	0.193	0.745	0.098	0.162	0.098	0.078	0.078	0.078	0.077

I have labeled the column headings ("C" through "X") and row number ("14") — your column headings and row number will depend on the columns and row where you put your numbers. Also, notice in box/cell C14 that the negative cost must be entered as a negative number. Boxes G14, H14, I14, J14, and K14 were squished together on this page to save space because they are all 0.000's.

STEP 4M. Next, find another empty cell and enter the following:

"= IRR (cell range, estimate)"

What the!? I know, it looks strange. For now, just trust me. For *Psych Thrill* this comes to:

"= IRR (C14:X14, 0.10)"

Include everything but the quotation marks. As you can see with *Psych Thrill*, I am telling Excel to compute an IRR using cells C14 through X14. The 0.1 is my best guess at what the IRR might be — Excel needs your best guess to get started. For your best guess pick a number between 0.01 to 0.11.

STEP 4N. Once Step 4M is done, you will end up with a *quarterly* IRR that you then have to turn into an *annual* IRR. With *Psych Thrill*, my quarterly IRR comes to:

quarterly IRR = IRR(C14:X14, 0.10) = 9.7%

To convert to an annual IRR do the following:

annual IRR = (1+quarterly IRR) x (1+quarterly IRR) x (1+quarterly IRR) x (1+quarterly IRR) – 1

If I substitute *Psych Thrill* numbers and step through the calculations it looks like:

= (1 + 9.7%) x (1 + 9.7%) x (1 + 9.7%) x (1 + 9.7%) – 1
= (1 + 0.097) x (1 + 0.097) x (1 + 0.097) x (1 + 0.097) – 1
= 1.097 x 1.097 x 1.097 x 1.097 – 1
= 44.8%

And there you go. You have your annual IRR (it comes out as 44.9% on the table because of rounding issues). On the table it is listed as "ANNUALIZED IRR."

STEP 4O. Just to firm up these wacky concepts we've discussed so far, do me a favor and read Appendix B's discussion of IRR versus ROI. Then move on to the next step.

STEP 4P. Examine your "ANNUALIZED IRR" for the "Medium Success" scenario. This is what you and potential investors will focus on as your forecasted IRR. While there are no hard-and-fast rules, ideally, it should fall in the 30%–50% range. This will put the investors' focus more on your filmmaking team's passion, integrity, and knowledge, than on returns that are too high or too low. Of course, any informed investor will know that the numbers are pretty meaningless as a way of predicting results. However, investors can't help but be distracted when it comes to returns that are too high or too low.

If your "Medium Success" IRR falls just outside of this range, either on the high side or the low side, I wouldn't worry too much. As low as 25% is okay and as high as 55% is okay. However, any further outside and you want to reconsider some of the assumptions in your Comparable Films Table or the size of your film's budget. As for your "High Success" and "Low Success" scenarios, it is okay for them to fall well outside the 30%–50% range. They are essentially designed to do so.

Appendix B will help you more if your returns are out of range.

STEP 4Q. Get out the champagne bottles! We're almost finished with the financials. In preparation for writing the text of this section, you will need to calculate what is called an "ROI multiple," or "return on investment multiple." It sounds scarier than it is.

Take your ROI, change it into a decimal, and add 1.0 to it. For instance, if your "NON-ANNUALIZED ROI" is 178%, first change it to 1.78. Then add 1.0 to it to get 2.78. Finally, add the letter "x" to it, 2.78x, and *shazam*! You've got your ROI multiple.

Investors sometimes like to discuss returns in terms of "multiples." For instance if your investment returned 5x, that means you might have invested $100,000 and received back $500,000. This is before your subtract out your initial $100,000 investment for a net return of $400,000.

In our 2.78x example, a $100,000 investment would have returned a total of $278,000. Do not confuse your ROI multiple with your ROI, they are different. See the appendix for why.

STEP 4R. FINALLY! School's out! Write the text for your investor projections. Follow the format and tone of the sample plans. As with the cash flow text, stay low key and to the point. The numbers you describe in the text will speak for themselves. You will notice in the sample plans how I incorporated the calculations from Step 4Q into the text. ROI can be a broad-ranging term, but including the multiple clarifies exactly the definition of ROI you are using.

STEP 4S. Great work! Look at all you've done. Really look at it. That is awesome. The hardest part is over. Congratulations!

SAMPLE FINANCIAL PROJECTIONS SECTIONS

FINANCIAL PROJECTIONS[1]
(*SCI-FI ROM*)

The box office gross for a single film is absolutely unpredictable, regardless of financial model used or the film's budget, genre, cast, time frame, etc. It is box office gross that drives the financial success or failure of a film.

domestic distributor advances

When a domestic distributor takes a keen interest in a film, it sometimes advances future revenues to the producer prior to the commencement of distribution. The advance can be in return for a buyout of all future revenues or only a portion. Public information on the exact details of such arrangements is nonexistent and most often limited to ballpark estimates of advance sizes. As a result, profitability estimates for comparable films and projections for *Sci-Fi Rom* assume no domestic distributor advances and assume distribution terms less favorable than most producers of a successful film would face at the outset of distribution.

comparable films

Table 1 estimates the profitability of certain successful films during the 3.25-year period immediately following the commencement of domestic theatrical release. Their commonalities are as follows:

> > never achieved beyond 600 screens in domestic (U.S. and Canadian) theatrical release.
> > opened on fewer than 15 screens domestically, except for *Pic E* which opened on 26.
> > budgets were at $5 million or less.
> > released domestically some time between 2000 – 2004.

---

[1] Taxation in the case of an LLC is pass-through, and thus, all estimates and projections of profits and returns exclude taxes.

These films illustrate the profit potential of a film such as *Sci-Fi Rom* for two reasons. Each one is a thought-provoking, character-driven piece with an upbeat tone and no significantly name actors. As a result, their audiences would be the likely audiences for *Sci-Fi Rom*. Additionally, these films demonstrate that even domestic releases that never go beyond a 600-screen domestic release can be profitable. Wider releases of films in this budget range do sometimes occur, often generating significant revenue. However, *Sci-Fi Rom* need not depend on such a release to turn an appreciable profit. Regarding foreign revenue, it is an estimate of the revenue that might have been generated by each picture had it first been sold under current foreign marketplace conditions. Foreign revenue is not broken out for each picture because foreign rights for successful independent films are often sold to a territory in multiple formats at one time. For example, the Argentinian rights to a film may consist of theatrical, DVD/home video, TV, and pay TV releases of it. Figures are readily available for distribution prices by territory, but to list each territory and/or break the figures down further into their component formats is neither practical nor necessary.

income projections

Table 2 forecasts three profitability scenarios for *Sci-Fi Rom*. The comparable films table averages illustrate the upper end of revenue potential for *Sci-Fi Rom* because the majority of the comparable films benefited from critical acclaim and, in some cases, awards. Such success is vital to *Sci-Fi Rom* achieving box office and business of the same caliber as its comparable films. Due to the fact that *Sci-Fi Rom* is experimental in nature (the piece is set in one location, shot in one day, and deals with XXXXXXXXX), the degree of audience and critical acceptance of it becomes exceptionally difficult to predict. As a result, its revenue projections are greatly scaled back from the comparable films table averages. The "Medium Success" scenario is a successful outcome based on 50% reductions to the box office and home video comparable films table averages (domestic pay TV revenues feed from the box office projection using a licensing percentage). The "Low Success" scenario is constructed on the fulfillment of an investor priority return of 20%, and "High Success" is a best-case scenario derived by adjusting the domestic box office and home video revenues upward in amounts equal to the difference between their "Medium" and "Low" numbers. According to the Financing section, the percentage of return recouped by investors after restoration of their initial investment and before profits are split evenly with Sci-Fi Rom LLC is to be 20% (a.k.a. the "priority return"). All projections in table 2 (domestic, foreign, and otherwise) should be taken as estimations only. There is no guarantee that these projections will actually be met by the film.

cash flow projections

Table 3 predicts the timing of sources and uses of cash from the "Medium Success" scenario on the income table and how that cash will flow back to investors. Cash flow projections for the "High" and "Low" scenarios are available on request and closely follow the timing of the printed scenario, only with different amounts. It cannot be overemphasized that the actual timing and structure of income will depend on marketplace conditions and contracts with distributors and any foreign sales agent and producer's rep of the film. There is no guarantee that such contracts will be obtained or as to what their terms will be. The figures therein are not a guarantee of actual performance.

investor projections

Table 4 forecasts the projected return to investors over 5.75 years under the three profitability scenarios highlighted in the income projections. "High Success" indicates a non-annualized return on investment (ROI) of 441% (or an ROI multiple of 5.41x) and an annualized internal rate of return (IRR) of 62.4%. The IRR derives directly from the corresponding cash flow scenario. "Medium Success" yields a 231% ROI (3.31x) and an IRR of 40.9% while "Low Success" meets the priority return to investors with an ROI of 20% (1.20x) and an IRR of 5.2%. Although successful films can generate revenues for many years and sometimes decades after their release, the vast majority of revenues (often nearly 100%) are returned within 3.25 years of the release date. As with table 3, table 4 is for reference only, and the figures therein are not a guarantee of actual performance.

Table 1: Successful Films Comparable to *Sci-Fi Rom*								
	Pic A	*Pic B*	*Pic C*	*Pic D*	*Pic E*	*Pic F*	*Pic G*	Average
DOMESTIC (U.S.)[1]								
Box Office Gross	$2.4	$5.7	$4.2	$2.9	$7.0	$4.4	$9.2	$5.1
Less Exhibitor Share[2]	$1.1	$2.7	$1.9	$1.4	$3.3	$2.1	$4.1	$2.4
Gross Film Rentals	$1.3	$3.1	$2.2	$1.5	$3.8	$2.4	$5.1	$2.8
Home Video Revenue	$2.0	$8.1	$6.6	$6.1	$17.9	$21.1	$9.9	$10.3
Pay TV Revenue	$1.1	$2.6	$1.8	$1.2	$1.8	$1.9	$2.5	$1.9
Gross Ancillary Revenue	$3.1	$10.6	$8.5	$7.3	$19.7	$23.0	$12.5	$12.1
Domestic Gross[3]	$4.4	$13.7	$10.7	$8.8	$23.5	$25.4	$17.5	$14.9
Less Distribution Fee (35%)	$1.5	$4.8	$3.7	$3.1	$8.2	$8.9	$6.1	$5.2
Less Prints & Advertising[4]	$0.5	$1.3	$1.1	$0.5	$1.2	$0.1	$1.8	$0.9
Less Other Distributor Costs[5]	$0.9	$2.7	$2.1	$1.8	$4.7	$5.1	$3.5	$3.0
Net Domestic Receipts	$1.5	$4.8	$3.7	$3.4	$9.4	$11.3	$6.1	$5.7
FOREIGN								
Foreign Gross[6]	$1.2	$1.2	$2.3	$1.2	$1.2	$2.3	$2.3	$1.6
Less Sales Agent Fee & Expenses (35%)[7]	$0.4	$0.4	$0.8	$0.4	$0.4	$0.8	$0.8	$0.6
Net Foreign Receipts	$0.8	$0.8	$1.5	$0.8	$0.8	$1.5	$1.5	$1.1
TOTAL								
TOTAL PRODUCER'S REP GROSS[8]	$2.2	$5.6	$5.2	$4.2	$10.1	$12.8	$7.6	$6.8
Less Producer's Rep Fee (15%)	$0.3	$0.8	$0.8	$0.6	$1.5	$1.9	$1.1	$1.0
TOTAL PRODUCER'S GROSS	$1.9	$4.7	$4.4	$3.6	$8.6	$10.9	$6.4	$5.8
Less Negative Cost[9]	$0.3	$0.5	$2.0	$0.2	$1.0	$2.0	$1.5	$1.1
NET INVESTOR/PRODUCER PROFIT	$1.6	$4.2	$2.4	$3.4	$7.6	$8.9	$4.9	$4.7

NOTES:

*This table estimates the profitability of past films and is in no manner a guarantee of future performance.

*Amounts in millions of dollars and convey revenues collected during the 3.25 years immediately after the domestic theatrical release date.

*All raw data except for 'Other Distributor Costs' and 'Foreign Gross' is provided by Baseline StudioSystems.

*To allow for uniform comparisons, distribution arrangements are assumed the same for each film; actual fee and revenue-sharing arrangements are privately held data.

*Totals from films first released internationally are modified as if first released domestically.

*'Foreign Gross' is calculated from "The Going Rate," American Film Market 2004, *The Hollywood Reporter*, Nov. 2-10, 2004; Canada excluded.

*Totals may not add due to rounding.

FOOTNOTES:

1: DOMESTIC - For 'Box Office Gross' and 'Prints & Advertising,' domestic refers to U.S. & Canada, for all other data points it refers only to U.S.

2: Exhibitor Share - Theater owners' share of the box office revenue.

3: Domestic Gross - Sum of 'Gross Film Rentals' and 'Gross Ancillary Revenue.'

4: Prints & Advertising (P&A) - Cost of the marketing campaign and copies made of the original negative ('prints') for the theatrical release.

5: Other Distributor Costs - Expenses outside of P&A for which the distributor is reimbursed such as residuals and DVD manufacturing, marketing, and distribution costs.

6: Foreign Gross - Canada excluded; money received from advances by foreign distributors for the right to distribute in all formats; per territory data available.

7: Sales Agent - Markets to and collects advances from foreign distributors. Residuals are included as part of expenses.

8: Producer's Rep - Seeks out and negotiates domestic distribution and sales agent agreements.

9: Negative Cost - Costs incurred to shoot the film and create the negative off of which all copies of the film are made; also known as the 'budget' of the film.

Table 2: Projected Income for *Sci-Fi Rom*			
	Low Success	Medium Success	High Success
DOMESTIC (U.S.)[1]			
Box Office Gross	$0.5	$2.6	$4.6
Less Exhibitor Share (47%)	$0.2	$1.2	$2.2
Gross Film Rentals	$0.3	$1.4	$2.5
Home Video Revenue	$0.9	$5.1	$9.3
Pay TV Revenue	$0.2	$1.0	$1.8
Gross Ancillary Revenue	$1.1	$6.1	$11.1
Domestic Gross	$1.4	$7.5	$13.6
Less Distribution Fee (35%)	$0.5	$2.6	$4.8
Less Prints & Advertising	$0.1	$0.5	$0.8
Less Other Distributor Costs	$0.3	$1.5	$2.7
Net Domestic Receipts	$0.5	$2.9	$5.3

FOREIGN			
Foreign Gross	$0.3	$0.4	$0.6
Less Sales Agent Fee & Expenses (35%)	$0.1	$0.1	$0.2
Net Foreign Receipts	$0.2	$0.3	$0.4

TOTAL			
TOTAL PRODUCER'S REP GROSS	$0.7	$3.2	$5.7
Less Producer's Rep Fee (15%)	$0.1	$0.5	$0.8
TOTAL PRODUCER'S GROSS	$0.6	$2.7	$4.8
Less Negative Cost	$0.5	$0.5	$0.5
NET INVESTOR/PRODUCER PROFIT	$0.1	$2.2	$4.3

NOTES:

*This table reflects estimates of future performance that are in no manner a guarantee of future performance.

*Amounts in millions of dollars and convey revenues collected during the 3.25 years immediately after the domestic theatrical release date.

*Distribution arrangements follow those of the comparable films table; actual fee and revenue-sharing arrangements will vary depending on parties involved, desirability of the film, and market conditions.

*Foreign Gross figures based upon "The Going Rate," American Film Market 2004, *The Hollywood Reporter*, Nov. 2-10, 2004; Canada excluded.

*Totals may not add due to rounding.

FOOTNOTES:

1: DOMESTIC - For 'Box Office Gross' and 'Prints & Advertising,' domestic refers to U.S. & Canada, for all other data points it refers only to U.S.

Table 3: Projected Cash Flow for Sci-Fi Rom LLC (Medium)

	YEAR 1				YEAR 2				YEAR 3			
	Quarter 1	Quarter 2	Quarter 3	Quarter 4	Quarter 1	Quarter 2	Quarter 3	Quarter 4	Quarter 1	Quarter 2	Quarter 3	Quarter 4
Sci-Fi Rom												
Negative Cost[1]	$ (0.170)	$ (0.135)	$ (0.130)	$ (0.065)								
Gross Film Rentals											$ 0.616	$ 0.725
Home Video Revenue												
Pay TV Revenue												
Distribution Fee											$ (0.215)	$ (0.254)
Prints & Advertising											$ (0.209)	$ (0.247)
Other Distributor Costs											$ (0.123)	$ (0.145)
Dom Subtotal											$ *0.068*	$ *0.080*
Foreign Gross												
Sales Agent Fee & Costs												
Frgn Subtotal												
Producer's Rep Fee											$ *(0.010)*	$ *(0.012)*
TOTAL[2]	$ (0.170)	$ (0.135)	$ (0.130)	$ (0.065)	$ -	$ -	$ -	$ -	$ -	$ -	$ 0.057	$ 0.068
RUNNING TOTAL	$ (0.170)	$ (0.305)	$ (0.435)	$ (0.500)	$ (0.500)	$ (0.500)	$ (0.500)	$ (0.500)	$ (0.500)	$ (0.500)	$ (0.443)	$ (0.375)
RETURNED TO INVESTORS[3]	$ -	$ -	$ -	$ -	$ -	$ -	$ -	$ -	$ -	$ -	$ 0.057	$ 0.068
CUMULATIVE RETURNED	$ -	$ -	$ -	$ -	$ -	$ -	$ -	$ -	$ -	$ -	$ 0.057	$ 0.125

NOTES:
*This table reflects estimates of the timing and structure of income returned to investors and is in no manner a guarantee of the amounts or timing of such returns. Actual timing and structure depend on market conditions and contracts with involved parties (e.g., distributors, sales agent, producer's rep, etc.).
*Amounts in millions of dollars.
*Theatrical distribution is assumed to commence 1.5 years after the completion of postproduction. Actual release date will be determined by the distributor.
*A small amount of ancillary revenue is likely to occur beyond the film's 3.25-year revenue window with the agreed split between producer and investors still in effect.
*Totals may not add due to rounding.

FOOTNOTES:
1: Negative Cost - Reflects timing of the negative cost and is to take 6.5 weeks preproduction, 1 day principal photography, and 10.5 months postproduction.
2: Total - Sum of 'Negative Cost,' 'Dom Subtotal,' 'Frgn Subtotal,' and 'Producer's Rep Fee.'
3: Returned to Investors - Cash from 'Total' row returned to investors. Assumes 120% of initial investment returned, then remaining cash split 50/50 with Sci-Fi Rom LLC.

Table 3 (cont'd): Projected Cash Flow for Sci-Fi Rom LLC (Medium)

	YEAR 4				YEAR 5				YEAR 6		
	Quarter 1	Quarter 2	Quarter 3	Quarter 4	Quarter 1	Quarter 2	Quarter 3	Quarter 4	Quarter 1	Quarter2	Quarter 3
Sci-Fi Rom											
Negative Cost[1]											
Gross Film Rentals	$ 0.027	$ 0.282	$ 0.141	$ 0.141	$ 0.141	$ 0.141	$ 0.141	$ 0.113	$ 0.113	$ 0.113	$ 0.110
Home Video Revenue	$ 3.691										
Pay TV Revenue				$ 0.998							
Distribution Fee	$ (1.302)	$ (0.099)	$ (0.049)	$ (0.399)	$ (0.049)	$ (0.049)	$ (0.049)	$ (0.039)	$ (0.039)	$ (0.039)	$ (0.039)
Prints & Advertising	$ (0.009)										
Other Distributor Costs	$ (0.744)	$ (0.056)	$ (0.028)	$ (0.228)	$ (0.028)	$ (0.028)	$ (0.028)	$ (0.023)	$ (0.023)	$ (0.023)	$ (0.022)
Dom Subtotal	$ 1.664	$ 0.127	$ 0.063	$ 0.513	$ 0.063	$ 0.063	$ 0.063	$ 0.051	$ 0.051	$ 0.051	$ 0.050
Foreign Gross	$ 0.128	$ 0.128	$ 0.064	$ 0.064		$ 0.043					
Sales Agent Fee & Costs	$ (0.045)	$ (0.045)	$ (0.022)	$ (0.022)		$ (0.015)					
Frgn Subtotal	$ 0.083	$ 0.083	$ 0.042	$ 0.042		$ 0.028					
Producer's Rep Fee	$ (0.262)	$ (0.031)	$ (0.016)	$ (0.083)	$ (0.010)	$ (0.014)	$ (0.010)	$ (0.008)	$ (0.008)	$ (0.008)	$ (0.007)
TOTAL[2]	$ 1.485	$ 0.178	$ 0.089	$ 0.471	$ 0.054	$ 0.077	$ 0.054	$ 0.043	$ 0.043	$ 0.043	$ 0.042
RUNNING TOTAL	$ 1.110	$ 1.289	$ 1.378	$ 1.849	$ 1.903	$ 1.980	$ 2.034	$ 2.077	$ 2.120	$ 2.164	$ 2.206
RETURNED TO INVESTORS[3]	$ 0.980	$ 0.089	$ 0.045	$ 0.236	$ 0.027	$ 0.039	$ 0.027	$ 0.022	$ 0.022	$ 0.022	$ 0.021
CUMULATIVE RETURNED	$ 1.105	$ 1.194	$ 1.239	$ 1.474	$ 1.501	$ 1.540	$ 1.567	$ 1.589	$ 1.610	$ 1.632	$ 1.653

Table 4: Projected Investor Returns from Sci-Fi Rom LLC			
	Low Success	Medium Success	High Success
Total Cash Returned to Investors/Producer[1]	$0.6	$2.7	$4.8
Less Negative Cost	$0.5	$0.5	$0.5
Less Investor Priority Return[2]	$0.1	$0.1	$0.1
Adjusted Investor/Producer Profit	$0.0	$2.1	$4.2
Investor 50% Share of Adjusted	$0.0	$1.1	$2.1
Plus Investor Priority Return	$0.1	$0.1	$0.1
Plus Negative Cost	$0.5	$0.5	$0.5
TOTAL CASH RETURNED TO INVESTORS	$0.6	$1.7	$2.7
Amount Invested by Investors	$0.5	$0.5	$0.5
NET INVESTOR RETURN[3]	$0.1	$1.2	$2.2
NET RETURN PER $25,000 UNIT[4]	$ 5,000	$ 57,644	$ 110,222
NON-ANNUALIZED ROI[5]	20%	231%	441%
ANNUALIZED IRR[6]	5.2%	40.9%	62.4%

NOTES:

*This table reflects estimates of future returns to investors and is in no way a guarantee of future returns to investors.

*Totals may not add due to rounding.

FOOTNOTES:

1: Total Cash Ret. to Inv./Producer - All revenues generated by Sci-Fi Rom LLC prior to disbursement to investors (i.e., sum of all positive 'TOTAL' amounts from cash flow).

2: Investor Priority Return - 20% of the Negative Cost that is returned to investors after repayment of the Negative Cost but before profits are split with Sci-Fi Rom LLC.

3: Net Investor Return - The total cash returned to investors minus the amount invested by investors (i.e., minus the Negative Cost).

4: Net Return per $25,000 unit - The return earned on a single LLC unit beyond the initial investment amount, as expressed in $1 increments instead of $1,000,000 increments.

5: Non-annualized ROI - The return on investment as calculated by dividing the Net Investor Return by the Negative Cost (i.e., by the 'Amount Invested by Investors').

6: Annualized IRR (Internal Rate of Return) - The yearly rate of return on the initial investment given the timing of income in the projected cash flow. Actual timing and structure of income depend on market conditions and contracts with involved parties (e.g., distributors, sales agent, producer's rep, etc.) and will affect the annualized IRR.

FINANCIAL PROJECTIONS[1]
(*MASS H-COM*)

The box office gross for a single film is absolutely unpredictable, regardless of financial model used or the film's budget, genre, cast, time frame, etc. It is box office gross that drives the financial success or failure of a film.

domestic distributor advances
When a domestic distributor takes a keen interest in a film, it sometimes advances future revenues to the producer prior to the commencement of distribution. The advance can be in return for a buyout of all future revenues or only a portion. Public information on the exact details of such arrangements is nonexistent and most often limited to ballpark estimates of advance sizes. As a result, profitability estimates for comparable films and projections for *Mass H-Com* assume no domestic distributor advances and assume distribution terms less favorable than most producers of a successful film would face at the outset of distribution.

comparable films
Table 1 estimates the profitability of certain successful films during the 3.25-year period immediately following the commencement of domestic theatrical release. Their commonalities are as follows:
> rated R or NC-17.
> never achieved beyond 600 screens in domestic (U.S. and Canadian) theatrical release.
> opened on fewer than 15 screens domestically, except for *Pic E* which opened on 26.
> budgets were at $5 million or less.
> released domestically some time between 2000 – 2004.

These films illustrate the profit potential of a film such as *Mass H-Com* for two reasons. Although most of these films were helped in the box office by awards, *Mass H-Com* arguably appeals to a larger audience initially than each of these films did at the height of its popularity. *Pic Q* and *Pic N* are possible exceptions, as these films were immensely popular. Secondly, we see that films never reaching beyond a 600-screen domestic release can be profitable. *Pic Q*,

---

[1] Taxation in the case of an LLC is pass-through, and thus, all estimates and projections of profits and returns exclude taxes.

despite being a documentary, and *Pic N* illustrate the upper end of revenue potential films with a limited opening and overall release can achieve. There are other films that share the characteristics above but have achieved a much wider overall release and thus, profitability. However, listing them on these tables would excessively skew comparable film profitability. Regarding foreign revenue, it is an estimate of the revenue that might have been generated by each picture had it first been sold under current foreign marketplace conditions. Foreign revenue is not broken out for each picture because foreign rights for successful independent films are often sold to a territory in multiple formats at one time. For example, the Argentinian rights to a film may consist of theatrical, DVD/home video, TV, and pay TV releases of it. Figures are readily available for distribution prices by territory, but to list each territory and/or break the figures down further into their component formats is neither practical nor necessary.

income projections

Table 2 forecasts three profitability scenarios for *Mass H-Com*. *Mass H-Com* has a potentially wide appeal. At the same time, it has an exceptionally low budget due to the cost savings of shooting in the director's hometown. These two factors, very large target audience and very low negative cost, combine to produce large returns even when using projections, such as the "Medium Success" scenario, considered conservative in the context of the comparable films table. The "Medium Success" scenario is a successful outcome corresponding to the comparable films table average box office and home video revenues (domestic pay TV revenues feed from the box office projection using a licensing percentage). The "Low Success" scenario is constructed with the fulfillment of an investor priority return of 20%, and "High Success" is a best-case scenario derived by adjusting the domestic box office and home video revenues upward in amounts equal to the difference between their "Medium" and "Low" numbers. In the "High" scenario the home video gross is capped at the highest home video gross from the comparable films table; and according to the Financing section, the percentage of return recouped by investors after restoration of their initial investment and before profits are split evenly with Mass H-Com LLC is to be 20% (a.k.a. the "priority return"). All projections in table 2 (domestic, foreign, and otherwise) should be taken as estimations only. There is no guarantee that these projections will actually be met by the film.

cash flow projections

Table 3 predicts the timing of sources and uses of cash from the "Medium Success" scenario on the income table and how that cash will flow back to investors. Cash flow projections for the "High" and "Low" scenarios are available on request and closely follow the timing of the printed scenario, only with different amounts. It cannot be overemphasized that the actual timing and structure of income will depend on marketplace conditions and contracts with distributors and any foreign sales agent and producer's rep of the film. There is no guarantee that such contracts will be obtained or as to what their terms will be. The figures therein are not a guarantee of actual performance.

investor projections

Table 4 forecasts the projected return to investors over 5.25 years under the three profitability scenarios highlighted in the income projections. "High Success" indicates a non-annualized return on investment (ROI) of 468% (or an ROI multiple of 5.68x) and an annualized internal rate of return (IRR) of 75.9%. The IRR derives directly from the corresponding cash flow scenario. "Medium Success" yields a 248% ROI (3.48x) and an IRR of 50.1%, while "Low Success" meets the priority return to investors with an ROI of 20% (1.20x) and an IRR of 5.9%. Although successful films can generate revenues for many years and sometimes decades after their release, the vast majority of revenues (often nearly 100%) are returned within 3.25 years of the release date. As with table 3, table 4 is for reference only, and the figures therein are not a guarantee of actual performance.

Table 1: Successful Films Comparable to *Mass H-Com*

	Pic B	Pic S	Pic Q	Pic E	Pic M	Pic R	Pic N	Pic G	Pic K	Average
DOMESTIC (U.S.)[1]										
Box Office Gross	$5.7	$3.8	$21.2	$7.0	$8.8	$5.3	$25.5	$9.2	$3.6	$10.0
Less Exhibitor Share[2]	$2.7	$1.8	$9.9	$3.3	$4.1	$2.5	$11.9	$4.1	$1.7	$4.6
Gross Film Rentals	$3.1	$2.0	$11.4	$3.8	$4.7	$2.8	$13.7	$5.1	$1.9	$5.4
Home Video Revenue	$8.1	$4.6	$17.9	$17.9	$26.8	$9.9	$15.2	$9.9	$19.2	$14.4
Pay TV Revenue	$2.6	$1.0	$5.5	$1.8	$2.2	$1.3	$6.5	$2.5	$0.9	$2.7
Gross Ancillary Revenue	$10.6	$5.6	$23.3	$19.7	$29.1	$11.2	$21.8	$12.5	$20.1	$17.1
Domestic Gross[3]	$13.7	$7.7	$34.7	$23.5	$33.8	$14.1	$35.4	$17.5	$22.0	$22.5
Less Distribution Fee (35%)	$4.8	$2.7	$12.1	$8.2	$11.8	$4.9	$12.4	$6.1	$7.7	$7.9
Less Prints & Advertising[4]	$1.3	$1.4	$1.7	$1.2	$5.6	$2.3	$12.8	$1.8	$2.0	$3.3
Less Other Distributor Costs[5]	$2.7	$1.5	$6.9	$4.7	$6.8	$2.8	$7.1	$3.5	$4.4	$4.5
Net Domestic Receipts	$4.8	$2.0	$13.9	$9.4	$9.6	$4.1	$3.1	$6.1	$7.9	$6.8
FOREIGN										
Foreign Gross[6]	$1.2	$1.2	$2.3	$1.2	$2.3	$4.7	$4.7	$2.3	$4.7	$2.7
Less Sales Agent Fee & Expenses (35%)[7]	$0.4	$0.4	$0.8	$0.4	$0.8	$1.6	$1.6	$0.8	$1.6	$1.0
Net Foreign Receipts	$0.8	$0.8	$1.5	$0.8	$1.5	$3.1	$3.1	$1.5	$3.1	$1.8
TOTAL										
TOTAL PRODUCER'S REP GROSS[8]	$5.6	$2.8	$15.4	$10.1	$11.1	$7.1	$6.2	$7.6	$11.0	$8.5
Less Producer's Rep Fee (15%)	$0.8	$0.4	$2.3	$1.5	$1.7	$1.1	$0.9	$1.1	$1.6	$1.3
TOTAL PRODUCER'S GROSS	$4.7	$2.4	$13.1	$8.6	$9.4	$6.1	$5.3	$6.4	$9.3	$7.3
Less Negative Cost[9]	$0.5	$0.3	$3.0	$1.0	$3.0	$5.0	$5.0	$1.5	$4.5	$2.6
NET INVESTOR/PRODUCER PROFIT	$4.2	$2.1	$10.1	$7.6	$6.4	$1.1	$0.3	$4.9	$4.8	$4.6

NOTES:

*This table estimates the profitability of past films and is in no manner a guarantee of future performance.

*Amounts in millions of dollars and convey revenues collected during the 3.25 years immediately after the domestic theatrical release date.

*All raw data except for 'Other Distributor Costs' and 'Foreign Gross' is provided by Baseline StudioSystems.

*To allow for uniform comparisons, distribution arrangements are assumed the same for each film; actual fee and revenue-sharing arrangements are privately held data.

*Totals from films first released internationally are modified as if first released domestically.

*'Foreign Gross' is calculated from "'The Going Rate," American Film Market 2004, *The Hollywood Reporter*, Nov. 2-10, 2004; Canada excluded.

*Totals may not add due to rounding.

FOOTNOTES:

1: DOMESTIC - For 'Box Office Gross' and 'Prints & Advertising,' domestic refers to U.S. & Canada, for all other data points it refers only to U.S.

2: Exhibitor Share - Theater owners' share of the box office revenue.

3: Domestic Gross - Sum of 'Gross Film Rentals' and 'Gross Ancillary Revenue.'

4: Prints & Advertising (P&A) - Cost of the marketing campaign and copies made of the original negative ('prints') for the theatrical release.

5: Other Distributor Costs - Expenses outside of P&A for which the distributor is reimbursed such as residuals and DVD manufacturing, marketing, and distribution costs.

6: Foreign Gross - Canada excluded; money received from advances by foreign distributors for the right to distribute in all formats; per territory data available.

7: Sales Agent - Markets to and collects advances from foreign distributors. Residuals are included as part of expenses.

8: Producer's Rep - Seeks out and negotiates domestic distribution and sales agent agreements.

9: Negative Cost - Costs incurred to shoot the film and create the negative off of which all copies of the film are made; also known as the 'budget' of the film.

Table 2: Projected Income for *Mass H-Com*	Low Success	Medium Success	High Success
DOMESTIC (U.S.)[1]			
Box Office Gross	$1.0	$10.0	$19.1
Less Exhibitor Share (46%)	$0.5	$4.6	$8.8
Gross Film Rentals	**$0.5**	**$5.4**	**$10.2**
Home Video Revenue	$1.4	$14.4	$26.8
Pay TV Revenue	$0.3	$2.8	$5.3
Gross Ancillary Revenue	**$1.8**	**$17.2**	**$32.2**
Domestic Gross	**$2.3**	**$22.6**	**$42.4**
Less Distribution Fee (35%)	$0.8	$7.9	$14.8
Less Prints & Advertising	$0.4	$3.5	$6.7
Less Other Distributor Costs	$0.5	$4.5	$8.5
Net Domestic Receipts	**$0.7**	**$6.6**	**$12.4**

FOREIGN			
Foreign Gross	**$1.6**	**$2.3**	**$3.1**
Less Sales Agent Fee & Expenses (35%)	$0.5	$0.8	$1.1
Net Foreign Receipts	**$1.0**	**$1.5**	**$2.0**

TOTAL			
TOTAL PRODUCER'S REP GROSS	**$1.7**	**$8.1**	**$14.3**
Less Producer's Rep Fee (15%)	$0.3	$1.2	$2.2
TOTAL PRODUCER'S GROSS	**$1.4**	**$6.9**	**$12.2**
Less Negative Cost	$1.2	$1.2	$1.2
NET INVESTOR/PRODUCER PROFIT	**$0.2**	**$5.7**	**$11.0**

NOTES:

*This table reflects estimates of future performance that are in no manner a guarantee of future performance.

*Amounts in millions of dollars and convey revenues collected during the 3.25 years immediately after the domestic theatrical release date.

*Distribution arrangements follow those of the comparable films table; actual fee and revenue-sharing arrangements will vary depending on parties involved, desirability of the film, and market conditions.

*Foreign Gross figures based upon "The Going Rate," American Film Market 2004, *The Hollywood Reporter*, Nov. 2-10, 2004; Canada excluded.

*Totals may not add due to rounding.

FOOTNOTES:

1: DOMESTIC - For 'Box Office Gross' and 'Prints & Advertising,' domestic refers to U.S. & Canada, for all other data points it refers only to U.S.

Table 3: Projected Cash Flow for Mass H-Com LLC (Medium)

Mass H-Com	YEAR 1				YEAR 2				YEAR 3			
	Quarter 1	Quarter 2	Quarter 3	Quarter 4	Quarter 1	Quarter 2	Quarter 3	Quarter 4	Quarter 1	Quarter 2	Quarter 3	Quarter 4
Negative Cost[1]	$ (0.840)	$ (0.120)	$ (0.120)	$ (0.120)								
Gross Film Rentals									$ 2.422	$ 2.853	$ 0.108	
Home Video Revenue											$ 10.368	$ 0.792
Pay TV Revenue												
Distribution Fee									$ (0.848)	$ (0.999)	$ (3.666)	$ (0.277)
Prints & Advertising									$ (1.590)	$ (1.873)	$ (0.071)	
Other Distributor Costs									$ (0.484)	$ (0.571)	$ (2.095)	$ (0.158)
Dom Subtotal[2]									$ (0.500)	$ (0.589)	$ 3.554	$ 0.356
Foreign Gross											$ 0.691	$ 0.691
Sales Agent Fee & Costs											$ (0.242)	$ (0.242)
Frgn Subtotal											$ 0.449	$ 0.449
Producer's Rep Fee											$ (0.600)	$ (0.121)
TOTAL[3]	$ (0.840)	$ (0.120)	$ (0.120)	$ (0.120)	$ -	$ -	$ -	$ -	$ -	$ -	$ 3.402	$ 0.685
RUNNING TOTAL	$ (0.840)	$ (0.960)	$ (1.080)	$ (1.200)	$ (1.200)	$ (1.200)	$ (1.200)	$ (1.200)	$ (1.200)	$ (1.200)	$ 2.202	$ 2.887
RETURNED TO INVESTORS[4]	$ -	$ -	$ -	$ -	$ -	$ -	$ -	$ -	$ -	$ -	$ 2.421	$ 0.342
CUMULATIVE RETURNED	$ -	$ -	$ -	$ -	$ -	$ -	$ -	$ -	$ -	$ -	$ 2.421	$ 2.763

NOTES:

*This table reflects estimates of the timing and structure of income returned to investors and is in no manner a guarantee of the amounts or timing of such returns. Actual timing and structure depend on market conditions and contracts with involved parties (e.g., distributors, sales agent, producer's rep, etc.).

*Amounts in millions of dollars.

*Theatrical distribution is assumed to commence one year after the completion of postproduction. Actual release date will be determined by the distributor.

*A small amount of ancillary revenue is likely to occur beyond the film's 3.25-year revenue window with the agreed split between producer and investors still in effect.

*Totals may not add due to rounding.

FOOTNOTES:

1: Negative Cost - Reflects timing of the negative cost and is to take 6.5 weeks preproduction, 6.5 weeks principal photography, and 9 months postproduction.

2: Year 3, Quarters 1 & 2 subtotals are carried forward and charged against Year 3, Quarter 3 subtotal.

3: Total - Sum of 'Negative Cost,' 'Dom Subtotal,' 'Frgn Subtotal,' and 'Producer's Rep Fee.'

4: Returned to Investors - Cash from 'Total' row returned to investors. Assumes 120% of initial investment returned, then remaining cash split 50/50 with Mass H-Com LLC.

Table 3 (cont'd): Projected Cash Flow for Mass H-Com LLC (Medium)

	YEAR 4				YEAR 5				YEAR 6
	Quarter 1	Quarter 2	Quarter 3	Quarter 4	Quarter 1	Quarter 2	Quarter 3	Quarter 4	Quarter 1
Mass H-Com									
Negative Cost[1]									
Gross Film Rentals									
Home Video Revenue	$ 0.396	$ 0.396	$ 0.396	$ 0.396	$ 0.396	$ 0.317	$ 0.317	$ 0.317	$ 0.310
Pay TV Revenue		$ 2.793							
Distribution Fee	$ (0.139)	$ (1.116)	$ (0.139)	$ (0.139)	$ (0.139)	$ (0.111)	$ (0.111)	$ (0.111)	$ (0.108)
Prints & Advertising									
Other Distributor Costs	$ (0.079)	$ (0.638)	$ (0.079)	$ (0.079)	$ (0.079)	$ (0.063)	$ (0.063)	$ (0.063)	$ (0.062)
Dom Subtotal[2]	*$ 0.178*	*$ 1.435*	*$ 0.178*	*$ 0.178*	*$ 0.178*	*$ 0.143*	*$ 0.143*	*$ 0.143*	*$ 0.139*
Foreign Gross	$ 0.345	$ 0.345		$ 0.230					
Sales Agent Fee & Costs	$ (0.121)	$ (0.121)		$ (0.081)					
Frgn Subtotal	*$ 0.224*	*$ 0.224*		*$ 0.150*					
Producer's Rep Fee	*$ (0.060)*	*$ (0.249)*	*$ (0.027)*	*$ (0.049)*	*$ (0.027)*	*$ (0.021)*	*$ (0.021)*	*$ (0.021)*	*$ (0.021)*
TOTAL[3]	$ 0.342	$ 1.410	$ 0.151	$ 0.279	$ 0.151	$ 0.121	$ 0.121	$ 0.121	$ 0.118
RUNNING TOTAL	$ 3.229	$ 4.640	$ 4.791	$ 5.070	$ 5.221	$ 5.342	$ 5.464	$ 5.585	$ 5.703
RETURNED TO INVESTORS[4]	$ 0.171	$ 0.705	$ 0.076	$ 0.139	$ 0.076	$ 0.061	$ 0.061	$ 0.061	$ 0.059
CUMULATIVE RETURNED	$ 2.935	$ 3.640	$ 3.716	$ 3.855	$ 3.931	$ 3.991	$ 4.052	$ 4.112	$ 4.172

Table 4: Projected Investor Returns from Mass H-Com LLC			
	Low Success	Medium Success	High Success
Total Cash Returned to Investors/Producer[1]	$1.4	$6.9	$12.2
Less Negative Cost	$1.2	$1.2	$1.2
Less Investor Priority Return[2]	$0.2	$0.2	$0.2
Adjusted Investor/Producer Profit	$0.0	$5.5	$10.7
Investor 50% Share of Adjusted	$0.0	$2.7	$5.4
Plus Investor Priority Return	$0.2	$0.2	$0.2
Plus Negative Cost	$1.2	$1.2	$1.2
TOTAL CASH RETURNED TO INVESTORS	$1.4	$4.2	$6.8
Amount Invested by Investors	$1.2	$1.2	$1.2
NET INVESTOR RETURN[3]	$0.2	$3.0	$5.6
NET RETURN PER $50,000 UNIT[4]	$ 10,000	$ 123,817	$ 233,925
NON-ANNUALIZED ROI[5]	20%	248%	468%
ANNUALIZED IRR[6]	5.9%	50.1%	75.9%

NOTES:

*This table reflects estimates of future returns to investors and is in no way a guarantee of future returns to investors.

*Totals may not add due to rounding.

FOOTNOTES:

1: Total Cash Ret. to Inv./Producer - All revenues generated by Mass H-Com LLC prior to disbursement to investors (i.e., sum of all positive 'TOTAL' amounts from cash flow).

2: Investor Priority Return - 20% of the Negative Cost that is returned to investors after repayment of the Negative Cost but before profits are split with Mass H-Com LLC.

3: Net Investor Return - The total cash returned to investors minus the amount invested by investors (i.e., minus the Negative Cost).

4: Net Return per $50,000 unit - The return earned on a single LLC unit beyond the initial investment amount, as expressed in $1 increments instead of $1,000,000 increments.

5: Non-annualized ROI - The return on investment as calculated by dividing the Net Investor Return by the Negative Cost (i.e., by the 'Amount Invested by Investors').

6: Annualized IRR (Internal Rate of Return) - The yearly rate of return on the initial investment given the timing of income in the projected cash flow. Actual timing and structure of income depend on market conditions and contracts with involved parties (e.g., distributors, sales agent, producer's rep, etc.) and will affect the annualized IRR.

2 MARKET ANALYSIS & MARKETING STRATEGY

HOW TO DO THE MARKET ANALYSIS & MARKETING STRATEGY SECTION

The purpose of this section is to describe who is going see to your film and how you and your distributor are going to reach those people. In doing this, you will be describing the two sections of the movie industry where your film will operate: the independent film sector, and within that, the genre or sub-genre that your project falls under. Ideally, you are making the argument that both of these arenas are healthy and ripe for making money. If they are unhealthy, then at the very least, you are giving the reasons for why your film will be the exception. Let's get started!

STEP 5. DESCRIBE HOW INDEPENDENT FILMS ARE DOING (... BE HONEST).

Unfortunately, direct numbers on the independent film market are rare and expensive to come by, mostly because there is no single definition of which films are "independent" and which are not. So any person or company collecting data on the market uses up a lot of time and energy doing so, and then charges for it. Sometimes in the press you will see data on independent films, but with no definition of what is meant by "independent." All of this means you are going to have to put in some time and effort into doing your own analysis. I'll give you several strategies.

One is to do what I did in the sample texts (see the end of the chapter). I found articles on the theaters where independent films were playing and reported on how those theaters were doing. Naturally, if the independent film market is doing well, then so must be these theaters. Appendix B has some resources on theater news for those of you in Los Angeles, in addition to some info on independent films of mass appeal. Since the time the sample plans were made, major exhibitors have also made commitments to screens dedicated to independent and independent-style pictures

Another strategy for tracking the independent film market is to get a list of the top domestic films (independent or not) that were released on 1000 screens or fewer (see Step 1A in Appendix B for a reminder about screen count). Do so for the past two or three years. Such a list is published every year in the fall by *Daily Variety*. Or you could request lists of such films from Baseline StudioSystems, though you might have to pay a bit. Next, go through the list and identify which of the films are independent (see Step 1C again for how to do this). Remember, our definition of "independent" includes some films that are distributed by studios, just not financed by them. Then, add up the box offices of the top 30 or so independent films from each year and compare the totals across years. See if you notice any trends. (Step 8 will do a similar kind of analysis, except looking at year-to-year changes in genres.) You could also complete the same sort of process except starting with a list of the top films with budgets under $5 million, or whatever budget range you were working with on your Comparable Films Table. That way you could easily include films that went to more than 1000 screens. In the end you are hoping for a positive trend.

Yet another alternative is to measure the year-to-year box office totals of films against which your film will directly compete, namely, specialty films. And you would do so without removing the non-independent films. There is no exact definition of "specialty films," but it generally refers to films, independent or not, reaching 1000 screens or fewer domestically. Of course there are exceptions, such as breakout hits like *Little Miss Sunshine* or *Juno*, both of which smashed through the 1000-screen barrier (despite never having had such expectations), or *The Constant Gardener*, which opened on over 1300 screens. How to examine all specialty films can be tricky. Using the *Daily Variety* limited release list, you omit the major breakouts and films like *The Constant Gardener*. If you restrict yourself to films with only a limited opening, you omit exceptions that are not quite the exceptions they used to be, such as *The Prairie Home Companion*, which opened on 760 screens, or *The Constant Gardener*. However you do it, use a specific definition for what you mean by "specialty films" and compare the box office total of the top 30 or so from year to year.

Finally, you could always cite how many Oscar nominees are independent and non-independent films. However, this has more to do with prestige than with the health of the independent film industry.

What if you can't help but find crappy news? Well, then point to the few films that did do well. Perhaps those were the only good films of the year. Better yet, maybe your film has a lot in common with those films, or maybe the market is so tough that only the exceptional films are doing well, and, of course, your film will be exceptional. Perhaps the market is just overstuffed with not-so-great films. You can also try some of the tips from the Industry Overview chapter (Chapter 7) to help frame any bad news in a positive light. There is always a silver lining, and you should always try to point to it in tough times. (Of course, it may the back of a gorilla that's about to maul you, but that's beside the point.)

STEP 6. PREACH THE IMPORTANCE OF WORD-OF-MOUTH.

Low-budget independents live and die by word-of-mouth. Their distributors do not have the luxury of blasting ads across newspapers and television and in effect buying part of their box office gross (spend enough on ads and people will come). Instead, independents rely on audiences reacting favorably to them and spreading the word to friends, who come and see a movie and spread the word to their friends, who come and do the same, and so on and so forth until people are onto the next movie and stop showing up. You must make this point to the reader.

You will notice that my sample plans include no comparable films whose opening screen counts went beyond 15 (except for one). As a result, my focus is on the more typical theatrical release scenario for a low-budget independent: open on a small number of screens and use positive word-of-mouth to generate enough interest and revenue to expand onto more screens (and thus, theaters).

There is the contrasting scenario, however, where some low-budget independents open on hundreds of screens right away. This tactic, while still not the norm, has become slightly less uncommon than in the earlier part of the decade (early 2000s) due to the crowded release schedule faced by distributors, especially during awards season (August to November, though more officially regarded as September, the Telluride Film Festival, until the end of the year). Low-budget independents face such competition for moviegoer attention from new openings every weekend that sometimes a distributor decides that opening on hundreds of screens, or opening on a small number and then quickly expanding to hundreds of screens, will reach the audience more quickly than the more typical platform/gradual release. Of course such a method can, and often does, backfire when the audience in fact does not like the piece; it then dies a quicker death.

If your comparable films reflect such wider-opening films, even just one, mention it as an example of an alternative to the more traditional platform release (a.k.a. slow roll out) and how opening more aggressively attempts to capture the audience right away, as opposed to gradually building it up. Because of my sample comparable films, I was able to use them and make a table for *Sci-Fi Rom* and *Mass H-Com* demonstrating the premise of limited release. *Psych Thrill* had too few comparable films to do so. If you wish to make a similar table, remember to leave off, and explain in the text, any of your exceptions that opened very wide.

STEP 7. TALK ABOUT HOW INDEPENDENT FILMS ARE MARKETED.

Next, describe the general approach you will recommend in the marketing of your film. And by the way, it should match the general approach used to market all independent films. Please don't say anything zany like tattooing the name of your film on Little Joey's forehead. What you see in the sample plans for this step is still pretty much how indies are marketed. Of course, the online part of it has become much more sophisticated, but even that still fights for the same goal, firing up that word-of-mouth. Ultimately your distributor will have the final word on the marketing of your picture (we point this out clearly later on in the plan), so all your can do is make recommendations. But if your recommendations are well informed, your investor will feel more comfortable, and any distributor that later deals with you will be more likely to listen.

You can update the info in the sample plans by scouring for articles on the websites of *Variety* and *The Hollywood Reporter*. Information on the marketing of low-budget independents should not be hard to find. You can especially expand on the Internet marketing of films, where more highly targeted campaigns are being launched via the creation of online communities on MySpace and Facebook. In the end, however, remember, while the methods may change, the general strategy of marketing for low-budget indies will not: generate interest through grassroots marketing efforts. Doing so maximizes the bang for the buck that distributors of low-budget fare get out of their limited marketing budgets. If you are in Los Angeles, also use the Margaret Herrick Library's "Advertising for Films" and "Marketing" clipping files, as well as the production clipping files for the films on your Comparable Films Table.

STEP 8. WHAT'S YOUR TARGET AUDIENCE AND HOW WILL YOU REACH THEM?

Here you carve out exactly who will come to see your film and how you will apply the general marketing strategy to reaching them. This is one of the few parts of the business plan where you can take a more relaxed approach to highlighting the good things about your project. You can compare it to films not in the same budget class as your own, and you can make specific marketing recommendations for which you may ultimately have no input. The strict rules of film comparison were used in the Financial Projections section, but by relaxing those requirements here, you can start with a general sense of your target audience, then narrow that sense down as the section proceeds.

In the sample plans I talked about how genres were doing in general by referencing a great report that *The Hollywood Reporter* used to publish every summer/fall called "Film 500." As luck would have it, they stopped publishing it in 2007. Luckily, you can still talk about how genres are doing from year-to-year by using any one of the numerous year-end top film lists and doing some calculations on your own. Stick to domestic lists only (U.S. and Canada). I've done so using *Weekly Variety's* yearly "Top 250" list:

TABLE 2.1: Each genre's share of the top 100 domestic box office*					
	2004	2005	2006	2007	2008
	% of Whole	% of Whole	% of Whole	% of Whole	% of Whole
Action	23.6%	20.0%	21.6%	32.3%	33.2%
Animation	15.2%	8.2%	16.1%	13.6%	12.3%
Comedy	16.7%	16.1%	20.7%	15.6%	18.8%
Documentary	1.5%	1.0%	0.0%	0.3%	0.0%
Drama	18.4%	15.5%	20.2%	7.1%	12.1%
Family	1.9%	9.1%	7.2%	7.9%	1.6%
Fantasy	6.9%	7.2%	1.7%	7.3%	4.0%
Horror	6.1%	6.9%	5.6%	5.3%	3.0%
Musical	0.0%	0.9%	0.5%	2.9%	4.3%
Romance	4.7%	4.9%	3.3%	3.0%	5.1%
Sci-fi	0.0%	6.9%	0.0%	0.0%	1.4%
Thriller	5.3%	3.3%	3.1%	4.1%	4.3%
Western	0.0%	0.0%	0.0%	0.7%	0.0%

*Source: Author's manipulation of *Weekly Variety* "Top 250," January 2004, 2005, 2006, 2007, 2008.

For each year, I grouped the top 100 films on the list by genre, added up the total box office of those genres, and checked what percentage each genre was of the top 100. For instance, one year you might have seven features in the top 100 that classify as "Animated." Then when you add up their grosses the total might come to $0.5 billion. If the total grosses of all the top 100 films on the list are $5 billion, then the Animated genre would be 10% of the gross of that year's top 100 films ($0.5 billion/$5 billion = 10%). It seems like it may take awhile to do all this, but the time goes surprisingly fast. And if you don't know a film, you can check IMDb or any of the numerous film guides out there for a description of it.

Then, in your discussion of target audience, it can be helpful to discuss how particular genres have either grown or shrunk. You can measure growth from year to year over the latest two years or across all the years that you have tracked. See Appendix B for how to calculate a growth or decline (a.k.a. a "percentage change").

Another tool you can use in describing an audience is a report put out every year by the MPAA entitled the "Movie Attendance Survey." The MPAA (Motion Picture Association of America) is a trade association representing the interests of the six major studios. The report is published every year and can be obtained for free at the MPAA's website under the "Research and Statistics" heading (*www.mpaa.org/researchstatistics.asp*) or referenced in the Current Statistics binder at the Margaret Herrick Library. It has great statistics on the general characteristics of moviegoers and can be especially useful for helping to discuss the target audience of your film if it has mass appeal.

Take a look at the sample texts for some ideas on how you might want to complete the writing of this step. Among other things, they will demonstrate how to apply your general marketing strategies to hitting your film's audience. You will also see why it is important to do the financial section first, since it gives you a strong sense of the specific type of audience your film is going for. Appendix B has a little bit more to add on *Mass H-Com*'s section.

SAMPLE MARKET ANALYSIS & MARKETING STRATEGY SECTIONS

MARKET ANALYSIS & MARKETING STRATEGY*
(Sci-Fi Rom)

exhibitors

Low-budget independent films are generally shown in two types of movie theaters, specialty theaters or non-specialty theaters. Specialty theaters generally consist of one to five screens and cater to niche audiences while non-specialty theaters frequently have more screens and cater to much wider audiences. Studio films are much more likely to be found in a non-specialty theater. Over the past five years the number of specialty theaters has increased, as has the number of non-specialty theaters willing to show low-budget independent films. In fact, Landmark Theatres, the nation's oldest and largest chain of specialty theaters, committed in August 2003 to adding 21 screens to its circuit in cities such as Atlanta, Georgia; Washington, D.C.; and Edina, Minnesota. Landmark was subsequently purchased by dot-com billionaires Mark Cuban and Todd Wagner, who have made plans to revamp one if its West Los Angeles sites into the nation's largest specialty theater (with 14 screens), in addition to renovating many other Landmark sites. In early 2002, Southern California-based Pacific Theaters opened its ArcLight venue in Hollywood where, in the summer of 2003, seven of this multiplex's 14 screens were regularly playing films typically found in specialty theaters. The theater went on to achieve such success by February 2004 that Pacific Theaters announced it would proceed with plans to replicate the ArcLight in 40 additional markets.[1] These large capital outlays for specialty screens illustrate exhibitor confidence in the potential market for high caliber independent films such as *Sci-Fi Rom*.

---

*Any box office numbers or release patterns quoted in the remainder of the business plan refer to the domestic market (U.S. & Canada) unless otherwise noted.

[1] Nicole Sperling, "Crowded Art House," *The Hollywood Reporter,* August 5, 2003; Lorenza Munoz, "Botox for the Bijou," *Los Angeles Times*, February 15, 2004.

word-of-mouth

As with most low-budget independent films, any company that domestically dis-tributes *Sci-Fi Rom* will likely open it on a very limited number of specialty theater screens and use the proceeds from those screens to pay for wider theatrical release of the film. *Sci-Fi Rom* will rely heavily on word-of-mouth for its initial suc-cess. This word-of-mouth is essential to films that open with a limited release. Witness the extreme examples of *The Blair Witch Project* in 1999 and *My Big Fat Greek Wedding* in 2002. *Blair Witch* opened on one screen and went on to gross $140 million. *Wedding* opened on 108 screens, high for the typical independent film but very low by studio standards, and used positive word-of-mouth to extend its theatrical run to 47 weeks and $241 million. Though these two films show extremely exceptional results, other recent and more grounded independent pictures have also relied on initial world-of-mouth to achieve successful grosses, as the following table illustrates:

Recent independents with successful grosses:			
Film (release year)	Opening Screens	Budget* ($ mil)	Box Office* ($ mil)
Pic A (2003)	6	$ 0.3	$ 2.4
Pic B (2003)	3	$ 0.5	$ 5.7
Pic D (2002)	6	$ 0.2	$ 2.9
Pic E (2002)	26	$ 1.0	$ 7.0
Pic F (2002)	3	$ 2.0	$ 4.4
Pic G (2000)	8	$ 1.5	$ 9.2

*Source: Baseline StudioSystems

It is worth noting that each of the films appearing on the table never reached more than 600 screens. To do so is rare for a low-budget independent.[2]

general marketing strategy

Once a suitable domestic distributor is found, we will recommend that marketing begin with targeted screenings and Internet exposure, followed by local promo-tions. These screenings will target audiences most likely to take an interest in the film and feature follow-up discussions with key members of the project such as the writer/director, producer, and actors. As an example, the distributors for *Thirteen* (2003), an R-rated limited release concerning adolescent issues, raised awareness of their film by focusing on screenings to school counselors, teen psychologists, and members of Congress, Planned Parenthood, and The

---

[2] *Weekly Variety* box office charts, 1999 – 2003; and *IMDb.com*.

Brookings Institution.[3] The result was a successful theatrical release of $4.6 million domestically over a production budget of $XXXXXXX.[4] Two other examples are the films *Osama* (2004) and *The Fog of War* (2003). The initial target audience for each film was a narrow slice of the total market, and thus, early on in the marketing campaigns screenings were arranged with members of these slices.[5] Ultimately, *Osama* went on to gross $1.1 million on a budget of $0.3 million and *Fog* went on to $4.0 million on an approximate budget of $2.0 million.[6] Internet exposure can also be effective in reaching a film's target audience. Such exposure was the cornerstone of *The Blair Witch Project*'s initial marketing campaign. Visitors at websites frequented by the target audience were directed to the film's website where new information was repeatedly posted to ensure the return of these initial visitors. Studio spending on Internet exposure further highlights the importance of online marketing. Such spending by Motion Picture Association of America members (seven studios) climbed nearly 50% in 2003 to a level even with the height of the dot-com bubble.[7]

Once it is decided in what city or cities the film will debut, local promotions will also be advised. These promotions can be with businesses ranging from large corporations to diners catering to a film's primary audience and willing to provide a prize or host an event. The allure of these promotions is that expenses are limited to fliers and postcards because the promoter picks up the tab for whatever product or service it is providing. The marketing team for *My Big Fat Greek Wedding* spent months using promotions to repeatedly target the same bridal salons, Greek diners, and Greek Orthodox churches in New York City. Marketers for *Pic P* (9 initial screens, $3.5 million budget, $20.8 million gross) set up promotions with restaurants throughout NYC. The total cost of these promotions rarely exceeds $20,000 yet yields a measurable return, as *Wedding* and *Pic P* illustrate.[8] The overall goal with these marketing strategies is to begin significant word-of-mouth about a film. Once word-of-mouth spreads, the resulting revenues can be used to pay for more traditional publicity, such as media buys and publicists.

---

[3] Beth Pinsker, "Other People's Money," *Daily Variety*, August 18, 2003.

[4] *IMDb.com*; Baseline StudioSystems.

[5] Stephen Galloway, "How They Did It," *The Hollywood Reporter*, May 18, 2004.

[6] *Weekly Variety* box office charts, 2003–2004; *IMDb.com*; Dave Calhoun, "Story-telling Beyond the Veil," *The Times* (London), February 12, 2004; Kathy A. McDonald, "The Fog of War," *Daily Variety*, December 12, 2003.

[7] Ben Fritz, "Another banner year," *Daily Variety*, May 10, 2004.

[8] XXXXXXXXXX.

target audience & specific marketing strategy

Because *Sci-Fi Rom* is characterized as a science fiction romance, its market will draw on members of the movie-going public who frequent each of these types of films. Out of twelve movie genres during the release years 2000–2003 inclusive, science fiction experienced the third largest growth in box office share (behind musical and family), expanding 149%. In 2003 it comprised 11.5% of the box office at $1.0 billion. While romance films have varied little over the four years in terms of box office share (hovering around 3.4%), two romantic comedies breached the top 25 films of 2003 in terms of ticket sales: *Something's Gotta Give* at $124 million and *How to Lose a Guy in 10 Days* at $106 million (2004 figures not available until August 2005).[9] Both of these films were studio films with budgets well over $10 million. Nonetheless, these numbers illustrate that a market exists for a science fiction romance. However, because *Sci-Fi Rom* features no significantly name actors, is experimental in nature (to be shot entirely in one location in one day), and is very character-driven (its actors' performances drive the piece), its market dramatically shrinks to an audience who enjoys the aforementioned genres but also desires intellectually challenging, upbeat material. In fact, the very characteristics that narrow the film's market are highly valued by members of this audience group. This group consists of patrons to specialty theaters who enjoy low-budget, upbeat, character-driven independent films, both foreign and homegrown. The group also provides a substantial market for films such as *Sci-Fi Rom*, as the following table illustrates:

Films comparable to *Sci-Fi Rom*:			
Film (release year)	Foreign language?	Box Office* ($ mil)	Budget* ($ mil)
Pic G (2000)	No	$ 9.2	$ 1.5
Pic E (2002)	No	$ 7.0	$ 1.0
Pic B (2003)	No	$ 5.7	$ 0.5
Pic F (2002)	Yes	$ 4.4	$ 2.0
Pic C (2002)	Yes	$ 4.2	$ 2.0
Pic D (2002)	No	$ 2.9	$ 0.2
Pic A (2003)	No	$ 2.4	$ 0.3

*Source: Baseline StudioSystems

[9] Calculations and numbers based on "Film 500," *The Hollywood Reporter*, August 2001, 2002, 2003, 2004; and "U.S. Entertainment Industry: 2006 Market Statistics" by Motion Picture Association Worldwide Market Research & Analysis, Motion Picture Association, Sherman Oaks, California, *http://www. mpaa.org*; "release year" refers to the fact that a film can be released in a given year but still earn box office revenue in the following year (as with many year-end releases).

Each of these films is low-budget, upbeat, character-driven, and does not feature actors who were significant names at the time of its release. Because many pictures in specialty theaters share these characteristics, the target demographic for *Sci-Fi Rom* can be best described as specialty theater patrons favoring upbeat material. The films on the table are further highlighted in the financial section.

The many different aspects of *Sci-Fi Rom* create a breadth of opportunities for targeted screenings. Because of the remarkable fact that it will be shot in one day, the film can be screened at film societies. Due to the fact that it deals with XXXXXXXX and other matters of science fiction, science fiction fan clubs, book clubs, and conventions can be targeted. Furthermore, because the film is a romance, it can also be screened at regional women's book clubs dealing with highly intellectual material. Regarding Internet marketing, sites we will recommend targeting are those centered on the same types of clubs, societies, and conventions where the screenings should occur. It bears mentioning that studios have found marketing on the Internet especially useful when dealing with pictures in the science fiction and horror genres.[10] In terms of promotions, we will suggest partnering primarily with restaurants catering to specialty theater patrons. The narrow market for *Sci-Fi Rom* suggests that promotions might not pay off with more specific targeting.

---

[10] Ben Fritz, "'Net heads finally get some respect," *Weekly Variety*, April 12, 2004.

MARKET ANALYSIS & MARKETING STRATEGY*
(*Mass H-Com*)

exhibitors

Low-budget independent films are generally shown in two types of movie the-aters: specialty theaters or non-specialty theaters. Specialty theaters generally consist of one to five screens and cater to niche audiences, while non-specialty theaters frequently have more screens and cater to much wider audiences. While specialty theaters generally cater to niche audiences, they do carry independent films, and sometimes studio films, of mass appeal. However, studio films are much more likely to be found in a non-specialty theater. Over the past five years the number of specialty theaters has increased, as has the number of non-spe-cialty theaters willing to show low-budget independent films. In fact, Landmark Theatres, the nation's oldest and largest chain of specialty theaters, committed in August 2003 to adding 21 screens to its circuit in cities such as Atlanta, Georgia; Washington, D.C.; and Edina, Minnesota. Landmark was subsequently purchased by dot-com billionaires Mark Cuban and Todd Wagner, who have made plans to revamp one if its West Los Angeles sites into the nation's largest specialty theater (with 14 screens), in addition to renovating many other Landmark sites. In early 2002, Southern California-based Pacific Theaters opened its ArcLight venue in Hollywood where, in the summer of 2003, seven of this multiplex's 14 screens were regularly playing films typically found in specialty theaters. The theater went on to achieve such success by February 2004 that Pacific Theaters announced it would proceed with plans to replicate the ArcLight in 40 additional markets.[1] These large capital outlays for specialty screens illustrate exhibitor confidence in the potential market for high caliber independent films such as *Mass H-Com*.

word-of-mouth

As with most low-budget independent films, any company that domestically distrib-utes *Mass H-Com* will likely open it on a very limited number of specialty theater screens and use the proceeds from those screens to pay for wider theatrical release

---

*Any box office numbers or release patterns quoted in the remainder of the business plan refer to the domestic market (U.S. & Canada) unless otherwise noted.

[1] Nicole Sperling, "Crowded Art House," *The Hollywood Reporter*, August 5, 2003; Lorenza Munoz, "Botox for the Bijou," *Los Angeles Times*, February 15, 2004.

of the film. *Mass H-Com* will rely heavily on word-of-mouth for its initial success. This word-of-mouth is essential to films that open with a limited release. Witness the extreme examples of *The Blair Witch Project* in 1999 and *My Big Fat Greek Wedding* in 2002. *Blair Witch* opened on one screen and went on to gross $140 million. *Wedding* opened on 108 screens, high for the typical independent film but very low by studio standards, and used positive word-of-mouth to extend its theatrical run to 47 weeks and $241 million. Though these two films show extremely exceptional results, other recent independent pictures have also relied on initial word-of-mouth to achieve successful grosses, as the following table illustrates:

Recent independents with successful grosses:			
Film (release year)	Opening Screens	Budget* ($ mil)	Box Office* ($ mil)
Pic B (2003)	3	$ 0.5	$ 5.7
Pic Q (2002)	8	$ 3.0	$ 21.2
Pic E (2002)	26	$ 1.0	$ 7.0
Pic M (2001)	6	$ 3.0	$ 8.8
Pic N (2001)	11	$ 5.0	$ 25.5
Pic G (2000)	8	$ 1.5	$ 9.2

*Source: Baseline StudioSystems

It is worth noting that each of the films appearing on the table never reached more than 600 screens. To do so is rare for a low-budget independent.[2]

general marketing strategy

Once a suitable domestic distributor is found, we will recommend that marketing begin with targeted screenings and Internet exposure, followed by local promotions. These screenings will target audiences most likely to take an interest in the film and feature follow-up discussions with key members of the project such as the writer/director, producers, and actors. As an example, the distributors for *Thirteen* (2003), an R-rated limited release concerning adolescent issues, raised awareness of their film by focusing on screenings to school counselors, teen psychologists, and members of Congress, Planned Parenthood, and The Brookings Institution.[3] The result was a successful theatrical release of $4.6

---

[2] *Weekly Variety* box office charts, 1999–2003; and *IMDb.com*.
[3] Beth Pinsker, "Other People's Money," *Daily Variety*, August 18, 2003.

million domestically over a production budget of $XXXXXXX.[4] Two other examples are the films *Osama* (2004) and *The Fog of War* (2003). The initial target audience for each film was a narrow slice of the total market, and thus, early on in the marketing campaigns screenings were arranged with members of these slices.[5] Ultimately, *Osama* went on to gross $1.1 million on a budget of $0.3 million and *Fog* went on to $4.0 million on an approximate budget of $2.0 million.[6] Internet exposure can also be effective in reaching a film's target audience. Such exposure was the cornerstone of the horror picture *The Blair Witch Project's* initial marketing campaign. Visitors at websites frequented by the target audience were directed to the film's website where new information was repeatedly posted to ensure the return of these initial visitors. Studio spending on Internet exposure further highlights the importance of online marketing. Such spending by Motion Picture Association of America members (seven studios) climbed nearly 50% in 2003 to a level even with the height of the dot-com bubble.[7]

Once it is decided in what city or cities the film will debut, local promotions will also be advised. These promotions can be with businesses ranging from large corporations to diners catering to a film's primary audience and willing to provide a prize or host an event. The allure of these promotions is that expenses are limited to fliers and postcards because the promoter picks up the tab for whatever product or service it is providing. The marketing team for *My Big Fat Greek Wedding* spent months using promotions to repeatedly target the same bridal salons, Greek diners, and Greek Orthodox churches in New York City. Marketers for *Pic P* (9 initial screens, $3.5 million budget, $20.8 million gross) set up promotions with restaurants throughout NYC. The total cost of these promotions rarely exceeds $20,000 yet yields a measurable return, as *Wedding* and *Pic P* illustrate.[8] The overall goal with these marketing strategies is to begin significant word-of-mouth about a film. Once word-of-mouth spreads, the resulting revenues can be used to pay for more traditional publicity, such as media buys and publicists.

[4] *IMDb.com*; Baseline StudioSystems.

[5] Stephen Galloway, "How They Did It," *The Hollywood Reporter*, May 18, 2004.

[6] *Weekly Variety* box office charts, 2003–2004; *IMDb.com*; Dave Calhoun, "Story-telling Beyond the Veil," *The Times* (London), February 12, 2004; Kathy A. McDonald, "The Fog of War," *Daily Variety*, December 12, 2003.

[7] Ben Fritz, "Another banner year," *Daily Variety*, May 10, 2004.

[8] XXXXXXXXXXX.

target audience & specific marketing strategy

The largest section of the movie-going public in 2003 was 12-to-29-year-olds, representing 48% of box office admissions.[9] *Mass H-Com* will target this demographic because of the genres it draws upon. During the release years 2000–2003 inclusive, comedy was the largest grossing genre in the domestic box office ($2.3 billion in 2003), and out of the twelve measured genres only five experienced growth in box office share with horror placing fourth at 126%.[10] Members of the 12-to-29 demographic are the primary audience group for horror films.[11] They also frequently occupy the same role for comedies. *Mass H-Com* is a horror-comedy. The most successful example to date of this blended genre is the *Scary Movie* franchise that began in 2000. It was geared toward 12-to-29-year-olds and grossed a combined total of $338 million with its three pictures.[12] These films centered on making fun of contemporary horror and pop-culture films; whereas *Mass H-Com* does not. It is rather characterized by humor and horror that derive directly from the storyline. It should be noted that *Mass H-Com* will have an R rating and this may restrict some parts of the 12-to-29 demographic during its theatrical run. History has shown, however, that a popular movie with an R rating can perform and do so extremely well. Eight of the twelve films mentioned thus far in this section of the business plan are rated R, including horror film *The Blair Witch Project*. In fact, six of the top 25 grossing films in 2003 were rated R, in contrast to only one in 2002.[13]

Because *Mass H-Com* is also a horror, two trends within this genre should further benefit the film's potential market. For the one-year period from June 2003 through May 2004, among domestic horror films that grossed $2.0 million or more, one in every five featured zombies, versus none in 2002/2003 and only one zombie release in 2001/2002.[14] In fact, two major zombie releases this past

---

[9] "2003 U.S. Movie Attendance Study" by Motion Picture Association Worldwide Market Research.

[10] Calculations and numbers based on "Film 500," *The Hollywood Reporter*, August 2001, 2002, 2003, 2004; and "U.S. Entertainment Industry: 2006 Market Statistics" by Motion Picture Association Worldwide Market Research & Analysis; "release year" refers to the fact that a film can be released in a given year but still earn box office revenue in the following year (as with many year-end releases).

[11] Patrick Goldstein, "A horror a week will keep fans screaming," *Los Angeles Times*, September 2, 2003; John Dempsey, "Gore Galore in 2004," *Daily Variety*, September 22, 2003; Lorenza Munoz, "The female fear factor," *Los Angeles Times*, November 8, 2003.

[12] *Weekly Variety* box office charts, 2000–2004; *IMDb.com*.

[13] "U.S. Entertainment Industry: 2003 MPA Market Statistics" by Motion Picture Association Worldwide Market Research.

[14] Calculation based on data from *Weekly Variety* "Top 250" of the year lists and *IMDb.com*.

fall, *Resident Evil 2* and the horror-comedy *Shaun of the Dead*, registered over $50 million and $13 million respectively.[15] *Mass H-Com*'s plot heavily features zombies. The other beneficial horror trend is increased violence and gore. This trend is more qualitative and can be demonstrated by examining the content of horror films since spring 2003. These films have been more bloody and raw than their immediate predecessors and can be viewed as a backlash against a style of horror that was born in the mid 1990s with the *Scream* franchise. This franchise and its subsequent influence emphasized jokes and self-referencing over gore and violence.[16] *Mass H-Com*'s plot does not self-reference the horror genre, and while obviously featuring jokes, it does not do so at the expense of gore and violence. Despite having these popular horror film elements, *Mass H-Com* remains unique as a horror because of its story line, XXXXXXXX battle for survival XXXXXXXXXXXXXXXXXXXXXXXXXX. Furthermore, because of the film's rare blend of broad and subtle humor, this storyline also renders it unique as a comedy. Its broader comedy will be much in the vein of *Dude, Where's My Car?* and should attract younger members of the 12-to-29 age group. While at the same time, its subtle wit will provide an added appeal to older members. *Dude* grossed $46 million in the U.S alone.[17]

We will recommend targeted screenings of *Mass H-Com* focused on horror fan clubs and conventions, as well as universities. Follow-up discussions with members of the project should prove especially useful because of the presence of significantly name actor XXXXXXXX. His renown in the horror genre, only to be heightened by the release of his next film on over 2,500 screens, should greatly increase interest in these screenings. It will also serve as an invaluable tool in generating interest for the picture on the Internet. Sites we will recommend targeting are fan sites of horror films and fan sites of Mr. XXXXXXXXX. It bears mentioning that studios have found marketing on the Internet especially useful for horror films. For instance, Universal Studios focused much attention on the Internet when marketing its R-rated 2004 zombie release *Dawn of the Dead*.

---

[15] *IMDb.com.*

[16] Gina McIntyre, "Fright Club," *The Hollywood Reporter*, June 10, 2003; Susan King, "Movies put the R back in horror," *Los Angeles Times*, July 14, 2003; Matthew M. Ross, "Indie scare tactics," *Daily Variety*, August 18, 2003.

[17] *IMDb.com.*

The film went on to gross nearly $60 million.[18] In terms of the promotions, we will suggest partnering with gothic dance clubs and bars, in addition to the owners of XXXXXXXXXXXX. For his role XXXXXXXXXXX, the readers of this periodical awarded Mr. XXXXXXXX Award for Best Supporting Actor. XXXXXXXX has been in circulation for XXXXXXXX years and is in close contact with Ms. XXXXXXXX regarding her previous feature XXXXXXXXXXXXXX.

---

[18] Stephen Galloway, "Logging On," *The Hollywood Reporter,* May 18, 2004; Ben Fritz, "'Net heads finally get some respect," *Weekly Variety*, April 12, 2004.

3 MOTION PICTURE DISTRIBUTION

HOW TO DO THE MOTION PICTURE DISTRIBUTION SECTION

In this section of the business plan you explain the distribution process, and mostly at the end of the section, explain how you plan to make your film a part of that process. To do this, you will need to read, read, read! Read as much as you can on distribution, and while all the information is swimming around in your head, summarize it. Some great resources to start with are:

Entertainment Industry Economics (7th edition) by Harold L. Vogel
(Cambridge and New York: Cambridge University Press, 2007)

The Insider's Guide to Independent Film Distribution by Stacey Parks
(Burlington and Oxford: Elsevier, 2007)

The Movie Business by Kelly Charles Crabb
(New York and London: Simon & Schuster, 2005)

Risky Business: Financing and Distributing Independent Films
by Mark Litwak
(Los Angeles: Silman-James Press, 2004)

Margaret Herrick Library clipping files: particularly "Independent Production" and "Independent Distribution," but also "Distribution."

You won't need to read every word from these sources, just the ones pertaining to distribution, though with the Parks book, you may want to read most of it. The clipping files (or articles from the Internet in their place) will give you a sense of current events in the distribution world. Be careful, however! The point here is not to read just enough so you can write a good section on distribution, but to become so well informed that you can answer distribution questions put to you by investors. Because distribution is such a large subject, you will inevitably leave stuff out of the business plan that your investors will later ask you about. If you can't answer those questions, it won't really matter what you wrote.

STEP 9. TELL THEM HOW YOUR MOVIE MAKES IT TO GRANDMA'S iPOD.

Provide an overview of the distribution process. Don't forget, the key assumption you are making in the plan is that your film will be sought after by distributors and distributed successfully. I say this because there are many differences between the ways in which a successful film, such as the ones on your Comparable Films Table, and unsuccessful ones, such as the vast majority of low-budget independents, are distributed. Chief among them is that, with unsuccessful ones, fractionalization of rights into separate formats is much more common. In other words, DVD rights are typically sold separately from broadcast rights and even theatrical rights, if a theatrical release even occurs. To keep your overview simple, focus on how the distribution process generally works for successful films. This means teaching the basics, which are by no means basic. You may end up writing and rewriting here more than at any other stage of the plan (except possibly the Executive Summary), but while you're tearing your hair out, know that that is usual.

Because the sample text is older (see the end of the chapter), mention of the Internet as a distribution format is lacking — Grandma could barely afford shoes, much less an iPod back then. While revenue from the Internet is too small to make forecasting it worthwhile, you should still mention it in your plan as a distribution format. Internet distribution typically occurs as part of other distribution windows, such as home video or premium cable. On a separate note, the underlined sentence in the sample text is there because, once your film is done, investors might not understand why you would engage in a theatrical release. They might view theatrical as a step that returns little or no money (as is often the case) and a step that just delays the receipt of later monies. The underlined statement refutes the view that theatrical release is just some nuisance and makes the point that it should not be easily ignored.

STEP 10. BREAK THE NEWS GENTLY:
YOU PAY THE CHARGES, DISTRIBUTORS MAKE THE DECISIONS.

This is one of the most shocking aspects of movie distribution to investors. They supply the money, take nearly all the risk, and then have to trust a distributor, whom they likely have never even met, to make all the important decisions about how to return that money. Not to mention the fact that the distributor will deduct expenses from any revenues *after* already rewarding itself with a fee off the top. Isn't this a great business? Unfortunately it's the truth, and while this step is actually quite short, it's also quite important. It prepares the investor for the road ahead.

First, briefly summarize the most recognizable distribution expense, Prints & Advertising (P&A), and how it, along with the distribution fee and any other expenses, are passed on to the producer. Discussing the P&A expense is important, because it will be the most recognizable category of expenses cutting into the profits of a successful film. For low-budget independent films, the total of other distribution expenses will often exceed the P&A because of the costs associated with DVDs, which is why DVD expenses are discussed as well. To find the current cost of a film print (a.k.a. the release print), you can reference the latest edition of *Entertainment Industry Economics* or directly contact the Los Angeles area offices of the makers of such prints, for instance Deluxe or Technicolor. For advertising rates in a newspaper you will need to contact a major paper such as the *Los Angeles Times* or the *New York Times* and ask for a quote on a quarter page ad in their film section. Don't get too bogged down in getting these quotes; you are just trying to give the investor a general idea of how big P&A expenses can get. DVD expenses can be found in news articles or the latest editions of Harold L. Vogel's and John J. Lee Jr./Rob Holt's books (see Appendix C).

An important omission in the sample texts is the movement of theaters towards digital projectors (so called "d-cinema") — not a significant development when the texts were written, but definitely something to consider now. While d-cinema is not pervasive, all signs are that it will be in the next two or three years. You may want to mention the fact that some independent films no longer need prints because they can be shown in theaters that have digital projectors. This will one day cut down on print costs significantly.

Next, you want to lay out the bottom line when it comes to distributors: they will have final say when it comes to marketing, since they will be paying for it before any money is made. Also mention the fact that in order to get distribution you may need to change certain aspects of the film at the distributor's request. In other words, the director's, and perhaps the investor's, final vision of the project may not end up the same as the distributor's, if making money is the ultimate goal. Some investors are unaware that you, as the producer and manager of your business entity, ultimately give the most important part of the filmmaking process to the distributor. Don't let this come as a surprise!

Before we finish this step, take a quick look back at the sample texts and where I discussed the typical low-budget independent release (under "distributor control"). If your comparable films have no opening weekend screen limit because some of them had wider releases, it still helps to mention the more typical opening of a low-budget independent (I mentioned 15 screens in the sample texts). Then you can possibly provide a brief mention of the less common wider release.

STEP 11. DESCRIBE INDEPENDENT FILM DISTRIBUTORS (NICELY).

Given what we just covered, those distributors can seem like crooks, but one of the reasons they charge so much and take so much of the power in the distribution process is because they bear a huge amount of risk. A series of failed films can easily put a distributor out of commission. So, as much as they screw us, the little old filmmaker, it sometimes helps to remember where they are coming from. Those punks! (Sorry, I couldn't help myself.) But now it's time to put hard feelings aside and paint a picture of independent film distributors.

The groups in which to put indie film distributors vary, mainly because the players in the indie market are constantly changing. In the sample texts, I employed a three-tier structure that was basically used by *The Hollywood Reporter* until 2006. Many people use a simpler system, classifying companies as either studio specialty divisions or not studio specialty divisions. People also use the term "mini-major," which can refer to studio subdivisions and large non-studio companies such as Lionsgate, Summit, and Overture. In the sample text, "mini-major" strictly referred to studio subdivisions. Whatever way you use to describe indie film distributors, stick to some version of Big, Medium, and Small. And please, don't just copy the sample text; it's out of date. Warner Independent was axed, and Paramount Classics was placed under Paramount Vantage, which was greatly scaled back. Warner Brothers never really appeared to have a strong interest in specialty films (remember, "specialty films" are either independent films or independent-style films) and Paramount Vantage appears to have marketed itself to death, spending too much on its films' P&A. The two paragraphs from the "distribution companies" section should be merged into a more straightforward account of who the players are.

To get a feel for how to group the distributors, *The Hollywood Reporter* and *Variety* put out several issues every year covering the indie sector. In August/September *The Hollywood Reporter* publishes a special issue entitled "Independent Producers & Distributors," while *Daily Variety* publishes a supplement in its "V Plus" section. Both publications also put out end-of-the-year assessments of the indie distributors. These occur sometime in early January. You can get an even better feel for things by looking at *Daily Variety's* annual limited release chart. It typically accompanies the fall indie film supplement and lists the top limited-release films (studio and non-studio) as well as their distributors.

Taking a look again at the sample text, the 2003 top 10 list I refer to in the "distribution companies" section does not adhere to our strict definition of independent films, in that it included studio subsidiaries that at least partly financed some of their films. However, the list gave a general idea of the state of independent film distributors. Trying to go through and group distributors based on the actual number of true independents they distribute, or paying someone else to do it, is too time consuming or expensive. That is why the footnote referencing the top distributors list was expanded.

STEP 12. WHAT DO THEY LOOK FOR IN A FILM?

Another short but important step. Describe what distributors look for in a project. The three criteria listed in the sample text (cast, genre, and storyline) are essentially the three criteria used by distributors to evaluate a project. Of course, if you have a name director attached (much less likely than having a significantly name actor), distributors may also be enticed. Be honest! If your project is lacking any of these elements, explain why it won't be an issue. Or explain why it will be an issue, but one that is quite likely to be overcome. Remember, investors hate surprises that were hidden by the filmmaker, and you will, too, if the result is a lawsuit.

As you'll see when you examine the sample texts' "distribution criteria," I say that these are "some of the main factors" affecting a distributor's decision to distribute. I do this because I hate to put anything in a business plan that appears to be a written-in-stone rule. Maybe I'm just being paranoid, but I want to cover myself in case some wild card factor becomes each distributor's main reason for not wanting the project. Then the investor can't turn and say, "But you said we'd get distribution if we satisfied these three requirements!"

STEP 13. WHAT'S YOUR STRATEGY FOR SNAGGING A DISTRIBUTOR?
– NO BEGGING.

There are umpteen ways in which to seek out distributors for a film. So that you don't double the length of your plan explaining all of them, stick to the underlying assumption of the entire plan: your film will be successful. This implies the project will attract the attention of all levels of distributors and ultimately land with one capable of delivering at least the "Low Success" scenario you have projected for box office revenues. With a focus on films of this sort, the path to seeking out distributors becomes much more narrow, like the path laid out in the sample texts.

Turning to the sample texts, the first thing to be aware of is that the quoted producer's rep and sales agent fees are current. Secondly, notice that for *Mass H-Com*, the festivals I chose to target were different from those of *Sci-Fi Rom* and *Psych Thrill*. This was mainly because of the picture's comedic elements. American comedy does not usually translate well in the foreign markets, unless it is very physical or somehow otherwise universal. You will also see that for *Mass H-Com* I took out the examples of advances just covering a film's negative cost because two of the examples were sold at Cannes, a European festival not to be targeted by *Mass H-Com*. While we're on the topic of festivals, Mark Litwak and Stacey Parks give opinions in their books on what the top festivals for distribution are, with Litwak providing an in-depth description of several. More descriptions can be found in books solely focused on film festivals (search Amazon for the authors Chris Gore or Chris Holland). Any of these are a good starting point for doing some more research on your own. Your comparable films and general distribution research will also give you a feel for the top festivals.

Finally, the last paragraph of the sample texts is very important. It basically relates the ugly truth about independent films: unless your film makes it to a major festival or gets picked up by a top producer's rep, your already tough prospects of reaping a return on your film become even tougher. The major festivals themselves are already littered with films that will ultimately lose money, not to mention the projects that were turned away. Once you have exhausted your options for finding a top-tier festival and/or producer's rep, your workload increases, your potential returns decrease, and your focus becomes just getting back your investors' initial investment. (There are exceptions, of course, as the film *What the #$*! Do We (K)now?* demonstrates.) For a great discussion of the various ways to get that money back, read Parks' book.

SAMPLE MOTION PICTURE DISTRIBUTION SECTION

MOTION PICTURE DISTRIBUTION
(*Sci-Fi Rom, Mass H-Com, Psych Thrill*)

distribution overview

Distribution of an independent film involves licensing its rights to a distribution company or companies for a specified length of time. During this time each distributor further licenses the film to various markets. Markets are divided into geographical regions. These regions can be described as broadly as domestic (U.S. and Canadian) and foreign or as specifically as Belgian and Argentinian. Markets are also divided into formats, such as theatrical, DVD/home video, and TV. "Format" refers to the way in which a movie can be viewed. The theatrical market includes all public movie theaters; the DVD/home video market includes DVDs for sale and rental; and the television market includes network, syndication, cable/satellite, pay-per-view, and video-on-demand. Other formats for which rights can be licensed include soundtrack, novelization, merchandising, and showings of the film not entirely open to the public, such as for the airlines, armed forces, and campuses. For films with solid commercial prospects, a distributor will typically acquire the rights for all formats and do so within a specific country or countries. For example, a company that acquires or has been licensed the "German rights" to a film has the right to release the film in Germany in all the aforementioned formats. Domestically this is also the case, with U.S. and Canadian rights acquired together as a block. <u>Revenues in all domestic formats and foreign markets are driven by the success of the domestic theatrical release</u>. As such, a domestic theatrical release is often viewed as a reasonable investment despite the fact that in most cases theatrical release profits are minimal. It establishes audience awareness of a film. Theatrical release in foreign markets may or may not occur depending on genre, market conditions, and the like. Regardless, the timing of film distribution in the domestic market generally follows the chart below:

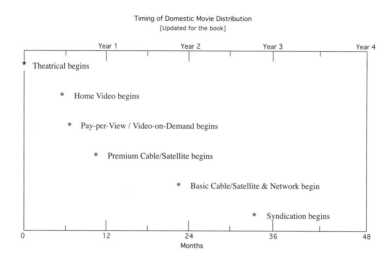

distributor expenses and fees

Prints and Advertising (P&A) are the most recognizable of distribution expenses. Once a final version of a film is completed and ready for theatrical distribution, a copy of this version is made from which all other copies, known as "prints," are created. One print costing approximately $1500 domestically must be made for each screen on which the film is being shown during any given weekend. Advertising is much more expensive. The cost of a quarter page ad in a major newspaper can be over $10,000 per day. If a film such as *Sci-Fi Rom/Mass H-Com/Psych Thrill* achieves a domestic theatrical release on 100–600 screens, the P&A costs could approach or even exceed the film's budget. Often, an even larger, but less recognizable, expense for low-budget independent films is the cost of manufacturing, marketing, and distributing DVDs. These costs can exceed $4.00 per DVD on a wholesale price of $15–$18. Returning to the topic of P&A, some low-budget films take it upon themselves to raise and spend P&A funds. We will not take this approach because P&A expenditure is the specialty of distributors and would be most efficiently handled by them.

Each distributor is responsible for collecting the revenue generated by its markets. After doing so, the distributor subtracts its distribution fee, followed by expenses (including P&A costs for any theatrical release), and remits the remaining portion to the producer. The fee is a percentage of the total revenue and depends upon the nature of the producer-distributor contract. These contracts vary widely from project to project, but should they arise, will be negotiated by Sci-Fi Rom/Mass H-Com/Psych Thrill LLC and its lawyers to maximize investor profits. It bears mentioning again that revenues in all other markets are driven by the success of the domestic theatrical release, because it establishes audience awareness for the film. This area is where especially close attention and effort will be paid in trying to find a quality distributor for *Sci-Fi Rom/Mass H-Com/Psych Thrill*.

distributor control

Before agreeing on a contract, the distributor may request any number of changes to a film itself, ranging from length to music to style of editing. These requests will only be met if we feel they serve to maximize investor profits. Once the contract is signed, the distributor has control over a film's marketing. In the case of a film with solid commercial prospects where the distributor has been licensed all format rights, the distributor also has control over the film's theatrical release pattern. The distributor will determine in which city or cities and in how many theaters the movie should open. Typically with independent films of a similar budget to *Sci-Fi Rom/Mass H-Com/Psych Thrill*, initial domestic release occurs on fewer than 15 screens, sometimes as few as one, and then spreads to more theaters when proceeds are high enough to pay for more prints and advertising. With regard to marketing, the distributor will determine to whom and how to market the picture, including with which newspapers and radio and television channels to advertise. Because so much control is exercised by distributors, we will take the utmost care in assuring our views on how the film should be marketed and released are represented in any distribution contract. The overriding concern in any agreement will be maximizing investor profit, and we will make the full use of our lawyers and their experience in this field in efforts to do so.

distribution companies [Remember, this is from a plan in late 2004!]

Domestic distribution companies in the independent film industry can be divided into three groups: studio subsidiaries (also known as "mini-majors"), stand-alones, and mini-distributors. Studio subsidiaries are a testament to the health of the independent film sector. Their parents, the studios, have recognized the potential profit of these films and created their own specialty divisions to distribute them. Recently, Warner Brothers became the seventh major studio to do so by establishing Warner Independent Pictures in 2003. Stand-alone distributors and mini-distributors are not subdivisions of a studio.

The mini-majors clearly have the domestic distribution power. When looking at independent film distributors with the top 2003 theatrical grosses, mini-majors held six of the top ten spots, including positions one through five.[1] Because of their attachment to studios, the mini-majors have more experience and deeper financial resources with which to acquire, promote, and release films. While we intend to go after the mini-majors, stand-alone distributors provide another attractive option. They held the remaining positions in the top ten with stand-alone Lionsgate outperforming mini-majors Sony Pictures Classics and Paramount Classics (Paramount was outperformed by three other stand-alones as well).[2] Mini-distributors have a more difficult time successfully distributing films due to their small size and somewhat limited power. Nevertheless, Zeitgeist, Manhattan Pictures, and ThinkFilm were examples of such companies able to keep their top 2003 releases in theaters for over sixteen weeks.[3] Additionally, these companies look for good films with which to establish themselves. In terms of foreign distribution, a mini-major or stand-alone has the capacity to distribute internationally or refer a film to a foreign sales agent (who in turn licenses the film to foreign distributors). Mini-distributors may or may not. We will focus on trying to obtain domestic distribution with companies that have foreign capacity or contacts. It is worth noting the terms "foreign sales agent" and "foreign distributor" are sometimes used interchangeably.

---

[1] Ian Mohr, "Indies Fly High," *The Hollywood Reporter*, January 7, 2004; note that some of these totals, especially those of the mini-majors, may also include pictures at least partially financed by studios; however, as a general proxy of independent film distribution power, the table is reliable.

[2] Ibid.

[3] *Weekly Variety* box office charts, 1999–2003; *IMDb.com*.

distribution criteria (Sci-Fi Rom)

Distributors seek films with at least one recognizable cast member, an exploitable genre or market segment, and a storyline that is original. These are some of the main factors influencing a distributor's decision to acquire the rights to a film. While *Sci-Fi Rom* will contain no cast member whose name alone carries innate audience appeal, its target audience often supports movies without such talent. This audience consists of specialty theater patrons favoring upbeat fare. The film's absolutely unique storyline of XXXXXXXXXXXXXXXXXXXXXXXXXXXXXXXXX XXXXXXX, yielding a feature film set in one location and shot in one day, should spark major interest among this market segment. As a result, *Sci-Fi Rom* is well positioned to maximize its chances for garnering distribution.

distribution criteria (Psych Thrill)

Distributors seek films with at least one recognizable cast member, an exploitable genre or market segment, and a storyline that is original. These are some of the main factors influencing a distributor's decision to acquire the rights to a film. *Psych Thrill* will feature at least one actor whose name carries innate audience appeal. Furthermore, it will do so in a genre (psychological thriller) that has a great potential for generating revenues, as the performances of the low-budget independent *Pic N* and the studio-budgeted *Silence of the Lambs* franchise illustrate. Finally, *Psych Thrill* contains the unique story line of a XXX XXXXXXXXXXXXXXXXXXXXXXXXXXXXXXXXXXXXXXXXXXXXXXX. These qualities of the project will maximize its chances for garnering distribution.

distribution criteria (Mass H-Com)

Distributors seek films with at least one recognizable cast member, an exploitable genre or market segment, and a storyline that is original. These are some of the main factors influencing a distributor's decision to acquire the rights to a film. One of the leads in *Mass H-Com* will be played by XXXXXXXXX, whose name carries innate audience appeal, especially among the demographic of the audience for horror films. The film itself is a horror-comedy with horror elements that capitalize on recent trends in the horror industry and comedic elements that appeal to both fans of subtle and broad humor. These genre elements increase its attractiveness to the largest demographic of moviegoers, 12-to-29-year-olds. Also, *Mass H-Com* carries the unique story line of a XXXXXXXXXXXXXXXXXXXXXXXXX XXXXXXXXXXXXXXXXXXXXXXXXXXXXXX. In their entirety, these qualities of *Mass H-Com* will maximize its chances for garnering distribution.

strategy for attaining distribution (Sci-Fi Rom)

We will implement a three-step approach to attaining distribution. First, we will submit the film to top-tier film festivals such as Sundance, Berlin, Tribeca, Cannes, and Toronto. At major festivals such as these, all levels of distributors attend screenings arranged for festival attendees. In the ideal scenario, distributors at these screenings take such keen interest in a film that a bidding war ensues, in which distributors bid against one another for domestic and foreign rights in all formats. These bidding wars, while extremely rare, can result in exorbitant advances being paid to the producers (and thus investors) of a film well before distribution commences. Recent examples include *Pic B* (2003), *Pic A* (2003), and *Pic D* (2002), which sold in the neighborhood of $1.5 million, $3.5 million, and $5 million on respective budgets of $0.5 million, $0.3 million, and $0.2 million.[4] Additional examples, also very rare, are films that were sold at festivals (a.k.a. delivered advances) closer to the vicinity of their negative costs, including *Pic Q* (2002), *Pic E* (2002), and *Pic M* (2001), which sold in the neighborhood of $3 million, $1 million, and $4 million respectively.[5] Simultaneous to festival submissions, we will submit the film to top producer's representatives, otherwise known as producer's reps, for representation. For a fee ranging from 10%–15% of all revenues returned from a film to the producer, the top producer's reps use their contacts with distributors to secure and negotiate domestic and international distribution for a film. They do so by helping films gain entrance to one of the top-tier festivals and/or positioning distributors against one another at such a festival to induce a bidding war. Sometimes producer's reps will not take on a film until after it has gained acceptance to a festival, and in other cases they can secure distribution for a film prior to or independent of a festival appearance. Once domestic distribution in all formats is secured via a film festival, via a producer's rep, or both, the third step in attaining distribution will be to seek out a foreign sales agent to license the film to any remaining foreign territories. The foreign sales agent, sometimes referred to as a foreign distributor, may be referred or hired by a producer's rep and will attend various film markets throughout the year in

---

[4] XXXXXXXXXXXXXXXXXXXXXXXXXXXXXXXXXXXXXXXXXXXXXXXXXXXXXXXXXXXXXXXXXXXXXXXXXXX XXXXXXXXX.
[5] XXXXXXXXXXXXXXXXXXXXXXXXXXXXXXXXXXXXXXXXXXXXXXXXXXXXXXXXXXXXXXXXXXXXXXXXXXX XXXXXXXXXXXXXXXXXXXXXXXXXXXXXXXXXXXXXXXXXXXXXXXXXXXXXXXXXXXXXXXXXXXX.

Europe, America, and possibly elsewhere and license the film to distributors from certain geographical territories. These distributors pay an advance to the sales agent against which the agent charges a 10%–25% fee, deducts expenses, and remits the remaining portion to the producer or producer's rep.

Should top-tier festivals and producer's reps not take an interest in *Sci-Fi Rom*, as is the case with the vast majority of independent features, a second tier of festivals and approaches will be utilized with the goal of securing a domestic theatrical release. However, as each subsequent set of options becomes eliminated, the prospects for returning more than a film's principal investment, and the principal investment itself, decrease.

strategy for attaining distribution (Mass H-Com)

We will implement a three-step approach to attaining distribution. First, we will submit the film to top-tier American film festivals such as Sundance, Tribeca, Los Angeles, and AFI. At major festivals such as these, all levels of distributors attend screenings arranged for festival attendees. In the ideal scenario, distributors at these screenings take such keen interest in a film that a bidding war ensues in which distributors bid against one another for domestic and foreign rights in all formats. These bidding wars, while extremely rare, can result in exorbitant advances being paid to the producers (and thus investors) of a film well before distribution commences. Recent examples include *Pic B* (2003), *Pic A* (2003), and *Pic D* (2002) which sold in the neighborhood of $1.5 million, $3.5 million, and $5 million on respective budgets of $0.5 million, $0.3 million, and $0.2 million.[4] Simultaneous to festival submissions, we will submit the film to top producer's representatives, otherwise known as producer's reps, for representation. For a fee ranging from 10%–15% of all revenues returned from a film to the producer, the top producer's reps use their contacts with distributors to secure and negotiate domestic and international distribution for a film. They do so by helping films gain entrance to one of the top-tier festivals and/or positioning distributors against one another at such a festival to induce a bidding war. Sometimes

---

[4] XXXXXXXXXXXXXXXXXXXXXXXXXXXXXXXXXXXXXXXXXXXXXXXXXXXXXXXXXXXXXXXXXXXXXXXXXXXXXXXXXXXXXX XXXXXXXXX.

producer's reps will not take on a film until after it has gained acceptance to a festival, and in other cases they can secure distribution for a film prior to or independent of a festival appearance. Once domestic distribution in all formats is secured via a film festival, via a producer's rep, or both, the third step in attaining distribution will be to seek out a foreign sales agent to license the film to any remaining foreign territories. Low-budget American comedies do not translate well in the foreign market; however, low-budget horrors do, thus mitigating some of the negative effects of the film's comedy on potential foreign revenue. The foreign sales agent, sometimes referred to as a foreign distributor, may be referred or hired by a producer's rep and will attend various film markets throughout the year in Europe, America, and possibly elsewhere and license the film to distributors from certain geographical territories. These distributors pay an advance to the sales agent against which the agent charges a 10%–25% fee, deducts expenses, and remits the remaining portion to the producer or producer's rep.

Should top-tier festivals and producer's reps not take an interest in *Mass H-Com*, as is the case with the vast majority of independent features, a second tier of festivals and approaches will be utilized with the goal of securing a domestic theatrical release. However, as each subsequent set of options becomes eliminated, the prospects for returning more than a film's principal investment, and the principal investment itself, decrease.

⁴COMPANY DESCRIPTION

HOW TO DO THE COMPANY DESCRIPTION SECTION

Behind the Executive Summary and financial sections, this is the most important section of the business plan. Here you make clear the structure of the filmmaking company, who the key members of it are, and what their background is. Basically, you are saying, "Don't worry, your money is safe with us." DO NOT LIE OR EMBELLISH. Apart from it just being wrong, at any point in time after you start the project, if your investors find out, they will be able to sue your pants off. Be matter-of-fact, state the facts about what people have done, and be ready to prove your claims if necessary. Trying to sound fancy here, even if you are telling the truth, can come across as embellishment, and the last thing an investor wants to do is to hand off his or her money to people trying to sound better than they really are. If you and the people you are working with are not experienced filmmakers (doing short films counts as experience; ask any respectable director), stop writing a business plan and go out and get that experience! No one will trust his or her money to you. Would you give your money to a mechanic who's never fixed cars before?

STEP 14. IDENTIFY YOURSELF! (OR AT LEAST YOUR FILM'S BUSINESS ENTITY.)

Provide all details of the company apart from personnel. Specify the legal business entity being formed (LLC, S-Corp, etc.), when it will be or was formed, what its purpose is, a brief description of your film, the market to-ward which it is geared, its budget, its timetable for completion, and a brief description of the kind of distribution you are seeking (theatrical-based) and how that distribution might occur. Again, as with all the sections of this book, these are merely recommendations, but do describe the important aspects of your company and its film. With regard to the film's timetable for completion, make no promises. Instead use words like "we anticipate" or "we feel." Looking briefly at the sample text (end of the chapter), I say "one year" at the latest before distributors can examine the film because in each of my cash flows, I assigned one year for preproduction, principal photography, and postproduction. Overall, as you can see from the two sample texts (the other text being in the back of the book), this section can assume a somewhat standard form.

STEP 15. WHO'S ON YOUR TEAM?

List people affiliated with your project, and only list those who you are 99% certain will do the project. An investor will have the right to pull his or her money if somebody in this section pulls out. By the time you are handing a business plan to potential investors, you should at the very least have your producer(s), writer(s), and director. Other key members to include, *if you have them and they are experienced*, are the director of photography, editor, casting director, composer, and anyone else whose contribution to the project will be critical. If they don't have experience, it is best to leave them out of this section.

Regarding the cast, only mention specific names if they are significantly name actors and if they have committed with a letter of intent to the project. Letters of intent are extremely rare, but your entertainment attorney will draw one up if the opportunity presents itself. Otherwise, make no mention of specific cast members. My experience watching low-budget indie producers casting name talent is that the options vary from day to day and the decision is sometimes not made until the week, or days, before shooting. Listing an actor in your plan and not hiring them may cause friction with an investor who gets their hopes up, and friction is not what you need in the time leading up to the start of a shoot.

Examine the two sample texts to get a feel for this section. What is not readily apparent due to the XXXing out is that *Mass H-Com* is to be shot in a certain region of the country not necessarily known for films; as a result, I make sure to mention when a person has worked in, or had other ties to, that area of the country. With *Mass H-Com* I also make sure to mention projects that members of the team have worked on together. A past history of success as a team increases the likelihood it will happen again.

SAMPLE COMPANY DESCRIPTION SECTION

COMPANY DESCRIPTION
(*Mass H-Com*)

company details

Mass H-Com LLC is a Los Angeles, California-based manager-managed limited liability company to be founded once financing commences. The purpose of the LLC will be to produce, find distribution, and collect revenues for the full-length 35mm feature entitled, *Mass H-Com*. *Mass H-Com* consists of horror and comedic elements, characters, and themes geared toward the largest section of the U.S. movie-going public, 12-to-29-year-olds. Typically, films of this type are produced by studios, but we feel *Mass H-Com* can be made for a lower budget and at a higher story quality than the studio version. It will be budgeted at $1.2 million and we anticipate ready for distributors to examine no later than one year after financing is complete. Our focus will be to license the film to a domestic distributor that can garner a successful theatrical release. Such a release would drive the profitability of the film and likely begin in a limited number of specialty theaters. Specialty theaters generally consist of one to five screens and cater to, but are not restricted to, niche audiences. On positive word-of-mouth the film would spread to other theaters.

company personnel

XXXXXXXXXX, **manager/producer** — XXXXXXXXXX will serve as sole manager of Mass H-Com LLC. She is also the founder and sole owner of XXXXXXXXXXX, a production company now dedicated to the creation of high quality, well-written features that keep the writer's vision of the project intact. In the spring of XXXX the company produced three fully crewed short films in the span of two months and recently shifted gears to develop several full-length features to be shot over the next two years. Ms. XXXXX was also a founding member and Vice President of Production at XXXXXXXXXXXXXX, a film production company where she oversaw all aspects of physical and postproduction. During her time at XXXXXXXXXX Ms. XXXXXXX produced the short film XXXXXXXXXXXX directed by XXXXXXXXX. This short was shot professionally on 35mm film and used a full cast and crew including stunt choreographers, children, animals, XXXXXXXXXXXXXXX, and XXXXXXXXXXXXXXX. It has gone on to popular reception and awards during its tour of over 15 film festivals and counting. Through her various projects, Ms. XXXXXX has established valuable industry contacts that will be helpful in the production of *Mass H-Com*. These projects have also served as exceptional preparation to produce features.

XXXXXX, **producer** — XXXXXXX is an independent producer who began her career as an executive assistant XXXXXXXXXX, Executive Vice President of XXXXXXXXXXXXXXXX. For her time at XXXXXX she was awarded a XXXXXXXXXXXXXXXXXXXXXXXXXXXXX. After several years in Los Angeles, she returned to her home state of XXXXXX to produce independent films shot in the XXXXXXXX. Ms. XXXXXXXX's most recent credit was as Producer on the independent feature XXXXXXX. Shot in XXXXXXXXXX last summer, the film acquired worldwide DVD distribution during postproduction and left her with valuable resources in the state that will prove cost effective in creating *Mass H-Com*. She is currently teaming with Ms. XXXXXXXX to produce several independent feature films.

XXXXXXXXXXX, **writer/director** — XXXXXXXXXX began his film career as a student at XXXXXXX and XXXXXXXXXXXX. During his college tenure he successfully directed numerous shorts, one of which went on to win "Best Picture" at XXXXXXX Film Festival. After moving to Los Angeles in XXXX, he enrolled at XXXXXXX under the tutelage of XXXXXXXXX to learn directing from an actor's perspective. Mr. XXXXXX also wrote and directed XXXXXXX, produced by XXXXXXXXXX. The short has left him with valuable industry contacts from whom advice can be drawn upon during production of *Mass H-Com*. It is customary for directors to hone their craft on shorts, then make the jump to features. Examples range from Steven Soderbergh to Steven Spielberg. Mr. XXXXXX also served as a producer on XXXXXXXXXXXXXX.

XXXXXXX, **actor** — XXXXXXX has signed a letter of intent to play the lead role of XXXXXXX. He is most recognized for his starring role in XXXXXX, a horror XXXXXX, but his career has spanned nearly 50 years. During this time he has amassed over 100 separate credits ranging from the films XXXXXXXXX and XXXXXXX to the television shows XXXXXXX and XXXXXXXXXX. Mr. XXXXXX's next starring role will be as a lead in XXXXXXX, to open on over 2,500 screens in XXXXXXX of next year.

XXXXXXXX, **cinematographer** — XXXXXXXX is an award-winning cinematographer with 13 years experience and countless film and television credits, including XXXXXXX. In XXXXX and again in XXXXXXXXX, Mr. XXXXXXX was awarded the Artistic

Achievement in Cinematography award by the International Cinematographers Guild and Kodak. Mr. XXXXXXX has worked in commercials and music videos, in addition to mainstream and independent films. He was declared by XXXXXXXX XXXXXXXX, an established and reputable trade magazine, to be "One of ten cinematographers to watch for."

XXXXXXXX, **special make-up effects artist** — XXXXXXXX is the founder and owner of XXXXXXXXXXXXX , a company specializing in special make-up effects. The company was formed in XXXX and has worked on a handful of films, including XXXXXXXX in the summer of XXXX. Prior to XXXX, he worked as a member of the effects team at XXXXXXXX . While at XXXXXXXX he was involved with such studio films as XXXXXXXX, XXXXXXX, XXXX XXXXX, and XXXXXXX and such TV shows as XXXXX and XXXXXXXX.

XXXXXXX, **casting director** — XXXXXXX is currently Casting Executive for XXXXXXXX where she oversees XXXXX, XXXXXXXX, XXXXXXXX, and XXXX for XXXXXXXX and XXXXXXXXXXXX. She has cast shows including XXXXXXXXXX, XXXXX, XXXXXXXX, XXXXXXXXXXXX, and XXXXXXXX. Ms. XXXXXXXX also launched XXXXXXXX in XXXX specifically targeted at independent films. Her first endeavor, XXXXXXXX, launched the career of XXXXXXXX (XXXXXXXXXXX).

XXXXXXXX **LLP, legal consultant** — XXXXXXXXXX (XXX) is a full-service law firm with expertise in entertainment transactions and litigation. XXXXXXXXXX will assist Mass H-Com LLC in legal services involved with the formation, financing, physical production, and distribution of the film.

⁵PRODUCT DESCRIPTION

This is probably the simplest section to complete in your entire plan. The Product Description section is where you describe the product you will be selling; in your case the product is a movie. Elaborate on certain aspects of the picture such as story, locations, and if you're lucky enough to get the ever-so-rare written commitment, acting attachments.

STEP 16. WRITE A STORY SYNOPSIS FOR YOUR FILM.

Rely on your writer to help with this part. You can summarize the story in as much or as little detail as you would like. I would write it as if the investor has not yet read the script. That is, don't give away the ending, and leave enough other details out to leave the reader wanting more. That being said, do not omit details that would result in a heart attack at the screening, if the investor gave you money but never read the script. Yes, it is their responsibility to read the script, but an angry investor is an angry investor, whether the script was read or not. Details not to be omitted include controversial topics (drugs, abortion, etc.) or especially graphic scenes.

Let's examine the sample text. The first line is the quote that would appear at the bottom of the movie poster. It should be very short but capture the essence of the picture — vague, I know, but when read by someone familiar with the movie, the person should say, "That says it all." The next line is what is known as the logline. The logline is a description of the movie in one sentence. A generalized formula for writing one might be, "The main character(s) must do X when Y has happened to/threatens him or her." In other words you briefly explain what the protagonist must do to compensate for the movie's inciting incident — ask a writer what I mean. There are other ways to look at the logline but again, it needs to describe your film in one sentence.

Next comes the actual synopsis, a one-page description of your film written in the manner first described above. In the different samples you'll notice an unchanged synopsis section. This is done to protect the original stories of the sample plans. Also take note of the sample footnote I provided. It's an example of letting the reader know that if an investment is made in this movie, this is the kind of movie that investment will be paying for. Again, you want no surprises for the investor regardless of whose responsibility it was to read the screenplay before investing.

STEP 17. DESCRIBE THE PROJECT'S OTHER IMPORTANT DETAILS.

Describe the film you are making in detail. You will end up repeating things you have already said in the Company Description, but that is okay. The more an investor remembers from your business plan, the better. Mention the project's rating, genre (or type), budget, target audience, writer, director, location, film stock (35mm, Super 16, High Def, etc.), casting details, and timing for completion of the film (when it will be ready for distributors to examine). In mentioning each of these things, expand on any that highlight the strengths of the project, such as a strong target audience, the director's experience, or fame of the cast. Incidentally, if you end up shooting on something other than 35mm, mention some other successful films that have shot in your format. A list of notable 16mm films can be found on Wikipedia (*www.wikipedia.org*) by searching the site with the phrase "Category:Films shot in Super 16." Make sure to double check the results with each film's IMDb "technical specs" page. Remember, only mention those significantly name actors that have a letter of intent to do the project (as mentioned before, you will hardly ever be able to get such a letter). Otherwise, leave their names to verbal discussions with investors, and remind investors that finding talent is a very fluid process. The only thing you can guarantee in your plan is that the person you cast will have been the lead in at least one domestically released feature that grossed $50 million or more in theaters.

Turning to the sample "project details" sections, you will notice that I do not mention the time of year each project plans to shoot, despite the fact that each sample project (apart from *Sci-Fi Rom*) was initially contingent on certain seasons. Excluding the shoot time is done to ensure maximum flexibility with shooting schedule. Sometimes events beyond your control may cause you to want to change the story so that it can be shot in another season. For instance, suppose you've just found your final investor, but it's too late for the season you want, and waiting another nine months until the season is just right might mean the money is no longer available. If changing the season does not greatly affect your story, your investors might be more willing to accept such a change, as long as you haven't played up in the plan how the film was meant for a specific season.

Another reason I like to avoid mentioning the desired timing of the shoot is that, if you start looking for monies in the spring for a shoot next winter, interested investors might put off talking with you until the fall, only to have lost interest by then. If they are interested and the timing is not listed in the plan, they are pretty much forced to start discussions with you right away, rather than waiting until the fall and forgetting about it. Any face time with an investor gives you a chance to stick out in his or her mind. There are exceptions to omitting the season of shooting until discussions with an investor. If your film is about the abominable snowman, you might as well mention the season. However, avoid mentioning specific months so that you don't have to run back to investors and double check if shooting in January is okay, even though you said December in the plan. Save returning to investors for more significant matters.

SAMPLE PRODUCT DESCRIPTION SECTION

PRODUCT DESCRIPTION*
(*Sci-Fi Rom, Mass H-Com, Psych Thrill*)

synopsis [example unconnected to sample films]

"Between a rock and a jelly-filled."

Forced by his distant mobster uncle to conceal $150,000, an out-of-work Finnish immigrant decides to open a donut shop only to find that popular donuts are not the best investment vehicle for laundering money.

Markku is down on his luck. His wife just died of a drug overdose and unless he can prove that he has a job, the INS will deport him back to Finland where he faces imprisonment by the new Socialist regime. Markku decides on the next best alternative... suicide.

Just as he has the noose fitted around his neck, a special delivery arrives at the door. Examining the package he notices it is from his uncle, a reputed Finnish mobster and otherwise unsavory character who regularly exports Finnish heroin to the neighborhood. Having given up selling since his wife's death, Markku sets the package aside and resumes his plans to travel to the afterlife. Suddenly, however, the noose breaks, landing him straight on top of the package. When he gets up, he notices the contents, $150,000, have exploded all over the room... along with a note.

Reading the note Markku finds a new purpose in life: he is to conceal the money for his uncle in a manner that will earn a high rate of return until his uncle can find a way to get to America. Not doing so will result in the loss of 90% of Markku's mental faculties.

Charged with a new lease on life, Markku decides to open a donut shop fueled by his deceased mother's ancient Finnish reindeer antler recipe.

---

*This movie will have scenes where the lead sleeps with and cuts to pieces reindeer. However, the scenes are comically portrayed as if the lead is doing so to a reindeer mascot suit with a person in it rather than to an actual reindeer. The focus of these scenes is a ridiculous, over-the-top portrayal of the inner angst faced by the main character.

Unfortunately for his uncle, the recipe is a hit and people from all around take notice of this little Finnish donut shop on the corner of Fletcher and Glendale, not the least of whom are the cops who can't get enough of the jelly-filled reindeer ears. The store becomes a community landmark and melting pot, and to complicate matters further, when neighborhood activists start to date the local cops, the results are explosive.

A call to arms is made to clean up the neighborhood and rid it of the pernicious Finnish heroin infestation. Fearing for his own life, Markku must learn what it is to be a Finnish man in American society. Can he give up his heritage and his life for a great American cause? Or will the fears and weaknesses that have plagued him all his life push him back into the mold of protecting his uncle? Whatever the decision, Markku promises to affect the reputation of Finnish Americans for generations to come. Who knew that the decision between jelly-filled and antler-filled would carry so much weight?

project details [Sci-Fi Rom]

Sci-Fi Rom is a PG-13 rated science fiction romance budgeted at $0.5 million and geared toward specialty theater audiences favoring upbeat fare. It is written and will be directed by XXXXXXXXXXX, a WGA member and playwright whose previous screenplay was sold to XXXXXXXXXXXX. Apart from the storyline, the uniqueness of this picture is the fact that it will be shot in one day and at a production quality characteristic of pictures that have secured distribution. Typically movies are filmed over the course of weeks, if not months. The project will be shot in Los Angeles using 35mm film, the same format used by movie studios on their projects. Casting will begin once financing is in place, and we anticipate the film to be ready for distributors to examine no later than one year after financing has been secured.

project details [Mass H-Com]

Mass H-Com is a mass-appeal R-rated horror-comedy budgeted at $1.2 million featuring both broad and subtle comedic elements. The target audience is 12-to-29-year-olds, the largest section of the U.S. movie-going public. It is written and will be directed by XXXXXXXXX, an award-winning short film director whose most recent project, XXXXXXXXXXXX, featured a cast including XXXXXX and XXXXXXXXXXXXXXXXXX and has gone on to popular reception and awards during its tour of over 15 film festivals and counting. A letter of intent to play one of the lead roles (XXXXXX) has been signed by horror film icon and significantly name actor XXXXXXXXXXXX. For the purposes of this business plan, a significantly name actor is one who has appeared in a leading role in at least one feature that has domestically grossed $50 million or above. For his role in XXXXXX he was awarded XXXXXXXXX Award for Best Supporting Actor by the readers of XXXXXX periodical in circulation for XXXXXX years. XXXXXX holds a starring role in the sequel, XXXXXX, to be released by XXXXXXXXXXXX on over 2,500 screens in XXXXXX. The remainder of casting will continue once financing is in place, followed by shooting on 35mm film, the same film stock used by major motion picture studios. Shooting will occur in XXXXXX hometown of XXXXXXXXXX, offering significant cost advantages in producing the film. We anticipate the project to be ready for examination by distributors no later than one year after financing has been secured.

project details [Psych Thrill]

Psych Thrill is an R-rated psychological thriller much in the vein of *Silence of the Lambs* meets *Pic N*. It is budgeted at $1.5 million and targets upscale young adults, college students, and specialty theater patrons, as well as other audiences that favor intelligent thrillers with richly developed characters. It is written and will be directed by XXXXXXXX, a Los Angeles-based actor. Casting will begin once financing is in place and consist of hiring at least one significantly name actor. For the purposes of this business plan, a significantly name actor is one who has appeared in a leading role in at least one feature that has domestically grossed $50 million or above. Shooting will occur in Louisiana due to the aptness of the location and significant cost savings of shooting there versus other locations; it will also be done on studio quality 35mm film. We anticipate the film to be ready for examination by distributors no later than one year after financing has been secured.

⁶FINANCING

HOW TO DO THE FINANCING SECTION

Possibly the shortest section of the entire plan, the Financing section tells the investor how you will be financing the film and how that financing will be paid back, if the film makes money. Unlike other sections, you do not want to give a general overview of how film financing works, unless of course your funds will be coming from several different sources, such as coproductions, presales, gap financing, etc. Describing financing sources other than the ones you are going for may create confusion and doubt for the reader. He or she may wonder why this project isn't good enough to receive presale agreements, even though you know full well that such agreements are rare these days. Or why other production companies do not want to share the risk by partnering with yours, even though you know full well your company can fully handle the load and your director lacks the track record for such a deal. Or the investor might ask if you could please re-explain gap financing and why it was in the plan in the first place. Get the picture? Investors will be overwhelmed, in all likelihood, by the mountain of information thrown at them already, so no need to complicate one of the most important parts. Also, if they read a lot of business plans and this is one of the first sections they turn to, they will appreciate your getting to the point.

STEP 18. BRIEFLY SCARE THE CRAP OUT OF THE INVESTOR (A.K.A. MINI-RISK STATEMENT).

Restate some of the points from your risk statement. Now, the risk statement is one of the first parts of your proposal, but in this book, it's not covered until later, in Chapter 9. So I'll save the in-depth discussion of risks until then. In the meantime, let's keep things brief. While you want to make the risks absolutely clear to the investor, it's okay here to omit some of the more bruising facts of the full-length risk statement. (You mean it gets worse? Yes.) If the investor has made it this far through your plan, no need to scare the daylights out of them a second time. Instead, you want a friendly, but still firm, reminder of what he or she is getting into. Some business plan writers omit this second "mini-risk statement," but by including it, you are taking every precaution to avoid the situation where an investor returns to you saying, "Gee, I didn't think it was *that* risky," in which case you may be in serious trouble. Playing devil's advocate, there is the chance that this is one of the first sections to which the investor turns, after having skipped the page-long risk statement in favor of reading the Executive Summary. If this is so, it might be worth including the omitted risks from the full-length risk statement. Feel free to do so.

STEP 19. EXPLAIN HOW YOU INTEND TO FUND THIS GAMBLE/FILM.

In the Company Description section you described the business entity you are forming in order to raise money for your film. Here you go into slightly more detail about that entity. In the case of the sample texts I explain the size of the LLC's investment units and reinforce some of the advantages, to be covered in the Industry Overview section, of funding a film via private equity; although in the Industry Overview section the term "independent movie making" will be used instead of specifically referencing private equity funding. Should you be participating in any coproductions, lay out exactly what the coproducers are providing, be it cash or services, and in the rare but fortunate instance of presales, mention the amount of funding these presales have generated. Obviously list any loan amounts here as well. If you are solely funding your film via cash given to you by investors, don't worry about these last three items I just mentioned.

STEP 20. EXPLAIN HOW YOU INTEND TO DISTRIBUTE THE WINNINGS.

Lay out exactly how monies generated by the film will be paid to investors. This information will be reiterated in a Private Placement Memorandum (PPM), should you end up using one. The PPM is an official document prepared by your lawyer that encompasses key information from your business plan, as well as other non-business-plan information, so that you can be in compliance with securities laws. Also, explain how profit participations will not affect money returned to an investor, since such participations will be paid out of the producer's share of profits; profit participations are when a member of the filmmaking team, be it an actor, high profile editor, etc., is promised some of the net profit. The only exception would be if you hired such a famous actor or director that part of their contract dictates that they receive a share of gross or adjusted gross, thus affecting the amount of money returned to investors. If you have such a talent attached to your project, you are likely in very good shape, but still must make investors aware of the deal. If later in the casting process you come upon such an actor who takes an interest in the project, you must go back and run the potential hiring by investors before altering the deal for which the investors signed up. Again, the scenario I just described is a good problem to have because it means a big star is interested in your project, and with a big star you are virtually guaranteed at least some form of distribution. Finally, lay out expectations for when accounting statements and any accompanying revenues may be received from the three parties responsible for such matters (distributors, foreign sales agents, and producer's reps). As with the rest of the plan, make no promises here, other than that you will remit funds and accounting statements within 30 days of when you receive them.

STEP 21. DEPICT THE UGLY TRUTH ABOUT RESIDUALS.

Check out the sample text under "residuals." Do not forget to mention this information. The content is pretty self-explanatory, not to mention depressing. If your film uses union talent, you are responsible for making sure any distributor or foreign sales agent agrees to pay residuals owed to talent. If you do not do so, the unions have the right to some serious legal action against you in the pursuit of their residuals. The real pain is that if your film is not highly sought after, you have little or no leverage to exert in forcing a distributor or foreign sales agent to accept residual responsibility. Your only real recourse in such a situation is if a distributor buys your copyright from you (that is, you no longer own the film), then you can pressure the distributor to pay residuals using an obscure provision from the Digital Millennium Copyright Act.[1] If you do not outright transfer your copyright, your recourse becomes murkier. (Incidentally, selling your

---

[1] For an in-depth discussion of this mode of recourse, read "Can the Digital Millennium Copyright Act Save the Day for Independent Filmmakers (and for the Rest of Hollywood)? *10th & Wolf* v. *ThinkFilm* and the Legal Obligation to Pay Residuals," by Larry Iser and Chad Fitzgerald of Kinsella Weitzman Iser Kump & Aldisert, *Intellectual Property Today*, November 2007, *www.iptoday.com/articles/2007-11-iser.asp*.

film's copyright to a sales agent would hardly, if ever, occur.) Note that the residuals a sales agent would pay would be only out of revenues collected by the sales agent (chiefly advances). For instance, if a film became a blockbuster DVD hit in Indonesia, but the sales agent was unable to collect the overages (the money beyond just advances), he or she would not pay the residuals theoretically owed on the overages.[2] The bottom line here is to inform investors that their interests will be second in line to residual recipients, if it happens that the producer is forced to pay residuals. Otherwise, residuals will be counted as part of distributor and sales agent expenses. Also, mention the necessity to first pay deferrals, should deferrals be planned for in your film (see Step 2G's entry in Appendix B).

---

[2] For an article on how the unions have attempted in the past to secure foreign residuals see Sharon Swart, "Guilds eye indies' overseas residuals," *Daily Variety,* July 26, 2001, *www.variety.com/article/VR 1117850271. html?categoryid=1013&cs=1.*

SAMPLE
FINANCING
SECTION

FINANCING
(*Sci-Fi Rom, Mass H-Com, Psych Thrill*)

risk statement

Movies are the most risky of assets. They are subject to production, distribution, company-specific, and general economic risks that can vastly hamper the forecasting of their results. Risks associated with *Sci-Fi Rom/Mass H-Com/Psych Thrill* (the "movie") include, but are not limited to, failure to complete production, failure to achieve distribution, ineffective distribution of the movie by a distributor, a distributor of the movie going bankrupt, extreme competition from other movies, failure of the public to accept the movie, inability of management and other persons to guide the movie through the marketplace, and general economic and market factors. When combined, these risks can drastically change the actual results versus the forecasted results posited in this business plan. This list of risk factors is by no means complete.

method of financing

Sci-Fi Rom/Mass H-Com/Psych Thrill LLC is seeking $0.5/$1.2/$1.5 million in equity capital (in units of $25,000/$50,000/$50,000) to finance the entire production budget of the motion picture *Sci-Fi Rom/Mass H-Com/Psych Thrill*. The use of private equity funding ensures that the advantages of making an independent film can be fully realized. Creative control centered in the hands of the director ensures a film free from the divisive influence of too many voices. Low overhead and extreme care in formulating the budget yield a higher potential return for investors. Greater creative control ultimately yields a higher potential return as well.

investor repayment

Money remitted to the LLC will first be returned to investors until their initial investment plus a 20% percentage of return (a so-called "priority return") is recouped. Payments will be proportionately distributed to investors according to their individual investment size and without preference to all investors simultaneously. Any remaining profits will be split evenly between Sci-Fi Rom/Mass H-Com/Psych Thrill LLC and investors. Sci-Fi Rom/Mass H-Com/Psych Thrill LLC may use a portion of its profits (after the split) to pay for profit participations agreed upon between it and various talent or crew, such as actors, composers, or producers.

Distributors and foreign sales agents typically produce accounting statements on a quarterly, or sometimes monthly, basis during the beginning of a distribution term and change to less frequent reports one or two years later. Reports and any concomitant revenues are often remitted to a producer's rep or producer within 30–45 days of their monthly, quarterly, semi-annual, or annual due date. Sci-Fi Rom/Mass H-Com/Psych Thrill LLC will deliver accounting statements and appropriate payments to investors within 30 days of the receipt of funds from a distributor, sales agent, or producer's rep. Producer's reps of successful films generally remit funds to producers within one to two weeks of their receipt from another party.

residuals

Residuals are payments made to union talent (actors, writers, etc.) out of revenues generated from post-theatrical exploitation of a movie. The producer is responsible for ensuring that a distributor or foreign sales agent makes these payments by including an assumption agreement in the language of any distribution or foreign sales agent deal. While successful pictures may not have substantial problems with distributors or foreign sales agents accepting and executing such agreements, pictures that are not highly sought after for distribution may face problems with distributors or foreign sales agents accepting responsibility for and paying residuals. In such cases it may be that monies returned from distributors or foreign sales agents for ancillary markets are first used to pay residuals and then used to pay investors.

⁷INDUSTRY OVERVIEW

The way to go about this portion of the plan is similar to the way you did the Movie Distribution section. Basically, read a lot and summarize what you have learned. In the end, you will want to describe some general aspects of the film industry: how a film is put together, how it gets into theaters, and who some of the major players in the industry are. Also you will need to distinguish between studio films and what you mean by independent films. Look up books and articles on the movie industry, and in the books check out their general descriptions of the industry.

Entertainment Industry Economics (7th Edition) by Harold L. Vogel, pages 73-74, and The Movie Business by Kelly Charles Crabb, pages 333-343, give good industry overviews. The Movie Business Book (3rd Edition) edited by Jason E. Squire, provides some great specifics, but beware that some of the information is out of date. If you are in Los Angeles, the "Motion Picture Industry (MPI)" and "Statistics" clipping files and the "Current Statistics" binder at the Margaret Herrick Library will get you up to speed with current developments. Many other helpful books exist; just keep in mind during your readings that definitions of terms such as "independent" and "mini-major," among others, vary across sources. You will need to clarify your definitions during the course of your plan.

STEP 22. PORTRAY THE WONDERFUL PROCESS OF MOVIEMAKING (WITHOUT THE BLOOD & SWEAT).

Briefly summarize the process of making and distributing a movie. I have done this in the sample text from the perspective of the producer, since that is the person in the world of independent film who is most responsible for guiding the ship. As much hell as moviemaking can be, keep your description detached and to the point, rather like a textbook. One thing to point out about the sample text, these days the "original negative" may not take the form of a cut negative (a "cut negative" being film, like the stuff found in a 35mm camera, that has been spliced together). Instead, it may take the form of a digital intermediate (DI) such as HDSR or D5. This allows a project to avoid the major expense of cutting a negative, which means that a film may be able to be screened for distributors and picked up for distribution without a negative ever being cut. Just something to keep in mind as you write your text and answer questions from investors.

STEP 23. STUDIO FILMS VS. INDEPENDENT FILMS.

Define what you mean by "studio film" and "independent film." Then highlight the main advantages and disadvantages of making films outside of the studio system. Don't forget the disadvantages. Investors need to know what they might be getting into, and finding out as the project goes down the toilet does not count. Warn them beforehand. Turning to the sample text, you might notice that the studio percentage of box office seems a little low. This is because 2004 was the year of the most successful independent film ever, *The Passion of the Christ*, whose share of the total box office to that point approached 8%. In any other given year most of that 8% would belong to the studios.

STEP 24. DESCRIBE THE CURRENT AND FUTURE STATE OF THE MOVIE INDUSTRY.

Again, you're going to have to read, read, read. Focus on the broader movie industry, saving discussions of the market for independent films for the Market Analysis & Marketing Strategy section. Useful online sources are *The Hollywood Reporter*, *Variety*, Video Business (*www.videobusiness.com*), and the Motion Picture Association of America (MPAA). Video Business is a company that tracks the home entertainment market, and the MPAA issues the annual U.S. Entertainment Industry Market Statistics report (*www.mpaa.org/researchstatistics.asp* — see the bottom of the web page). In the Margaret Herrick Library in Los Angeles, useful resources are the "Statistics," "Videodiscs," and "MPI" clipping files; the binder called "Current Statistics"; and recent copies of *Screen Digest*. Next, I'm going to give you a mix of tips for certain parts of this step.

A good source for the latest domestic box office total is the website of *The Hollywood Reporter*. If you type in "year-to-date" in the site's search box, one of the articles that will pop up is a weekly one quoting the latest box office figures for the year. These numbers are from Nielsen EDI, a company that specializes in box office statistics and is a sister company to *The Hollywood Reporter*. *Variety* has a particularly fantastic chart on its site that breaks out box office figures for sometimes well over 100 films released each week.

Frequently, articles about the industry will make predictions about the size of a market in the future. It's useful to translate these predictions into growth rates — you will notice these are the implied annual growth rates mentioned in the sample text. To do so, follow this next example. Suppose an article predicts the U.S. video-on-demand market will grow from $10 billion at the end of 2009 to $15 billion at the end of 2014 (these numbers are totally bogus by the way). For an implied annual growth rate you would do the following:

$$\text{implied annual growth} = (\$15 \text{ billion} / \$10 \text{ billion})^{\wedge}(1 / (2014 - 2009)) - 1$$
$$= (1.5)^{\wedge}(1 / 5) - 1$$
$$= (1.5)^{\wedge}(0.2) - 1$$
$$= 1.0844 - 1$$
$$= 0.0844$$
$$= 8.44\%$$

Don't freak out. Remember, the "/" means "divided by," and you want to do everything in the order I just did it. As for what the heck the " ^ " is, think of it like "to-the-power-of." For instance, 2^3 would be "two to-the-power-of three," or two cubed, or 2 x 2 x 2, or 8. Still confused? Just plug the above equation into Excel and you'll be fine. Going back to the example, if the video-on-demand market grew at 8.44% a year for the next five years, in 2014 it would be at $15 billion. Doing all this gives the numbers more meaning than just quoting large dollar amounts.

Now, here's the part about this step, and really the industry, that stinks. Home video numbers are a closely guarded secret. Even companies that specialize in reporting home video numbers don't really know what their actual value is. This stems mainly from the fact that the studios don't want a bunch of actors, writers, producers, etc. coming after them saying, "Hey! When you gave me my cut of the movie, you said the DVD only made this much! Now this magazine says it made *THIS MUCH*!!!" In the sample texts, I tried to cover for this with some figures available at the time for the top titles. Unfortunately, today, even figures for the top titles are hard to come by.

So what should you do with home video numbers (a.k.a. DVD numbers)? My best advice is to check the quarterly reports from the Video Business website. They include data on the entire DVD market, which unfortunately includes all kinds of things not related to recently released films, such as television seasons, foreign language TV shows, and movies from the '60s being released on DVD. However, as a general indication of where DVD revenues from recently released films are headed, the quarterly reports should do it. By quoting the general home video market as trending downward, upward, or staying the same, you will have done enough to indicate how new feature films released on DVD are doing. If an investor asks for more specific numbers, you can describe the difficulty in getting them, but that features (new and old) make up about two-thirds of home video revenue.[1]

Another thing to keep in mind about home video is that the market for DVDs has matured and is no longer expanding. This is because people are beginning to spend more money on digital delivery (such as online streaming and downloads) and cable video-on-demand. Also they are only just beginning to adopt the Blu-ray format as a new disc format. As a result, the home video market is actually shrinking — the sample text contains some of the first signs of this. In your plans, you need to paint the declining market in a positive light, and that positive light is that the U.S. home video revenue for a film often exceeds its box office gross, making home video the chief source of revenue for a film. Mention this against the backdrop of home video being expected to shrink so that the reader knows your year in question isn't some unexpected down year. Also mention that some of that revenue from DVDs is being diverted to the Internet/digital market for films, though clearly not in a 1:1 ratio to account for all of the lost DVD revenue.

Finally, what do you write if the industry is not doing so well, as it certainly does on occasion? In the articles that appear in early January during off years, you will find some reasons for why the numbers were bad. Use these especially if they make it sound like the industry couldn't

---

[1] Harold L. Vogel, *Entertainment Industry Economics: A Guide for Financial Analysis*, 7th ed., 129.

help but do poorly (for example, the bar was set unusually high by the previous year, a studio burned to the ground, etc.) Also, focus on positive statistics and studies, if there are any, though you won't be able to get away with omitting box office stats. If there were any major record breaking movies these might also be worth mentioning; perhaps you can make the point that the films themselves were bad, but that good films still did well. You might also briefly mention how independent films fared as a whole, if their market did well despite the overall industry picture. Keep any such independent film mentions brief, and say you will cover that section of the market in more depth in the Market Analysis & Marketing Strategy section. Of particular use during off years are the statements by the head of the MPAA made every March at or just before ShoWest, the industry's longest running annual convention for exhibitors and distributors. If anyone has an incentive to spin a bad year, it's the MPAA, and their spin can be a particularly useful way to describe an off year. The event is very well covered by media outlets such as *The Hollywood Reporter* and *Variety*. Check out Appendix B for a sample of what to write in an off year.

Last thing (I know, I already said "finally"), please don't mention MGM as a major studio. It's not. It is now owned by a consortium of investors, of which Sony is a 20% participant.

SAMPLE
INDUSTRY OVERVIEW
SECTION

INDUSTRY OVERVIEW
(*Sci-Fi Rom, Psych Thrill, Mass H-Com*)

production and distribution

There are four steps involved in the creation of any motion picture: development, preproduction, principal photography, and postproduction. The person who guides a film through these steps and beyond is the producer. During development the idea for a movie is hatched and developed into a screenplay. Money is raised to shoot the film and tentative commitments are entered into with crucial members of the cast and crew. Once these actions are taken and the main layout for the screenplay is established, the producer engages in what is known as "preproduction." At this time she finalizes contracts with the cast and crew, decides on locations, and sets the shooting order of the script. Then follows the actual shooting of the motion picture, known as "principal photography." During this phase the producer oversees the day-to-day operations of the film shoot, ensuring that they run smoothly. Following the successful completion of principal photography is postproduction. During this phase the movie is edited, sound and music established, special effects added, and a final version of the movie created in the form of an original negative. From this negative all other copies of the movie can be generated. The term "production" can be applied collectively to the steps described thus far (minus development) or solely to the step of principal photography. The former will be the definition used here.

Following the production of a movie is the process of distribution. A company or companies pays the producer for the right to release the movie in theaters, known as the "theatrical release," and various ancillary markets such as DVD/home video, free TV, and pay TV. Distribution to theaters and ancillary markets occurs both domestically (Canada and the U.S.) and internationally. Frequently distribution begins with a domestic theatrical release followed by further release into ancillary and foreign markets. The domestic theatrical release may occur on as many as 3000 movie screens or as few as one.

studio versus independent films

A movie can be financed by a studio or other entities. The major studios (a.k.a. "studios") as defined by the Motion Picture Association of America are Sony Pictures Entertainment/MGM, The Walt Disney Company, Warner Bros., Twentieth Century-Fox, Universal Studios, and Paramount Pictures. Generally, these are subdivisions of large, diversified corporations and are capable of producing and distributing 15–25 films annually worldwide. In fact, in the steps outlined above, a producer working for a studio does not get paid by a distributor for the rights to her film, because the studio already has a distribution division and owns the film. Studio films accounted for over 65% of U.S. box office revenue during the first six months of 2004 and are usually budgeted at well north of $10 million.[1] For the purposes of this business plan, those movies created with no funding from a U.S. studio are known as "independent films" and those with such funding and owned by a studio are "studio films." It is possible for an independent film to be distributed by a studio. Sci-Fi Rom/Mass H-Com/Psych Thrill will be an independent film financed through private equity raised by Sci-Fi Rom/Mass H-Com/Psych Thrill LLC.

There are several difficulties in shooting an independent versus a studio film. Apart from having to attract financing, the independent producer has to seek out one or more distributors. There is no guarantee that she will find distribution for her film. Another difficulty is that the success of the movie rests much more heavily on the skills and resources of the producer. A producer at a studio has a large and diverse network of advisors to consult regarding matters ranging from legal, accounting, and marketing to editing, shooting, and props. The independent producer does not. Finally, if an independent film exceeds its budget, it is often extremely difficult to approach investors for more funds, and a movie may not ever reach completion. In contrast, a studio is very willing to bridge the gap between an estimated and actual budget in order to complete a film.

There are, however, several very significant advantages to independent movie making that Sci-Fi Rom/Mass H-Com/Psych Thrill LLC feels outweigh filmmaking

---

[1] Calculation based on totals from "US Spring Box Office Up 30 Per Cent" by Staff reporting data from ACNielsen/EDI, Screen Digest, July 2004.

within the studio system. The producer and director have much more creative control. While there are many advisers in a studio regarding non-creative matters, there are also many studio executives (often with a legal or financial background, not a creative one) who have heavy influence over a film's content. This can lead to a producer and director's vision of the story being far different from the final studio version, a version that may suffer from too many separate ideas implemented in one picture. Furthermore, the employees of a studio are needed for the operations of many other films as well as the upkeep of the studio and its many divisions. As a result, overhead for a studio film is often much higher than that for an independent film. The same holds true for budgets. Because a studio is very willing to fund a budget that has exceeded projections, the same care is not given to budgeting a studio picture as to an independent. These higher budgets and overhead reduce the final profits of a studio film [and in the case of a project such as *Sci-Fi Rom*, would prohibit the movie from being made due to its smaller, but nonetheless significant, audience size].

current and future trends

Currently domestic box office receipts lead 2003 totals by 2.4%.[2] In 2003 U.S. box office revenue dropped by only 0.3% from the all-time record high of $9.5 billion in 2002. Additionally, U.S. movie theater admissions reached the second highest level since 1957. The fact that 2003's numbers approached those of 2002 was, in the words of one industry CEO, "a minor miracle" and came amid competition from 67% of American households with basic cable, 56% with Internet access, 42% with DVD devices, 36% with premium cable, and 18% with satellite dishes.[3] While these percentages represent competition to box office figures, they also serve as a boon to ancillary receipts. Ancillary receipts are revenue generated from non-box office sources such as DVD/home video and pay TV. Due arguably in large part to poorer movie quality, mid-year revenue from the top 15 DVD/home video titles was down 10.5% compared to the same time period in 2003. However, this same revenue total exceeded the box office total

[2] Nielsen EDI, Inc., December 12, 2004, *www.nielsenedi.com/charts/seasonal.html*.
[3] "U.S. Entertainment Industry: 2003 MPA Market Statistics" by Motion Picture Association Worldwide Market Research; Carl DiOrio, "Mouse wore the top hat in flat 2003," *Daily Variety*, January 5, 2004.

of these films by nearly 10%, as opposed to only 1.4% in 2003.[4] Regarding the cable and satellite TV market, it is expected to reach a size of $122.2 billion in 2008 from a total of $83.5 billion in 2003, implying an annual growth rate of 7.9%.[5] In addition to this ancillary expansion, projected U.S. box office figures for 2007 imply annual growth of approximately 6%.[6] Independent films similar to *Sci-Fi Rom/Mass H-Com/Psych Thrill* generate the vast majority of their revenue from domestic sources. Nonetheless, global film revenue is expected to reach approximately $108 billion in 2008, up from $75.3 billion in 2003, implying an annual growth rate of 7.5%.[7]

---

[4] Comparisons based on calculations using data from Video Business's online site: *www.videobusiness. com/info/CA621777.html.*

[5] Staff, "US: communications and entertainment media forecasts by sector," *Screen Digest*, August 2004, reporting data from Veronis Suhler.

[6] Staff, "Study: U.S. b.o. will top $10 bil in '06," *The Hollywood Reporter*, January 27, 2004; implied growth rate calculated from article statistics.

[7] Georg Szalai, "Global media on the rise," *The Hollywood Reporter,* June 29, 2004; implied growth rate calculated from article statistics.

8 EXECUTIVE SUMMARY

HOW TO DO THE EXECUTIVE SUMMARY

Good news! You've made it to the second-to-last section of your plan. Bad news: doing this section will be very difficult, because it will be nearly the last step and you will be sick of writing the plan. HANG IN THERE! After the Information and Risk Statement (which investors may skip), this will be the first thing they read. Do a good job of it, because it will be your sole chance in the plan to make a first impression. Here you summarize the entire business plan on one page.

STEP 25. RESTATE THE WHOLE PLAN... IN ONE PAGE.

Unfortunately there is no hard and fast set of guidelines to executing this page. Basically you want to take the important points from each section and highlight them here. Keep education about the basics of the industry to a minimum; instead, you want to devote your time on this page to making a case for why the film should get financed. Oftentimes investors read through the Executive Summary, turn to the Financial Projections, and then check on the experience of the company personnel. If they go any further, you're lucky. Also, keep the summary to a page. It makes it more convenient for the reader. (The samples are more than a page because of the small 6x9 size of this book. Sorry!)

I recommend taking some time to read through the sample plans and comparing their Executive Summaries (ESs) to the rest of their plans. This will give you a feel for what to do. Concerning the ES of my sample plans, the "management team" paragraph corresponds to the Company Description section of the business plan, "funding requirement & projected returns" corresponds to the Financing and Financial Projections sections, and the remaining ES sections (minus the intro) correspond to their matching titles in the body of the plan. The reason I use "management team" instead of "Company Description" is because I want to focus on who is guiding the ship, so to speak, especially since the structure of the company is mentioned in the introductory statement and covered more in depth in the "funding requirement & projected returns" section.

Why not just list an ES section corresponding exactly to, and entitled the same as, each section in the rest of the plan? You could, as long the end result is the same: communicating clearly and concisely why the investor should invest with you.

SAMPLE
EXECUTIVE SUMMARIES

EXECUTIVE SUMMARY
(*Sci-Fi Rom*)

introductory statement **[synopsis of unrelated film inserted]**

Sci-Fi Rom LLC is being formed for the sole purpose of producing and seeking distribution for the full-length feature film *Sci-Fi Rom*. *Sci-Fi Rom* is a science fiction romance budgeted at $0.5 million that follows a [Finnish immigrant balancing instincts of self-preservation against desires to do right by his illegally financed donut shop.] Designed to be shot in one day (unheard of for a feature), the project marks the directorial debut of XXXXXXXX, a member of the Writers Guild whose previous script sold to XXXXXXXXXXXXX. We anticipate the film to be ready for distributors to examine no later than one year after the full receipt of financing. The management team's efforts in producing *Sci-Fi Rom* will yield substantial budgeting and creative advantages without which, as would occur with a major motion picture studio, the project would never be made. These advantages should translate into a significant profit opportunity for Sci-Fi Rom LLC.

management team

XXXXXXXXXX will serve as the sole manager of Sci-Fi Rom LLC. She is the sole founder and owner of a film production company as well, and has assembled a team of filmmakers with the industry experience necessary to fully realize the potential of this project. Having cut her teeth on other films, Ms. XXXXXXX stands ready to make *Sci-Fi Rom* in a way that is most appealing to potential distributors.

product description **[synopsis of unrelated film inserted]**

"Between a rock and a jelly-filled." *Sci-Fi Rom* is a PG-13 science fiction romance centered on [Markku, a Finnish immigrant forced to conceal and grow his mobster uncle's $150,000 in cash. After opening a local donut shop, Markku finds his donuts selling at a blistering pace and must balance his uncle's threats and desires with his own new-found success.] Designed to be shot in one day and at a production quality characteristic of pictures having secured distribution, *Sci-Fi Rom* should greatly distinguish itself from past, present, and future efforts in both the science fiction and romance genres.

industry overview

2003 U.S. box office receipts fell much less than expected (0.3%) from the all-time record high of $9.5 billion set in 2002. Receipts currently exceed year-to-date 2003 totals by 2.4%. Beyond theaters, the DVD/home entertainment market often yields revenue totals in excess of box office grosses, and while the cable and satellite TV market yields less, it is expected to grow at 7.9% per annum from $83.5 billion in 2003 to $122.2 billion in 2008. Overall, worldwide film revenue is expected to reach approximately $108 billion in 2008, growing at an annual rate of 7.5%. Those movies with no production funding from a U.S. studio, such as *Sci-Fi Rom*, are known as "independent films." Independent films benefit from lower budgets and greater creative freedom than the typical studio picture.

market analysis & marketing strategy

Over the past five years large capital outlays have been made to increase the number of movie screens showing low-budget independent films. *Sci-Fi Rom* will capitalize on this trend by appealing to moviegoers who favor upbeat, character-driven independent films, both foreign and homegrown. This audience has a history of generating significant revenue for production companies. To spark interest among this group, *Sci-Fi Rom* will rely heavily on initial word-of-mouth most likely generated via targeted screenings, Internet exposure, and grass-roots promotions. Any domestic distributor that acquires the rights to the film will likely open it in a limited number of specialty theaters and expand the release to more theaters on positive word-of-mouth.

motion picture distribution

The domestic theatrical release is the single most important event in determining the future revenue stream of a motion picture. It establishes audience awareness for a film. For this reason Sci-Fi Rom LLC will place the utmost importance on seeking a U.S. theatrical distributor whose marketing plan and release strategy will establish this awareness. Three of the main factors influencing a distributor's decision to acquire a film are the presence of at least one significantly name actor, the exploitability of genre or market segment, and the originality of the story. *Sci-Fi Rom* exhibits the latter two traits, while the absence of the first is balanced by the fact that the film targets a market segment where the presence of such actors is not essential to success. Distributors should not face a difficult decision when examining this project.

funding requirement & projected returns

Sci-Fi Rom LLC is seeking equity investment of $0.5 million through the issuance of 20 units of membership in the limited liability company valued at $25,000 per unit. Under a successful outcome over a 5.75 year period beginning with the completion of financing, the projected return on the investment is 231% or $1,152,886 above the initial $0.5 million (an ROI multiple of 3.31x). This translates into a yearly internal rate of return of 40.9% based on cash flow projections. Films with comparable budgets, initial release patterns, and similar audiences demonstrate that such returns are possible.

EXECUTIVE SUMMARY
(*Mass H-Com*)

introductory statement

Mass H-Com LLC is being formed for the sole purpose of producing and seeking distribution for the full-length feature film *Mass H-Com*. *Mass H-Com* is a mass-appeal horror-comedy budgeted at $2.6 million that follows an odd group of XXXXXXXX in their battle for survival XXXXXXXXXXXXXXXXXXXXXXXXXXXXXXXXXX XXXXXXXXXXXXXXXXX. The picture will mark the feature-length directorial debut of XXXXXXX, an award-winning short film director, and will be filmed in his hometown of XXXXXXXXX. A letter of intent to play one of the lead roles has been signed by horror-film icon XXXXXXX. We anticipate *Mass H-Com* to be ready for distributors to examine no later than one year after the full receipt of financing. The management team's efforts in producing *Mass H-Com* will yield substantial budgeting and creative advantages over having this picture made by a major motion picture studio. These advantages should translate into a significant profit opportunity for Mass H-Com LLC.

management team

XXXXXXX will serve as the sole manager of Mass H-Com LLC. She is the sole founder and owner of a film production company as well, and has assembled a team of filmmakers that includes five lead members who have each worked together at one time or another. Overseeing this experienced unit, Ms. XXXXXXX stands ready to make *Mass H-Com* in a way that is most appealing to potential distributors.

product description

"XXXXXXXXXXXXXXXXXXXXXXXXXXXXXX ." *Mass H-Com* is an R-rated horror-comedy centered on the battle for survival by XXXXXXXXXXXXXXXXXXXXXXXXXXXXXXXXXXXXXXXXXX XXXXXXXXXXXXXXXXXXX . One of the leads has already been filled by XXXXXXXXXXXXX whose next starring role will be in the film XXXXXXXXXXX to be released across 2500 screens in XXXXXXX . The gore and violence of *Mass H-Com* are interlaced with broad and subtle comedic elements yielding an effort that should be greatly distinguished from past, present, and future efforts in the horror-comedy genre.

industry overview

2003 U.S. box office receipts fell much less than expected (0.3%) from the all-time record high of $9.5 billion set in 2002. Receipts currently exceed year-to-date 2003 totals by 2.4%. Beyond theaters, the DVD/home entertainment market often yields revenue totals in excess of box office grosses, and while the cable and satellite TV market yields less, it is expected to grow at 7.9% per annum from $83.5 billion in 2003 to $122.2 billion in 2008. Overall, worldwide film revenue is expected to reach approximately $108 billion in 2008, growing at an annual rate of 7.5%. Those movies with no production funding from a U.S. studio, such as *Mass H-Com*, are known as "independent films." Independent films benefit from lower budgets and greater creative freedom than the typical studio picture.

market analysis & marketing strategy

48% of the movie-going public in 2003 was 12-to-29-year-olds, the primary audience for *Mass H-Com*. The word-of-mouth generated by this age group has the power to make or break even the most marketed of studio pictures. Should a distributor acquire rights to *Mass H-Com*, we will recommend an initial marketing strategy relying heavily on screenings, Internet exposure, and grass-roots promotions. These should prove especially effective with the presence of Mr. XXXXX and the fact that one of the producers has a close relationship with XXXXXXXXXX, a periodical dedicated to XXXXXXX for XXXX years. Zombie films themselves have recently experienced a growth in popularity and frequency with two recent studio examples, *Resident Evil 2* and *Dawn of the Dead*, each grossing over $50 million.

motion picture distribution

The domestic theatrical release is the single most important event in determining the future revenue stream of a motion picture. It establishes audience awareness for a film. Three of the main factors influencing a distributor's decision to acquire a film are presence of at least one significantly name actor, exploitability of genre or market segment, and originality of the story. *Mass H-Com* will feature actor XXXXXXXXXX whose name carries innate audience appeal. The film contains horror and comedic subject matter appealing to the largest demographic of moviegoers, 12-to-29-year-olds. Finally, it is the unique story of XXXXXXXXX battle for survival XXXXXXXXXXXXXX. Distributors should not face a difficult decision when examining this film.

funding requirement & projected returns

Mass H-Com LLC is seeking equity investment of $1.2 million through the issuance of 24 units of membership in the limited liability company valued at $50,000 per unit. Under a successful outcome over a 5.25 year period beginning with the completion of financing, the projected return on the investment is 248% or $2,971,618 above the initial $1.2 million (an ROI multiple of 3.48x). This translates into a yearly internal rate of return of 50.1% based on cash flow projections. Films with comparable budgets, initial release patterns, but narrower target audiences demonstrate that such returns are possible.

9 INFORMATION AND RISK STATEMENT

There's a reason the first section of a business plan isn't described until this part of the book: It is depressing! The odds against you when it comes to making a movie of any kind are overwhelming. This part of the plan is where you explain why.

STEP 26. LEGAL JUNK (A.K.A. KEEPING YOU OUT OF JAIL).

I say the word junk, but that junk is gold when it comes to covering your you-know-what. The purpose of this step is to keep three entities happy: (1) the Securities and Exchange Commission (SEC), the governmental body responsible for regulating the U.S. investment community; (2) any state regulatory agencies with jurisdiction over the money-raising aspect of your film; and (3) the investor. Sometimes the investor may end up unhappy, but if you and your attorney have done this step (and, of course, the rest of your plan) correctly, that unhappiness will not result in a legitimate lawsuit, and that unhappiness will not spread to groups (1) and (2) who, by the way, have the power to put you in jail.

For this step, you and your attorney should write something that states clearly what your business plan is, what it is not, and what the reader and any regulators should expect out of your plan. The final version of what you write will likely differ from what you see in the sample text, but the sample text at least serves as a general guideline and talking point for some of the legal issues to consider when raising money for your film. So let's talk!

What follows is the sample text from the "for information only" section (see the end of the chapter) with a description of what it means:

This business plan (the "Business Plan") is for information only and is not an offer to sell or a solicitation of an offer to buy securities. The Business Plan is not a prospectus and is not a private placement memorandum. The Business Plan and its contents are not to be construed as legal, business, or tax advice.

The first sentence says that this business plan is not an offer to sell or a request for the reader to buy a stake in a company in which the reader would not take an active management position. The second sentence clarifies that the plan is neither of two official legal documents, a "prospectus" or a "private placement memorandum" (PPM), often used to make offers to sell or requests of a person to buy a stake in a company. Technically, a PPM is the applicable document for the types of offerings appropriate to the sample plans. Regardless, your own business plan will not be some kind of formal or informal offer to sell something to a reader; instead, it will be a detailed account of how you intend to make a successful feature film.

Assuming you are properly approaching investors with your business plan, your lawyer will come up with an official set of documents (possibly including a PPM) once a reader/potential investor expresses investment interest in your film. The third sentence is pretty self-explanatory. A plan for business is merely being presented, as opposed to advice on how the reader should take action on that plan.

The membership units discussed in the Business Plan will not be registered under the Securities Act of 1933. The exemption from registration will be claimed under Regulation D created by the Securities and Exchange Commission.

Here is being detailed how the LLC units (a.k.a. membership units), which will one day be sold for investment in the LLC, will not be registered with the SEC. (See Step 4J in Appendix B for a reminder about LLCs.) Registration with the SEC is a time-consuming and rigorous affair. Technically, when you are privately raising money for a film, the transaction of the money being given to you is known as a "private placement." In order to avoid registration, you have to meet certain federal requirements laid out by the SEC; in the case of the sample text, these requirements are laid out in Regulation D. You can choose one out of three rules to follow under Regulation D (rule 504, 505, or 506). Which rule you choose will depend on your budget and advice from your lawyer. On a separate but related note, your lawyer will also inform you as to the restrictions you will have to follow regarding contacting people about your film investment.

They should be people with whom you, or someone else also in charge of the film, has a "pre-existing relationship," the SEC's definition of which can be a bit gray. However, it is safe to say that placing an ad in the Sunday paper or waiting until later that night to call people from the phonebook about a "wonderful investment opportunity" is a big No-No.

The membership units discussed in the Business Plan will be registered in accordance with the blue sky laws of any state with blue sky laws applicable to the membership units described in the Business Plan.

Now, although you may not have to register at the federal level (with the SEC), you may have to register at the state level because of laws known as "blue sky laws," created by some states. Basically, these states want to take extra precautions to make sure that you are not offering someone an investment as valuable as a piece of the blue sky. Artistically, the blue sky is very valuable; monetarily, not so much. The reader is being told here not to worry, and that any ultimate investments in the LLC will be registered with the appropriate authorities. The state an investor lives in will determine in which state to register an investment. For a comprehensive overview with plenty of specifics on private placements and the rules and procedures involved, see Chapter 6 entitled "Private Placements" in *Raising Capital* by Andrew J. Sherman, 2005.

The membership units discussed in the Business Plan will be restricted and as such will be prohibited from resale or distribution.

This sentence states that each of the LLC's investment units will be offered solely to the person who purchases the unit as a way of investing in this particular film, and not as some kind of unit that can be purchased and resold, or purchased and given to others, such as stock in a company.

Any prospective purchaser of the membership units described in the Business Plan will be required to demonstrate that (1) he or she has the sophistication, or has retained the services of an investment adviser with the sophistication, necessary to evaluate the membership units described herein, and that (2) he or she can afford the total loss of his or her investment.

Should a reader choose to one day invest in the film, he or she will need to demonstrate that he or she has, or has hired, someone with the financial wherewithal to understand the investment being made. This demonstration usually takes the form of answering a questionnaire prepared by your legal counsel. Establishing the reader's competence with financial matters is done to prevent a lawsuit on the premise that you enticed the reader into an investment he or she was not capable of truly understanding. (I know, you're not like Enron, but some people out there are.) In some cases, you may not have to establish an investor's competence, just that they are wealthy enough to invest. In the sample text I assure the reader that both will be done. You and your legal counsel will have to determine what is right for you. Part (2) references the wealth issue by telling the reader that the loss of all money invested in the film should not result in a crippling blow to a potential investor's financial well-being; in other words, investment should only be undertaken if an investor is well-off financially. Of course, you have no intention of losing all of an investor's money, but you need to take every precaution to protect an investor and yourself should that occur.

You will notice in Appendix A's sample plan that the issue of confidentiality is addressed. On the cover page is a statement listing expectations for the reader to keep the contents of the plan confidential. It can be addressed in the "for information only" section as well, or alone on the cover page, however you so choose. Either way, the point of it is that, naturally, you don't want your story idea out in the public for anyone who will listen. Despite copyright laws, proving theft of a script idea is downright difficult, even in what may seem like the most cut and dried cases. Also, you don't want copies of your business plan floating around, making it look like you are just distributing it willy-nilly. The "Copy Number" on the cover is for you to keep track of who is given which copy of the business plan (each person gets a number). It also serves to reinforce the point that you mean business when it comes to the plan's confidentiality and whereabouts.

STEP 27. SCARE THE CRAP OUT OF THE INVESTOR (A.K.A. FULL RISK STATEMENT).
Remember in the introduction to the book how I talked about the unpredictability of films? Well, this is the part of the plan where you explain at least some of the reasons why. You should absolutely do it with your attorney, or at least run your own risk statement by him or her.

Out of respect to potential investors, paint a complete picture of the gamble they face. If in doubt, don't leave it out. You will be more respected by your investors if you are candid with them. You may be sued by them if you are not. It's better that they face the ugly truth now rather than five years from now with an undistributed picture.

Regarding the sample risk statement, apart from the sentences in bold, there is some language in the first paragraph that is a little more conversational and loose than the typical risk statement. Discuss with your attorney whether you feel comfortable including it. Concerning the last sentence in the sample text, it is important to state something to that sentence's effect, because it would be impossible to list all the risk factors associated with a potential investment, even if it were a less risky, non-film investment.

For a detailed discussion of the statistics underlying film risk, most of it illuminated by the research of retired economist Dr. Arthur De Vany, see Appendix B.

SAMPLE INFORMATION
AND
RISK STATEMENT

INFORMATION AND RISK STATEMENT
(*Sci-Fi Rom, Mass H-Com, Psych Thrill*)

for information only

This business plan (the "Business Plan") is for information only and is not an offer to sell or a solicitation of an offer to buy securities. The Business Plan is not a prospectus and is not a private placement memorandum. The Business Plan and its contents are not to be construed as legal, business, or tax advice.

The membership units discussed in the Business Plan will not be registered under the Securities Act of 1933. The exemption from registration will be claimed under Regulation D created by the Securities and Exchange Commission.

The membership units discussed in the Business Plan will be registered in accordance with the blue sky laws of any state with blue sky laws applicable to the membership units described in the Business Plan.

The membership units discussed in the Business Plan will be restricted and as such will be prohibited from resale or distribution.

Any prospective purchaser of the membership units described in the Business Plan will be required to demonstrate that (1) he or she has the sophistication, or has retained the services of an investment adviser with the sophistication, necessary to evaluate the membership units described herein, and that (2) he or she can afford the total loss of his or her investment.

risk factors

Roughly 60%–70% of major movies lose money and roughly another 10% break even.[1] **Furthermore, using averages to predict the performance of a film, as this business plan does, is ineffective. The box office gross for a single film is absolutely unpredictable, regardless of financial model used or the film's budget, genre, cast, time frame, etc. It is box office gross that drives the financial success or failure of**

---

[1] Harold L. Vogel, *Entertainment Industry Economics: A Guide for Financial Analysis*, 7th ed., 65, 133.

a film. The statistical measurement of deviation from the mean, known as variance, is infinite for film box office gross. Thus, one can make a prediction about the box office gross of a film and one's confidence interval for doing so will be plus or minus infinity.[2] An analogy with a less extreme result would be a campaign poll showing that a candidate currently has 40% of the public's support with a margin of error of plus or minus 40% (rather than the customary plus or minus 5%). A single movie's performance, such as that of *Sci-Fi Rom/Mass H-Com/Psych Thrill*, is even less predictable than the public opinion in this sample poll, regardless of method used for prediction. Keep these facts in mind as you read this plan. Also keep in mind, however, that the statements thus far on box office unpredictability are based on empirical research that has not measured film performance as a function of the passion, integrity, and knowledge of the filmmakers coupled with the quality of the script. These are the variables an investor should ultimately consider when deciding to invest in a film. Unfortunately, no research supports this assertion.

Movies are among the most risky of assets. Risks involved in the creation and exploitation of *Sci-Fi Rom/Mass H-Com/Psych Thrill* (the "Motion Picture") can be grouped into four categories: Production, Distribution, Company-specific, and General Economic. Production-related risks include but are not limited to: (1) the Motion Picture requiring more financing than was originally anticipated and being unable to complete production until such financing is achieved; and (2) the final version of the Motion Picture being substantially different from and inferior to the originally conceived concept. Distribution related risks include but are not limited to: (1) the Motion Picture being unable to find a distributor and thus being unable to generate revenues; (2) the Motion Picture not receiving a theatrical release; (3) the Motion Picture receiving an ineffective theatrical release that neither serves to generate positive cash flow for the picture nor to increase awareness of the picture for ancillary markets; (4) a distributor of the Motion Picture deciding to put the interests of one or many pictures it is distributing ahead of the Motion Picture; (5) a distributor of the Motion Picture going bankrupt; (6) the inability of the Motion Picture to compete for public acceptance against the likes of numerous other pictures, many of which will be supported by advertising campaigns much larger than that of the Motion Picture; (7) the Motion Picture not being accepted by the public; and (8) the Motion Picture competing against alternate forms of entertainment such as gaming consoles, cable television, and online entertainment.

[2] Arthur De Vany, *Hollywood Economics: How Extreme Uncertainty Shapes the Film Industry* (London and New York: Routledge, 2004), 65-66, 262-264, 273-275.

Company-specific risks include but are not limited to: (1) Sci-Fi Rom/Mass H-Com/Psych Thrill LLC (the "Company") having only one piece of intellectual property, the Motion Picture, and having no other intellectual property from which to derive revenue; (2) the Company being a start-up and as such having no operational history; (3) the Company being a start-up and as such being subject to the risks common to all start-ups; (4) the Company relying on the expertise of management to guide it through the marketplace and the expertise of dozens of non-management persons (actors, distribution executives, postproduction companies, etc.) to successfully create and exploit the Motion Picture; and (5) there being no market for and no market likely to ever exist for the membership units discussed in the plan. General Economic risks include but are not limited to: (1) the introduction of new and competing forms of entertainment technologies; (2) the deterioration of general industry and marketplace conditions; (3) unfavorable interest rate movements; (4) unfavorable currency exchange rate fluctuations; and (5) general industry and market uncertainty.

One, many, or none of the risks mentioned above may result in the total loss of investment in the Motion Picture. The risk factors mentioned above do not include all possible risk factors.

¹⁰ COMPLETED PLAN

Another title for this chapter could have been "The End."

STEP 28. PUT IT IN THE RIGHT ORDER.
Here's the order in which to put all the sections you have written:

1. Information and Risk Statement
2. Executive Summary
3. Company Description
4. Product Description
5. Industry Overview
6. Market Analysis & Marketing Strategy
7. Motion Picture Distribution
8. Financing
9. Financial Projections

If you examine books on writing non-film business plans, you will notice some variation on how the above content is grouped, named, and ordered, but not too much. For instance, descriptions of the management team may fall near the end of a plan or descriptions of product distribution may be folded into other areas, such as an Operations or Marketing section. Whatever order you end up favoring, make sure it makes things easier, not harder, on the reader. Also, do keep distribution as its own section; highlighting critical and/or unusual parts of your business is one of the rules of business plan writing.

For reference, and also for a sample cover page, see the completed and ordered plan in Appendix A.

STEP 29. GET A GOOD LAWYER.

If you haven't already, get an entertainment attorney with expertise in the financing of independent films. I know, attorneys cost money, but getting sued costs more money. You may be able to find one who will defer a portion of your bills until the budget has been raised (don't forget to include these attorney fees in your budget!) or one who will work for lower fees in exchange for an equity stake in your film (a.k.a. they get a cut of the profits). Whatever the case, the proper attorney will help you tweak your business plan and advise you on how best to use it in a manner that complies with the law. The easiest way to find an attorney is to just ask around. Check with other independent filmmakers, check with independent filmmaking associations, or just keep an eye out for the ones quoted in the press or in books.

STEP 30. MAKE A GREAT FILM!

What you have just accomplished is something major. You have taken your creative concept and attached to it a business sense. You are now a deadly combination of business smarts and creative smarts. I know it sounds dramatic, but it is. The people who last in the motion picture industry are the ones who have a sound understanding of it, and a creative vision to boot. Congratulations. Now go out there and show them what a great film really is!

APPENDIX A: SAMPLE PLAN FOR *PSYCH THRILL*

PSYCH THRILL LLC
Business Plan

COPY NUMBER _____

XXXXXXXXXXXXX
1428 XXXXXXX St., #221
Los Angeles, California XXXXX
(213) 555-5555

TABLE OF CONTENTS

TOPIC	PAGE
INFORMATION AND RISK STATEMENT	130
EXECUTIVE SUMMARY	133
COMPANY DESCRIPTION	136
PRODUCT DESCRIPTION	138
INDUSTRY OVERVIEW	140
MARKET ANALYSIS & MARKETING STRATEGY	143
MOTION PICTURE DISTRIBUTION	147
FINANCING	153
FINANCIAL PROJECTIONS	155

INFORMATION AND RISK STATEMENT

for information only

This business plan (the "Business Plan") is for information only and is not an offer to sell or a solicitation of an offer to buy securities. The Business Plan is not a prospectus and is not a private placement memorandum. The Business Plan and its contents are not to be construed as legal, business, or tax advice.

The membership units discussed in the Business Plan will not be registered under the Securities Act of 1933. The exemption from registration will be claimed under Regulation D created by the Securities and Exchange Commission.

The membership units discussed in the Business Plan will be registered in accordance with the blue sky laws of any state with blue sky laws applicable to the membership units described in the Business Plan.

The membership units discussed in the Business Plan will be restricted and as such will be prohibited from resale or distribution.

Any prospective purchaser of the membership units described in the Business Plan will be required to demonstrate that (1) he or she has the sophistication, or has retained the services of an investment adviser with the sophistication, necessary to evaluate the membership units described herein, and that (2) he or she can afford the total loss of his or her investment.

risk factors

Roughly 60%–70% of major movies lose money and roughly another 10% break even.[1] **Furthermore, using averages to predict the performance of a film, as this business plan does, is ineffective. The box office gross for a single film is absolutely unpredictable, regardless of financial model used or the film's budget, genre, cast, time frame, etc. It is box office gross that drives the financial success or failure of a film.** The statistical measurement of deviation from the mean, known as variance, is infinite for film box office gross. Thus, one can make a prediction about the box office gross of a film and one's confidence interval for doing so will be

---

[1] Harold L. Vogel, *Entertainment Industry Economics: A Guide for Financial Analysis*, 7th ed., 65, 133.

plus or minus infinity.[2] An analogy with a less extreme result would be a campaign poll showing that a candidate currently has 40% of the public's support with a margin of error of plus or minus 40% (rather than the customary plus or minus 5%). A single movie's performance, such as that of *Psych Thrill*, is even less predictable than the public opinion in this sample poll, regardless of method used for prediction. Keep these facts in mind as you read this plan. Also keep in mind, however, that the statements thus far on box office unpredictability are based on empirical research that has not measured film performance as a function of the passion, integrity, and knowledge of the filmmakers coupled with the quality of the script. These are the variables an investor should ultimately consider when deciding to invest in a film. Unfortunately, no research supports this assertion.

Movies are among the most risky of assets. Risks involved in the creation and exploitation of *Psych Thrill* (the "Motion Picture") can be grouped into four categories: Production, Distribution, Company-specific, and General Economic. Production-related risks include but are not limited to: (1) the Motion Picture requiring more financing than was originally anticipated and being unable to complete production until such financing is achieved; and (2) the final version of the Motion Picture being substantially different from and inferior to the originally conceived concept. Distribution related risks include but are not limited to: (1) the Motion Picture being unable to find a distributor and thus being unable to generate revenues; (2) the Motion Picture not receiving a theatrical release; (3) the Motion Picture receiving an ineffective theatrical release that neither serves to generate positive cash flow for the picture nor to increase awareness of the picture for ancillary markets; (4) a distributor of the Motion Picture deciding to put the interests of one or many pictures it is distributing ahead of the Motion Picture; (5) a distributor of the Motion Picture going bankrupt; (6) the inability of the Motion Picture to compete for public acceptance against the likes of numerous other pictures, many of which will be supported by advertising campaigns much larger than that of the Motion Picture; (7) the Motion Picture not being accepted by the public; and (8) the Motion Picture competing against alternate forms of entertainment such as gaming consoles, cable television, and online entertainment.

---

[2] Arthur De Vany, *Hollywood Economics: How Extreme Uncertainty Shapes the Film Industry*, 65-66, 262-264, 273-275.

Company-specific risks include but are not limited to: (1) Psych Thrill LLC (the "Company") having only one piece of intellectual property, the Motion Picture, and having no other intellectual property from which to derive revenue; (2) the Company being a start-up and as such having no operational history; (3) the Company being a start-up and as such being subject to the risks common to all start-ups; (4) the Company relying on the expertise of management to guide it through the marketplace and the expertise of dozens of non-management persons (actors, distribution executives, postproduction companies, etc.) to successfully create and exploit the Motion Picture; and (5) there being no market for and no market likely to ever exist for the membership units discussed in the plan. General Economic risks include but are not limited to: (1) the introduction of new and competing forms of entertainment technologies; (2) the deterioration of general industry and marketplace conditions; (3) unfavorable interest rate movements; (4) unfavorable currency exchange rate fluctuations; and (5) general industry and market uncertainty.

One, many, or none of the risks mentioned above may result in the total loss of investment in the Motion Picture. The risk factors mentioned above do not include all possible risk factors.

EXECUTIVE SUMMARY

introductory statement

Psych Thrill LLC is being formed for the sole purpose of producing and seeking distribution for the full-length feature film *Psych Thrill*. *Psych Thrill* is a psychological thriller budgeted at $1.5 million that follows XXXXXXX piecing together his XXXXXXX in order to XXXXXXXXXXXXXXX. The project marks the directorial debut of XXXXXXX, a veteran actor with numerous television and movie credits under his belt. The place of his acting training, XXXXXXX, has also produced several successful actors-turned-director. We anticipate *Psych Thrill* to be ready for distributors to examine no later than one year after the full receipt of financing. The management team's efforts in producing *Psych Thrill* will yield substantial budgeting and creative advantages over having this picture made by a major motion picture studio. These advantages should translate into a significant profit opportunity for Psych Thrill LLC.

management team

XXXXXXX will serve as the sole manager of Psych Thrill LLC. She is the sole founder and owner of a film production company as well, and has assembled a team of filmmakers with the industry experience necessary to fully realize the potential of this project. Having cut her teeth on other films, Ms. XXXXXXX stands ready to make *Psych Thrill* in a way that is most appealing to potential distributors.

product description

"XXXXXXXXXXXXXXX." *Psych Thrill* is an R-rated psychological thriller centered on XXXXXXXXXXXXXXXXXXXX who falls XXXXXXXXXXXXX during a confrontation XXX XXXXXXXXXXXXXXXXXXXXXXXXXXXXXXXXXXXXXXXXXXXXXXXXXXXXXXXXXXXXXXXXXX XXXX that ultimately lead him into XXXXXXXXXXXXXXXXXXXX with consequences beyond what he could have imagined. Shooting will take place in Louisiana with at least one significantly name actor as a part of the cast.

industry overview

2003 U.S. box office receipts fell much less than expected (0.3%) from the all-time record high of $9.5 billion set in 2002. Receipts currently exceed year-to-date 2003 totals by 2.4%. Beyond theaters, the DVD/home entertainment market often yields revenue totals in excess of box office grosses, and while the cable and satellite TV market yields less, it is expected to grow at 7.9% per annum from $83.5 billion in 2003 to $122.2 billion in 2008. Overall, worldwide film revenue is expected to reach approximately $108 billion in 2008, growing at an annual rate of 7.5%. Those movies with no production funding from a U.S. studio, such as *Psych Thrill*, are known as "independent films." Independent films benefit from lower budgets and greater creative freedom than the typical studio picture.

market analysis & marketing strategy

The target audience for *Psych Thrill* is specialty theater patrons, upscale young adults, and college students. This group recently propelled the psychological thriller *Pic N*, also an independent film, to stellar box office results. Should a distributor acquire rights to *Psych Thrill*, we will recommend an initial marketing strategy relying heavily on screenings, Internet exposure, and grass-roots promotions. These will target universities, police associations, and fan sites devoted to thriller movies and any name actors in the project. Any domestic distributor that acquires the rights to the film will likely open it in a limited number of specialty theaters and expand the release to more theaters on positive word-of-mouth.

motion picture distribution

The domestic theatrical release is the single most important event in determining the future revenue stream of a motion picture. It establishes audience awareness for a film. For this reason Psych Thrill LLC will place the utmost importance on seeking a U.S. theatrical distributor whose marketing plan and release strategy will establish this awareness. Three of the main factors influencing a distributor's decision to acquire a film are presence of at least one significantly name actor, exploitability of genre or market segment, and originality of the story. *Psych Thrill* will feature at least one actor whose name carries innate audience appeal. Furthermore, it delivers an exploitable genre, as the performances of the low-budget independent *Pic N* and studio budgeted *Silence of the Lambs* franchise illustrate, in addition to delivering a unique story line.

funding requirement & projected returns

Psych Thrill LLC is seeking an initial equity investment of $1.5 million through the issuance of 30 units of membership in the limited liability company valued at $50,000 per unit. Under a successful outcome over a 5.25 year period beginning with the completion of financing, the projected return on the investment is 214% or $3,208,184 million above the initial $1.5 million (an ROI multiple of 3.14x). This translates into a yearly internal rate of return of 44.9% based on cash flow projections. Films with comparable budgets, initial release patterns, and similar or narrower audiences demonstrate that such returns are possible.

COMPANY DESCRIPTION

company details

Psych Thrill LLC is a Los Angeles, California-based manager-managed limited liability company to be founded once financing commences. The purpose of the LLC will be to produce, find distribution, and collect revenue for the full-length 35mm feature entitled, *Psych Thrill*. *Psych Thrill* is a psychological thriller geared toward specialty theater patrons, upscale young adults, and college students. In 2001, this target audience strongly supported another independently financed psychological thriller, *Pic N*, which went on to gross $25.5 million domestically on a budget of $5.0 million. *Psych Thrill* will be budgeted at $1.5 million and we anticipate ready for distributors to examine no later than one year after financing is complete. Our focus will be to license the film to a domestic distributor that can garner a successful theatrical release. Such a release would drive the profitability of the film and likely begin in a limited number of specialty theaters. Specialty theaters generally consist of one to five screens and cater to, but are not restricted to, niche audiences. On positive word-of-mouth the film would spread to other theaters.

company personnel

XXXXXXX **manager/producer** — XXXXXXX will serve as sole manager of Psych Thrill LLC. She is also the founder and sole owner of XXXXXX, a production company now dedicated to the creation of high quality, well-written features that keep the writer's vision of the project intact. In the spring of XXXX the company produced three fully crewed short films in the span of two months and recently shifted gears to develop several full-length features to be shot over the next two years. Ms. XXXXXXX was also a founding member and Vice President of Production at XXXXXXXXXX, a film production company where she oversaw all aspects of physical and postproduction. During her time at XXXXXXXXXX Ms. XXXXXXX produced the short film XXXXXXXXXXXXX. This short was shot professionally on 35mm film and used a full cast and crew including stunt choreographers, children, animals, XXXXXXXXXX, and XXXXXXXXXXXXXXXXXXXX. It has gone on to popular reception and awards during its tour of over 15 film festivals and counting. Through her various projects, Ms. XXXXXXX has established valuable industry contacts that will be helpful in the production of *Psych Thrill*. These projects have also served as exceptional preparation to produce features.

XXXXXXXX, **writer/director** — XXXXXXXX's background is in acting where he has made dozens of appearances on TV shows as a series regular or guest star and in feature films as a supporting character. The bulk of his training has occurred at XXXXXXXXXXXX, where other actors-turned-director have also trained, including XXXXXXXX and XXXXXXXX, each of whom had feature-length movies recently admitted to the Sundance Film Festival. Other actors who have experienced directing success include Mel Gibson, Tim Robbins, and Clint Eastwood.

XXXXXX, **cinematographer** — XXXXXXXX's cinematography credits include nine features, countless television commercials, and several short films. One of his short films, XXXXXXXXXX, was screened at the Toronto International Film Festival and Los Angeles Film Festival, among others. Three of his commercials have been nominated for Regional Emmys awarded by the National Academy of Television Arts & Sciences.

XXXXXXXXX, **postproduction supervisor** — XXXXXXXXX is currently post-production coordinator at the XXXX television show XXXXXXXX. She has been with the show for the past three seasons. Ms. XXXXXXXXX is also a member of the Producer's Guild of America where she serves on XXXXXXXXXXXXXXXXX. Prior to XXXXXXXX, Ms. XXXXXXX's work included serving as postproduction supervisor at XXXXXXXXX on XXXXXXXXXXXX shows simultaneously, XXXXXXXXX, XXXXXXXXX, XXXXXXXXX, and XXXXXXXXX.

XXXXXXXXX, **casting director** — XXXXXXXX has cast more than 20 independent feature films. She is currently working on XXXXXXXXXXXXXX slated to star XXXXXX and was responsible for the discovery of XXXXXXXX (XXXXXXXX) when she cast him in the critically acclaimed XXXXXXXXX. Ms. XXXXXXXXX has also cast such talents as XXXXXXXXX, XXXXXXXXX, XXXXXXXXX, XXXXXXXXX, XXXXXXXXX, and XXXXXXXXX.

XXXXXXXXXXXXXXX **LLP, legal consultant** — XXXXXXXXX (XXXXXXXXX) is a full-service law firm with expertise in entertainment transactions and litigation. XXXXXXXX will assist Psych Thrill LLC in legal services involved with the formation, financing, physical production, and distribution of *Psych Thrill*.

PRODUCT DESCRIPTION*

synopsis [example unconnected to *Psych Thrill*]
"Between a rock and a jelly-filled."

Forced by his distant mobster uncle to conceal $150,000, an out-of-work Finnish immigrant decides to open a donut shop only to find that popular donuts are not the best investment vehicle for laundering money.

Markku is down on his luck. His wife just died of a drug overdose and unless he can prove that he has a job, the INS will deport him back to Finland where he faces imprisonment by the new Socialist regime. Markku decides on the next best alternative… suicide.

Just as he has the noose fitted around his neck, a special delivery arrives at the door. Examining the package he notices it is from his uncle, a reputed Finnish mobster and otherwise unsavory character who regularly exports Finnish heroin to the neighborhood. Having given up selling since his wife's death, Markku sets the package aside and resumes his plans to travel to the afterlife. Suddenly however, the noose breaks, landing him straight on top of the package. When he gets up, he notices the contents, $150,000, have exploded all over the room… along with a note.

Reading the note Markku finds a new purpose in life: he is to conceal the money for his uncle in a manner that will earn a high rate of return until his uncle can find a way to get to America. Not doing so will result in the loss of 90% of Markku's mental faculties.

Charged with a new lease on life, Markku decides to open a donut shop fueled by his deceased mother's ancient Finnish reindeer antler recipe. Unfortunately for his uncle, the recipe is a hit, and people from all around take notice of this little Finnish donut shop on the corner of Fletcher and Glendale, not the least of whom are the cops who can't get enough of the jelly-filled reindeer ears. The store becomes a community landmark and melting pot, and to complicate matters further, when neighborhood activists start to date the local cops, the results are explosive.

---

*This movie will have scenes where the lead sleeps with and cuts to pieces reindeer. However, the scenes are comically portrayed as if the lead is doing so to a reindeer mascot suit with a person in it rather than to an actual reindeer. The focus of these scenes is a ridiculous, over-the-top portrayal of the inner angst faced by the main character.

A call to arms is made to clean up the neighborhood and rid it of the pernicious Finnish heroin infestation. Fearing for his own life, Markku must learn what it is to be a Finnish man in American society. Can he give up his heritage and his life for a great American cause? Or will the fears and weaknesses that have plagued him all his life push him back into the mold of protecting his uncle? Whatever the decision, Markku promises to affect the reputation of Finnish Americans for generations to come. Who knew that the decision between jelly-filled and antler-filled would carry so much weight.

project details

Psych Thrill is an R-rated psychological thriller much in the vein of *Silence of the Lambs* meets *Pic N*. It is budgeted at $1.5 million and targets upscale young adults, college students, and specialty theater patrons, as well as other audiences that favor intelligent thrillers with richly developed characters. It is written and will be directed by XXXXXXXX, a Los Angeles-based actor. Casting will begin once financing is in place and consist of hiring at least one significantly name actor. For the purposes of this business plan, a significantly name actor is one who has appeared in a leading role in at least one feature that has domestically grossed $50 million or above. Shooting will occur in Louisiana due to the aptness of the location and significant cost savings of shooting there versus other locations; it will also be done on studio quality 35mm film. We anticipate the film to be ready for examination by distributors no later than one year after financing has been secured.

INDUSTRY OVERVIEW

production and distribution

There are four steps involved in the creation of any motion picture: development, preproduction, principal photography, and postproduction. The person who guides a film through these steps and beyond is the producer. During development the idea for a movie is hatched and developed into a screenplay. Money is raised to shoot the film and tentative commitments are entered into with crucial members of the cast and crew. Once these actions are taken and the main layout for the screenplay is established, the producer engages in what is known as "preproduction." At this time she finalizes contracts with the cast and crew, decides on locations, and sets the shooting order of the script. Then follows the actual shooting of the motion picture, known as "principal photography." During this phase the producer oversees the day-to-day operations of the film shoot, ensuring that they run smoothly. Following the successful completion of principal photography is postproduction. During this phase the movie is edited, sound and music established, special effects added, and a final version of the movie created in the form of an original negative. From this negative all other copies of the movie can be generated. The term "production" can be applied collectively to the steps described thus far (minus development) or solely to the step of principal photography. The former will be the definition used here.

Following the production of a movie is the process of distribution. A company or companies pays the producer for the right to release the movie in theaters, known as the "theatrical release," and various ancillary markets such as DVD/home video, free TV, and pay TV. Distribution to theaters and ancillary markets occurs both domestically (Canada and the U.S.) and internationally. Frequently distribution begins with a domestic theatrical release followed by further release into ancillary and foreign markets. The domestic theatrical release may occur on as many as 3000 movie screens or as few as one.

studio versus independent films

A movie can be financed by a studio or other entities. The major studios (a.k.a. "studios") as defined by the Motion Picture Association of America are Sony Pictures Entertainment/MGM, The Walt Disney Company, Warner Bros., Twentieth Century-Fox, Universal Studios, and Paramount Pictures. Generally, these are subdivisions of large, diversified corporations and are capable of producing and distributing 15–25 films annually worldwide. In fact, in the steps outlined above a producer working for a studio does not get paid by a distributor for the rights to her film because the studio already has a distribution division and owns the film. Studio films accounted for over 65% of U.S. box office revenue during the first six months of 2004 and are usually budgeted at well north of $10 million.[1] For the purposes of this business plan, those movies created with no funding from a U.S. studio are known as "independent films" and those with such funding and owned by a studio are "studio films." It is possible for an independent film to be distributed by a studio. *Psych Thrill* will be an independent film financed through private equity raised by Psych Thrill LLC.

There are several difficulties in shooting an independent versus a studio film. Apart from having to attract financing, the independent producer has to seek out one or more distributors. There is no guarantee that she will find distribution for her film. Another difficulty is that the success of the movie rests much more heavily on the skills and resources of the producer. A producer at a studio has a large and diverse network of advisors to consult regarding matters ranging from legal, accounting, and marketing to editing, shooting, and props. The independent producer does not. Finally, if an independent film exceeds its budget it is often extremely difficult to approach investors for more funds, and a movie may not ever reach completion. In contrast, a studio is very willing to bridge the gap between an estimated and actual budget in order to complete a film.

There are, however, several very significant advantages to independent movie making that Psych Thrill LLC feels outweigh filmmaking within the studio system. The producer and director have much more creative control. While there are many advisers in a studio regarding non-creative matters, there are also many studio executives (often with a legal or financial background, not a creative one) who have heavy influence over a film's content. This can lead to a producer and director's vision of the story being far different from the final studio version, a version that may suffer from too many separate ideas implemented in one picture. Furthermore, the employees of a studio are needed for the operations of many other films as well as the upkeep of the studio and its many divisions. As a result, overhead for a studio film is often much higher than that for an independent film. The same holds true for budgets. Because a studio is very willing to fund a budget that has exceeded projections, the same care is not given to budgeting a

---

[1] Calculation based on totals from "US Spring Box Office Up 30 Per Cent" by Staff reporting data from ACNielsen/EDI, *Screen Digest*, July 2004.

studio picture as to an independent. These higher budgets and overhead reduce the final profits of a studio film.

current and future trends

Currently domestic box office receipts lead 2003 totals by 2.4%.[2] In 2003 U.S. box office revenue dropped by only 0.3% from the all-time record high of $9.5 billion in 2002. Additionally, U.S. movie theater admissions reached the second highest level since 1957. The fact that 2003's numbers approached those of 2002 was, in the words of one industry CEO, "a minor miracle" and came amid competition from 67% of American households with basic cable, 56% with Internet access, 42% with DVD devices, 36% with premium cable, and 18% with satellite dishes.[3] While these percentages represent competition to box office figures, they also serve as a boon to ancillary receipts. Ancillary receipts are revenue generated from non-box office sources such as DVD/home video and pay TV. Due arguably in large part to poorer movie quality, mid-year revenue from the top 15 DVD/home video titles was down 10.5% compared to the same time period in 2003. However, this same revenue total exceeded the box office total of these films by nearly 10%, as opposed to only 1.4% in 2003.[4] Regarding the cable and satellite TV market, it is expected to reach a size of $122.2 billion in 2008 from a total of $83.5 billion in 2003, implying an annual growth rate of 7.9%.[5] In addition to this ancillary expansion, projected U.S. box office figures for 2007 imply annual growth of approximately 6%.[6] Independent films similar to *Psych Thrill* generate the vast majority of their revenue from domestic sources. Nonetheless, global film revenue is expected to reach approximately $108 billion in 2008, up from $75.3 billion in 2003, implying an annual growth rate of 7.5%.[7]

---

[2] Nielsen EDI, Inc., December 12, 2004, *www.nielsenedi.com/charts/seasonal.html*.

[3] "U.S. Entertainment Industry: 2003 MPA Market Statistics" by Motion Picture Association Worldwide Market Research; Carl DiOrio, "Mouse wore the top hat in flat 2003," *Daily Variety*, January 5, 2004.

[4] Comparisons based on calculations using data from Video Business's online site: *www.videobusiness. com/info/CA621777.html*.

[5] Staff, "US: communications and entertainment media forecasts by sector," *Screen Digest*, August 2004, reporting data from Veronis Suhler.

[6] Staff, "Study: U.S. b.o. will top $10 bil in '06," *The Hollywood Reporter*, January 27, 2004; implied growth rate calculated from article statistics.

[7] Georg Szalai, "Global media on the rise," *The Hollywood Reporter*, June 29, 2004; implied growth rate calculated from article statistics.

MARKET ANALYSIS & MARKETING STRATEGY*

exhibitors

Low-budget independent films are generally shown in two types of movie theaters, specialty theaters or non-specialty theaters. Specialty theaters generally consist of one to five screens and cater to niche audiences while non-specialty theaters frequently have more screens and cater to much wider audiences. Studio films are much more likely to be found in a non-specialty theater. Over the past five years the number of specialty theaters has increased, as has the number of non-specialty theaters willing to show low-budget independent films. In fact, Landmark Theatres, the nation's oldest and largest chain of specialty theaters, committed in August 2003 to adding 21 screens to its circuit in cities such as Atlanta, Georgia; Washington, D.C.; and Edina, Minnesota. Landmark was subsequently purchased by dot-com billionaires Mark Cuban and Todd Wagner who have made plans to re-vamp one if its West Los Angeles sites into the nation's largest specialty theater (with 14 screens), in addition to renovating many other Landmark sites. In early 2002, Southern California-based Pacific Theaters opened its ArcLight venue in Hollywood where, in the summer of 2003, seven of this multiplex's 14 screens were regularly playing films typically found in specialty theaters. The theater went on to achieve such success by February 2004 that Pacific Theaters announced it would proceed with plans to replicate the ArcLight in 40 additional markets.[1] These large capital outlays for specialty screens illustrate exhibitor confidence in the potential market for high caliber independent films such as *Psych Thrill*.

word-of-mouth

As with most low-budget independent films, any company that domestically dis-tributes *Psych Thrill* will likely open it on a very limited number of specialty theater screens and use the proceeds from those screens to pay for wider theatrical release of the film. *Psych Thrill* will rely heavily on word-of-mouth for its initial suc-cess. This word-of-mouth is essential to films that open with a limited release. Witness the extreme examples of 1999's *The Blair Witch Project* and 2002's *My Big Fat Greek Wedding*. *Blair Witch* opened on one screen and went on to gross

---

*Any box office numbers or release patterns quoted in the remainder of the business plan refer to the domestic market (U.S. & Canada) unless otherwise noted.

[1] Nicole Sperling, "Crowded Art House," *The Hollywood Reporter*, August 5, 2003; Lorenza Munoz, "Botox for the Bijou," *Los Angeles Times*, February 15, 2004.

$140 million. *Wedding* opened on 108 screens, high for the typical independent film but very low by studio standards, and used positive word-of-mouth to extend its theatrical run to 47 weeks and $241 million.[2] Though not impossible, *Psych Thrill* will likely not approach these results. Nevertheless, they serve to illustrate the point that maximum theatrical success with this project will be reached only after positive word-of-mouth stemming from a limited initial release.

general marketing strategy

Once a suitable domestic distributor is found, we will recommend that marketing begin with targeted screenings and Internet exposure, followed by local promotions. These screenings will target audiences most likely to take an interest in the film and feature follow-up discussions with key members of the project such as the writer/director, producer, and actors. As an example, the distributors for *Thirteen* (2003), an R-rated limited release concerning adolescent issues, raised awareness of their film by focusing on screenings to school counselors, teen psychologists, and members of Congress, Planned Parenthood, and The Brookings Institution.[3] The result was a successful theatrical release of $4.6 million domestically over a production budget of $XXXXXXX.[4] Two other examples are the films *Osama* (2004) and *The Fog of War* (2003). The initial target audience for each film was a narrow slice of the total market, and thus, early on in the marketing campaigns, screenings were arranged with members of these slices.[5] Ultimately, *Osama* went on to gross $1.1 million on a budget of $0.3 million and *Fog* went on to $4.0 million on an approximate budget of $2.0 million.[6] Internet exposure can also be effective in reaching a film's target audience. Such exposure was the cornerstone of *The Blair Witch Project*'s initial marketing campaign. Visitors at websites frequented by the target audience were directed to the film's website where new information was repeatedly posted to ensure the return of these initial visitors. Studio spending on Internet exposure further highlights the importance of online marketing. Such spending by Motion Picture Association of America members (seven studios) climbed nearly 50% in 2003 to a level even with the height of the dot-com bubble.[7]

[2] *Weekly Variety* box office charts, 1999–2003; and *IMDb.com*.

[3] Beth Pinsker, "Other People's Money," *Daily Variety*, August 18, 2003.

[4] *IMDb.com*; Baseline StudioSystems.

[5] Stephen Galloway, "How They Did It," *The Hollywood Reporter*, May 18, 2004.

[6] *Weekly Variety* box office charts, 2003–2004; *IMDb.com*; Dave Calhoun, "Story-telling Beyond the Veil," *The Times* (London), February 12, 2004; Kathy A. McDonald, "The Fog of War," *Daily Variety*, December 12, 2003.

[7] Ben Fritz, "Another banner year," *Daily Variety*, May 10, 2004.

Once it is decided in what city or cities the film will debut, local promotions will also be advised. These promotions can be with businesses ranging from large corporations to diners catering to a film's primary audience and willing to provide a prize or host an event. The allure of these promotions is that expenses are limited to fliers and postcards because the promoter picks up the tab for whatever product or service it is providing. The marketing team for *My Big Fat Greek Wedding* spent months using promotions to repeatedly target the same bridal salons, Greek diners, and Greek Orthodox churches in New York City. Marketers for *Pic P* (nine initial screens, $3.5 million budget, $20.8 million gross) set up promotions with restaurants throughout NYC. The total cost of these promotions rarely exceeds $20,000 yet yields a measurable return, as *Wedding* and *Pic P* illustrate.[8] The overall goal with these marketing strategies is to begin significant word-of-mouth about a film. Once word-of-mouth spreads, the resulting revenues can be used to pay for more traditional publicity, such as media buys and publicists.

target audience & specific marketing strategy

Psych Thrill can be best described as a cross between the psychological thrillers *Pic N* and *Silence of the Lambs*. *Pic N* was a 2001 low-budget independent film that achieved a gross of $25.5 million on a budget of $5.0 million, and *Silence* was a 1991 studio film budgeted in the ballpark of $16 million grossing a total of $130 million. Its sequel and prequel (also studio pictures), *Hannibal* (2001) and *Red Dragon* (2002), grossed $165 and $92 million respectively.[9] The thriller genre has experienced a steady decline in box office share over the release years 2000–2003 inclusive but as *Pic N*, *Hannibal*, and *Red Dragon* illustrate, the demand for successful ones is still there.[10] The target audience for this film consists of the same types of moviegoers that went to see the thrillers already listed, especially *Pic N*, as its budget is in the same range as that for *Psych Thrill*. *Pic N*'s core audience was comprised of specialty theater patrons, upscale young

[8] XXXXXXXXXXXXXXXXXXXXXXXXX.

[9] Baseline StudioSystems; *Weekly Variety* box office charts, 2001–2002; *IMDb.com*.

[10] Calculations and numbers based on "Film 500," *The Hollywood Reporter,* August 2001, 2002, 2003, 2004; and "U.S. Entertainment Industry: 2006 Market Statistics" by Motion Picture Association Worldwide Market Research & Analysis; "release year" refers to the fact that a film can be released in a given year but still earn box office revenue in the following year (as with many year-end releases).

adults, and college students.[11] Two of the films listed in the Financial Projections section, *Pic L* and *Pic J*, were foreign, so it is conceivable that, all things equal, *Psych Thrill*'s market will exceed these two films' markets as *Psych Thrill* will obviously be an English speaking film in an English speaking territory (the US).

We will recommend targeted screenings that focus on universities and police associations (as the film is about XXXXXXXXXXXXXXXXXXXXXXXXXXXXXXX). The presence of at least one significantly name actor in the cast should provide even more appeal to the screenings and their follow-up discussions. Regarding Internet marketing, we will advise targeting fan sites devoted to thriller movies as well as those devoted to any name actors in the film. We will also recommend focusing on sites frequented by members of the age 21-to-29 demographic. Promotions will be advised with partners in university neighborhoods and bars catering to this same demographic.

---

[11] XXXXXXXXXXXXXXXXXXXXXXXXXXXXXXXXXXXXXXXXXXXXXXXXXXXXXXXXXXXXXXXXXXXXXXXXXXXXXXXX XXXXXXXXXXXXXXXXXXXXXXXXXXXX.

MOTION PICTURE DISTRIBUTION

distribution overview

Distribution of an independent film involves licensing its rights to a distribution company or companies for a specified length of time. During this time each distributor further licenses the film to various markets. Markets are divided into geographical regions. These regions can be described as broadly as domestic (U.S. and Canadian) and foreign or as specifically as Belgian and Argentinian. Markets are also divided into formats, such as theatrical, DVD/home video, and TV. "Format" refers to the way in which a movie can be viewed. The theatrical market includes all public movie theaters; the DVD/home video market includes DVDs for sale and rental; and the television market includes network, syndication, cable/satellite, pay-per-view, and video-on-demand. Other formats for which rights can be licensed include soundtrack, novelization, merchandising, and showings of the film not entirely open to the public, such as for the airlines, armed forces, and campuses. For films with solid commercial prospects, a distributor will typically acquire the rights for all formats and do so within a specific country or countries. For example, a company that acquires or has been licensed the "German rights" to a film has the right to release the film in Germany in all the aforementioned formats. Domestically this is also the case, with U.S. and Canadian rights acquired together as a block. <u>Revenues in all domestic formats and foreign markets are driven by the success of the domestic theatrical release</u>. As such, a domestic theatrical release is often viewed as a reasonable investment despite the fact that in most cases theatrical release profits are minimal. It establishes audience awareness of a film. Theatrical release in foreign markets may or may not occur depending on genre, market conditions, and the like. Regardless, the timing of film distribution in the domestic market generally follows the chart below:

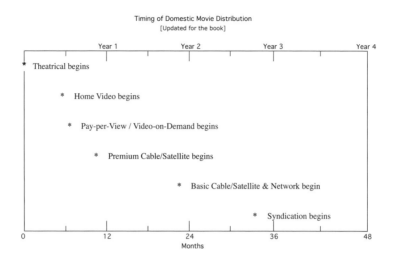

Timing of Domestic Movie Distribution
[Updated for the book]

Foreign markets often begin their releases shortly after domestic theatrical. Format order generally remains the same in these markets with variations occurring in timing and availability of release format.

distributor expenses and fees

Prints and Advertising (P&A) are the most recognizable of distribution expenses. Once a final version of a film is completed and ready for theatrical distribution, a copy of this version is made from which all other copies, known as "prints," are created. One print costing approximately $1500 domestically must be made for each screen on which the film is being shown during any given weekend. Advertising is much more expensive. The cost of a quarter page ad in a major newspaper can be over $10,000 per day. If a film such as *Psych Thrill* achieves a domestic theatrical release on 100–600 screens, the P&A costs could approach or even exceed the film's budget. Often, an even larger, but less recognizable, expense for low-budget independent films is the cost of manufacturing, marketing, and distributing DVDs. These costs can exceed $4.00 per DVD on a wholesale price of $15–$18. Returning to the topic of P&A, some low-budget films take it upon themselves to raise and spend P&A funds. We will not take this approach because P&A expenditure is the specialty of distributors and would be most efficiently handled by them.

Each distributor is responsible for collecting the revenue generated by its markets. After doing so, the distributor subtracts its distribution fee, followed by expenses (including P&A costs for any theatrical release), and remits the remaining portion to the producer. The fee is a percentage of the total revenue and depends upon the nature of the producer-distributor contract. These contracts vary widely from project to project, but should they arise, will be negotiated by Psych Thrill LLC and its lawyers to maximize investor profits. <u>It bears mentioning again that revenues in all other markets are driven by the success of the domestic theatrical release, because it establishes audience awareness for the film</u>. This area is where especially close attention and effort will be paid in trying to find a quality distributor for *Psych Thrill*.

distributor control

Before agreeing on a contract, the distributor may request any number of changes to a film itself, ranging from length to music to style of editing. These requests will only be met if we feel they serve to maximize investor profits. Once the contract is signed, the distributor has control over a film's marketing. In the case of a film with solid commercial prospects where the distributor has been licensed all format rights, the distributor also has control over the film's theatrical release pattern. The distributor will determine in which city or cities and in how many theaters the movie should open. Typically with independent films of a similar budget to *Psych Thrill*, initial domestic release occurs on fewer than 15 screens, sometimes as few as one, and then spreads to more theaters when proceeds are high enough to pay for more prints and advertising. With regard to marketing, the distributor will determine to whom and how to market the picture, including on which newspapers and radio and television channels to advertise. Because so much control is exercised by distributors, we will take the utmost care in assuring our views on how the film should be marketed and released are represented in any distribution contract. The overriding concern in any agreement will be maximizing investor profit, and we will make the full use of our lawyers and their experience in this field in efforts to do so.

distribution companies [Remember, this is from a plan in late 2004!]

Domestic distribution companies in the independent film industry can be divided into three groups: studio subsidiaries (also known as "mini-majors"), stand-alones, and mini-distributors. Studio subsidiaries are a testament to the health of the independent film sector. Their parents, the studios, have recognized the potential profit of these films and created their own specialty divisions to distribute them. Recently, Warner Brothers became the seventh major studio to do so by establishing Warner Independent Pictures in 2003. Stand-alone distributors and mini-distributors are not subdivisions of a studio.

The mini-majors clearly have the domestic distribution power. When looking at independent film distributors with the top 2003 theatrical grosses, mini-majors held six of the top ten spots, including positions one through five.[1] Because of their attachment to studios, the mini-majors have more experience and deeper financial resources with which to acquire, promote, and release films. While we intend to go after the mini-majors, stand-alone distributors provide another attractive option. They held the remaining positions in the top ten with stand-alone Lionsgate outperforming mini-majors Sony Pictures Classics and Paramount Classics. (Paramount was outperformed by three other stand-alones as well.)[2] Mini-distributors have a more difficult time successfully distributing films due to their small size and somewhat limited power. Nevertheless, Zeitgeist, Manhattan Pictures, and ThinkFilm were examples of such companies able to keep their top 2003 releases in theaters for over sixteen weeks.[3] Additionally, these companies look for good films with which to establish themselves. In terms of foreign distribution, a mini-major or stand-alone has the capacity to distribute internationally or refer a film to a foreign sales agent (who in turn licenses the film to foreign distributors). Mini-distributors may or may not. We will focus on trying to obtain domestic distribution with companies that have foreign capacity or contacts. It is worth noting the terms "foreign sales agent" and "foreign distributor" are sometimes used interchangeably.

distribution criteria

Distributors seek films with at least one recognizable cast member, an exploitable genre or market segment, and a storyline that is original. These are some of the main factors influencing a distributor's decision to acquire the rights to a film. *Psych Thrill* will feature at least one actor whose name carries innate audience appeal. Furthermore, it will do so in a genre (psychological thriller) that has

---

[1] Ian Mohr, "Indies Fly High," *The Hollywood Reporter*, January 7, 2004; note that some of these totals, especially those of the mini-majors, may also include pictures at least partially financed by studios; however, as a general proxy of independent film distribution power, the table is reliable.

[2] Ibid.

[3] *Weekly Variety* box office charts, 1999–2003; *IMDb.com*.

a great potential for generating revenues, as the performances of the low-budget independent *Pic N* and studio budgeted *Silence of the Lambs* franchise illustrate. Finally, *Psych Thrill* contains the unique story line of XXXXXXXXXXXXXXXXXXXXXXXX XXXXXXXXXXXXXXXXXXXXXXXXXXXXX. These qualities of the project will maximize its chances for garnering distribution.

strategy for attaining distribution

We will implement a three-step approach to attaining distribution. First, we will submit the film to top-tier film festivals such as Sundance, Berlin, Tribeca, Cannes, and Toronto. At major festivals such as these, all levels of distributors attend screenings arranged for festival attendees. In the ideal scenario, distributors at these screenings take such keen interest in a film that a bidding war ensues in which distributors bid against one another for domestic and foreign rights in all formats. These bidding wars, while extremely rare, can result in exorbitant advances being paid to the producers (and thus investors) of a film well before distribution commences. Recent examples include *Pic B* (2003), *Pic A* (2003), and *Pic D* (2002) which sold in the neighborhood of $1.5 million, $3.5 million, and $5 million on respective budgets of $0.5 million, $0.3 million, and $0.2 million.[4] Additional examples, also very rare, are films that were sold at festivals (a.k.a. delivered advances) closer to the vicinity of their negative costs, including *Pic Q* (2002), *Pic E* (2002), and *Pic M* (2001) which sold in the neighborhood of $3 million, $1 million, and $4 million respectively.[5] Simultaneous to festival submissions, we will submit the film to top producer's representatives, otherwise known as producer's reps, for representation. For a fee ranging from 10%–15% of all revenues returned from a film to the producer, the top producer's reps use their contacts with distributors to secure and negotiate domestic and international distribution for a film. They do so by helping films gain entrance to one of the top-tier festivals and/or positioning distributors against one another at such a festival to induce a bidding war. Sometimes producer's reps will not take on a film until after it has gained acceptance to a festival, and in other cases they can secure distribution for a film prior to or independent of a festival appearance. Once domestic distribution in all formats is secured via a film festival, via a producer's rep, or both, the third step in attaining distribution will be to seek out

---

[4] XXXXXXXXXXXXXXXXXXXXXXXXXXXXXXXXXXXXXXXXXXXXXXXXXXXXXXXXXXXXXXXXXXXXXXXXXXXXXXXXXXXXXXXXX
XXXXXXXXXXXXXXXXXXXXXXXXXXXXXXXXXXXXXXXXXXXXXXXXXX.

[5] XXXXXXXXXXXXXXXXXXXXXXXXXXXXXXXXXXXXXXXXXXXXXXXXXXXXXXXXXXXXXXXXXXXXXXXXXXXXXXXXXXXXXXXXX
XXXXXXXXXXXXXXXXXXXXXXXXXXXXXXXXXXXXXXXXXXXXXXXXXXXXXXXXXX.

a foreign sales agent to license the film to any remaining foreign territories. The foreign sales agent, sometimes referred to as a foreign distributor, may be referred or hired by a producer's rep and will attend various film markets throughout the year in Europe, America, and possibly elsewhere and license the film to distributors from certain geographical territories. These distributors pay an advance to the sales agent against which the agent charges a 10%–25% fee, deducts expenses, and remits the remaining portion to the producer or producer's rep.

Should top-tier festivals and producer's reps not take an interest in *Psych Thrill*, as is the case with the vast majority of independent features, a second tier of festivals and approaches will be utilized with the goal of securing a domestic theatrical release. However, as each subsequent set of options becomes eliminated, the prospects for returning more than a film's principal investment, and the principal investment itself, decrease.

FINANCING

risk statement

Movies are the most risky of assets. They are subject to production, distribution, company-specific, and general economic risks that can vastly hamper the forecasting of their results. Risks associated with *Psych Thrill* (the "movie") include but are not limited to failure to complete production, failure to achieve distribution, ineffective distribution of the movie by a distributor, a distributor of the movie going bankrupt, extreme competition from other movies, failure of the public to accept the movie, inability of management and other persons to guide the movie through the marketplace, and general economic and market factors. When combined, these risks can drastically change the actual results versus the forecasted results posited in this business plan. This list of risk factors is by no means complete.

method of financing

Psych Thrill LLC is seeking $1.5 million in equity capital (in units of $50,000) to finance the entire production budget of the motion picture *Psych Thrill*. The use of private equity funding ensures that the advantages of making an independent film can be fully realized. Creative control centered in the hands of the director ensures a film free from the divisive influence of too many voices. Low overhead and extreme care in formulating the budget yield a higher potential return for investors. Greater creative control ultimately yields a higher potential return as well.

investor repayment

Money remitted to the LLC will first be returned to investors until their initial investment plus a 20% percentage of return (a so-called "priority return") is recouped. Payments will be proportionately distributed to investors according to their individual investment size and without preference to all investors simultaneously. Any remaining profits will be split evenly between Psych Thrill LLC and investors. Psych Thrill LLC may use a portion of its profits (after the split) to pay for profit participations agreed upon between it and various talent or crew, such as actors, composers, or producers.

Distributors and foreign sales agents typically produce accounting statements on a quarterly, or sometimes monthly, basis during the beginning of a distribution term and change to less frequent reports one or two years later. Reports and any concomitant revenues are often remitted to a producer's rep or producer within 30–45 days of their monthly, quarterly, semi-annual, or annual due date. Psych Thrill LLC will deliver accounting statements and appropriate payments to investors within 30 days of the receipt of funds from a distributor, sales agent, or producer's rep. Producer's reps of successful films generally remit funds to producers within one to two weeks of their receipt from another party.

residuals

Residuals are payments made to union talent (actors, writers, etc.) out of revenues generated from post-theatrical exploitation of a movie. The producer is responsible for ensuring that a distributor or foreign sales agent makes these payments by including an assumption agreement in the language of any distribution or foreign sales agent deal. While successful pictures may not have substantial problems with distributors or foreign sales agents accepting and executing such agreements, pictures that are not highly sought after for distribution may face problems with distributors or foreign sales agents accepting responsibility for and paying residuals. In such cases it may be that monies returned from distributors or foreign sales agents for ancillary markets are first used to pay residuals and then used to pay investors.

FINANCIAL PROJECTIONS[1]

The box office gross for a single film is absolutely unpredictable, regardless of financial model used or the film's budget, genre, cast, time frame, etc. It is box office gross that drives the financial success or failure of a film.

domestic distributor advances

When a domestic distributor takes a keen interest in a film, it sometimes advances future revenues to the producer prior to the commencement of distribution. The advance can be in return for a buyout of all future revenues or only a portion. Public information on the exact details of such arrangements is nonexistent and most often limited to ballpark estimates of advance sizes. As a result, profitability estimates for comparable films and projections for *Psych Thrill* assume no domestic distributor advances and assume distribution terms less favorable than most producers of a successful film would face at the outset of distribution.

comparable films

Table 1 estimates the profitability of certain successful films during the two-year period immediately following the commencement of domestic theatrical release. Their commonalities are as follows:

> never achieved beyond 600 screens in domestic (U.S. and
>   Canadian) theatrical release.
> opened on fewer than 15 screens domestically.
> budgets were at $5 million or less.
> released domestically some time between 2000–2004.

These films illustrate the profit potential of a film such as *Psych Thrill* for two reasons. Each one has a rating of R or NC-17 and contains subject matter that is thrilling and/or handles the frailty of the human psyche. As a result, their audiences would be the likely audiences for *Psych Thrill* with *Pic N*, the film most similar to it, highlighting the very upper end of box office size for these audiences. Additionally, these films demonstrate that never reaching beyond a 600-screen

---

[1] Taxation in the case of an LLC is pass-through, and thus, all estimates and projections of profits and returns exclude taxes.

domestic release can be profitable. Wider releases of films in this budget range do sometimes occur, often generating significant revenue. However, *Psych Thrill* need not depend on such a release to turn an appreciable profit. Regarding foreign revenue, it is an estimate of the revenue that might have been generated by each picture had it first been sold under current foreign marketplace conditions. Foreign revenue is not broken out for each picture because foreign rights for successful independent films are often sold to a territory in multiple formats at one time. For example, the Argentinian rights to a film may consist of theatrical, DVD/home video, TV, and pay TV releases of it. Figures are readily available for distribution prices by territory, but to list each territory and/or break the figures down further into their component formats is neither practical nor necessary.

income projections

Table 2 forecasts three profitability scenarios for *Psych Thrill*. The revenues for the "Medium Success" scenario reflect the comparable films table averages. With the exception of home video, the comparable films averages are greatly boosted by a single movie, *Pic N*; however, this is acceptable as *Pic N* serves as a much closer representation of *Psych Thrill* than the other films on the table. This fact combined with *Psych Thrill*'s exceptionally low budget, partially a product as discussed of shooting in Louisiana, presents a large upside opportunity on returns. The "Low Success" scenario is constructed with the fulfillment of an investor priority return of 20%, and "High Success" is a best-case scenario derived by adjusting the domestic box office and home video revenues upward in amounts equal to the difference between their "Medium" and "Low" numbers. According to the Financing section, the percentage of return recouped by investors after restoration of their initial investment and before profits are split evenly with Psych Thrill LLC is to be 20% (a.k.a. the "priority return"). In the "High" scenario the home video gross is capped at the highest home video gross from the comparable films table. For all scenarios the domestic pay TV revenues feed from the box office projection using a licensing percentage. All projections in table 2 (domestic, foreign, and otherwise) should be taken as estimations only. There is no guarantee that these projections will actually be met by the film.

cash flow projections

Table 3 predicts the timing of sources and uses of cash from the "Medium Success" scenario on the income table and how that cash will flow back to investors. Cash flow projections for the "High" and "Low" scenarios are available on request and closely follow the timing of the printed scenario, only with different amounts. It cannot be overemphasized that the actual timing and structure of income will depend on marketplace conditions and contracts with distributors and any foreign sales agent and producer's rep of the film. There is no guarantee that such contracts will be obtained or as to what their terms will be. The figures therein are not a guarantee of actual performance.

investor projections

Table 4 forecasts the projected return to investors over 5.25 years under the three profitability scenarios highlighted in the income projections. "High Success" indicates a non-annualized return on investment (ROI) of 310% (or an ROI multiple of 4.10x) and an annualized internal rate of return (IRR) of 56.9%. The IRR derives directly from the corresponding cash flow scenario. "Medium Success" yields a 214% ROI (3.14x) and an IRR of 44.9%, while "Low Success" meets the priority return to investors with an ROI of 20% (1.20x) and an IRR of 5.9%. Although successful films can generate revenues for many years and sometimes decades after their release, the vast majority of revenues (often nearly 100%) are returned within 3.25 years of the release date. As with table 3, table 4 is for reference only, and the figures therein are not a guarantee of actual performance.

Table 1: Successful Films Comparable to *Psych Thrill*

	Pic L	Pic M	Pic J	Pic N	Pic K	Average
DOMESTIC (U.S.)[1]						
Box Office Gross	$1.2	$8.8	$5.4	$25.5	$3.6	$8.9
Less Exhibitor Share[2]	$0.6	$4.1	$2.5	$11.9	$1.7	$4.1
Gross Film Rentals	$0.7	$4.7	$2.9	$13.7	$1.9	$4.8
Home Video Revenue	$17.1	$26.8	$14.8	$15.2	$19.2	$18.6
Pay TV Revenue	$0.5	$2.2	$2.3	$6.5	$0.9	$2.5
Gross Ancillary Revenue	$17.6	$29.1	$17.1	$21.8	$20.1	$21.1
Domestic Gross[3]	$18.3	$33.8	$20.0	$35.4	$22.0	$25.9
Less Distribution Fee (35%)	$6.4	$11.8	$7.0	$12.4	$7.7	$9.1
Less Prints & Advertising[4]	$0.6	$5.6	$1.3	$12.8	$2.0	$4.5
Less Other Distributor Costs[5]	$3.7	$6.8	$4.0	$7.1	$4.4	$5.2
Net Domestic Receipts	$7.6	$9.6	$7.7	$3.1	$7.9	$7.2
FOREIGN						
Foreign Gross[6]	$1.2	$2.3	$2.3	$4.7	$4.7	$3.0
Less Sales Agent Fee & Expenses (35%)[7]	$0.4	$0.8	$0.8	$1.6	$1.6	$1.1
Net Foreign Receipts	$0.8	$1.5	$1.5	$3.1	$3.1	$2.0
TOTAL						
TOTAL PRODUCER'S REP GROSS[8]	$8.4	$11.1	$9.2	$6.2	$11.0	$9.2
Less Producer's Rep Fee (15%)	$1.3	$1.7	$1.4	$0.9	$1.6	$1.4
TOTAL PRODUCER'S GROSS	$7.1	$9.4	$7.8	$5.3	$9.3	$7.8
Less Negative Cost[9]	$1.0	$3.0	$2.0	$5.0	$4.5	$3.1
NET INVESTOR/PRODUCER PROFIT	$6.1	$6.4	$5.8	$0.3	$4.8	$4.7

NOTES:

*This table estimates the profitability of past films and is in no manner a guarantee of future performance.

*Amounts in millions of dollars and convey revenues collected during the 3.25 years immediately after the domestic theatrical release date.

*All raw data except for 'Other Distributor Costs' and 'Foreign Gross' is provided by Baseline StudioSystems.

*To allow for uniform comparisons, distribution arrangements are assumed the same for each film; actual fee and revenue-sharing arrangements are privately held data.

*Totals from films first released internationally are modified as if first released domestically.

*'Foreign Gross' is calculated from "The Going Rate," American Film Market 2004, *The Hollywood Reporter*, Nov. 2-10, 2004; Canada excluded.

*Totals may not add due to rounding.

FOOTNOTES:

1: DOMESTIC - For 'Box Office Gross' and 'Prints & Advertising,' domestic refers to U.S. & Canada, for all other data points it refers only to U.S.

2: Exhibitor Share - Theater owners' share of the box office revenue.

3: Domestic Gross - Sum of 'Gross Film Rentals' and 'Gross Ancillary Revenue.'

4: Prints & Advertising (P&A) - Cost of the marketing campaign and copies made of the original negative ('prints') for the theatrical release.

5: Other Distributor Costs - Expenses outside of P&A for which the distributor is reimbursed such as residuals and DVD manufacturing, marketing, and distribution costs.

6: Foreign Gross - Canada excluded; money received from advances by foreign distributors for the right to distribute in all formats; per territory data available.

7: Sales Agent - Markets to and collects advances from foreign distributors. Residuals are included as part of expenses.

8: Producer's Rep - Seeks out and negotiates domestic distribution and sales agent agreements.

9: Negative Cost - Costs incurred to shoot the film and create the negative off of which all copies of the film are made; also known as the 'budget' of the film.

Table 2: Projected Income for *Psych Thrill*	Low Success	Medium Success	High Success
DOMESTIC (U.S.)[1]			
Box Office Gross	$1.3	$8.9	$16.5
Less Exhibitor Share (46%)	$0.6	$4.1	$7.7
Gross Film Rentals	**$0.7**	**$4.8**	**$8.8**
Home Video Revenue	$2.7	$18.6	$26.8
Pay TV Revenue	$0.5	$2.9	$5.3
Gross Ancillary Revenue	**$3.2**	**$21.5**	**$32.2**
Domestic Gross	**$3.9**	**$26.3**	**$41.0**
Less Distribution Fee (35%)	$1.4	$9.2	$14.4
Less Prints & Advertising	$0.6	$4.4	$8.1
Less Other Distributor Costs	$0.8	$5.3	$8.2
Net Domestic Receipts	**$1.1**	**$7.5**	**$10.4**

FOREIGN			
Foreign Gross	**$1.6**	**$2.3**	**$3.1**
Less Sales Agent Fee & Expenses (35%)	$0.5	$0.8	$1.1
Net Foreign Receipts	**$1.0**	**$1.5**	**$2.0**

TOTAL			
TOTAL PRODUCER'S REP GROSS	**$2.1**	**$9.0**	**$12.4**
Less Producer's Rep Fee (15%)	$0.3	$1.3	$1.9
TOTAL PRODUCER'S GROSS	**$1.8**	**$7.6**	**$10.5**
Less Negative Cost	$1.5	$1.5	$1.5
NET INVESTOR/PRODUCER PROFIT	**$0.3**	**$6.1**	**$9.0**

NOTES:

*This table reflects estimates of future performance that are in no manner a guarantee of future performance.

*Amounts in millions of dollars and convey revenues collected during the 3.25 years immediately after the domestic theatrical release date.

*Distribution arrangements follow those of the comparable films table; actual fee and revenue-sharing arrangements will vary depending on parties involved, desirability of the film, and market conditions.

*Foreign Gross figures based upon "The Going Rate," American Film Market 2004, *The Hollywood Reporter*, Nov. 2-10, 2004; Canada excluded.

*Totals may not add due to rounding.

FOOTNOTES:

1: DOMESTIC - For 'Box Office Gross' and 'Prints & Advertising,' domestic refers to U.S. & Canada, for all other data points it refers only to U.S.

Table 3: Projected Cash Flow for Psych Thrill LLC (Medium)

	YEAR 1				YEAR 2				YEAR 3			
	Quarter 1	Quarter 2	Quarter 3	Quarter 4	Quarter 1	Quarter 2	Quarter 3	Quarter 4	Quarter 1	Quarter 2	Quarter 3	Quarter 4
Psych Thrill												
Negative Cost[1]	$ (1.050)	$ (0.150)	$ (0.150)	$ (0.150)								
Gross Film Rentals									$ 2.147	$ 2.528	$ 0.095	
Home Video Revenue											$ 13.418	$ 1.025
Pay TV Revenue												
Distribution Fee									$ (0.751)	$ (0.885)	$ (4.730)	$ (0.359)
Prints & Advertising									$ (1.965)	$ (2.314)	$ (0.087)	
Other Distributor Costs									$ (0.429)	$ (0.506)	$ (2.703)	$ (0.205)
Dom Subtotal[2]									*$ (0.999)*	*$ (1.176)*	*$ 3.819*	*$ 0.461*
Foreign Gross										$ 0.691	$ 0.691	$ 0.691
Sales Agent Fee & Costs										$ (0.242)	$ (0.242)	$ (0.242)
Frgn Subtotal										*$ 0.449*	*$ 0.449*	*$ 0.449*
Producer's Rep Fee											*$ (0.640)*	*$ (0.137)*
TOTAL[3]	$ (1.050)	$ (0.150)	$ (0.150)	$ (0.150)	$ -	$ -	$ -	$ -	$ -	$ -	$ 3.627	$ 0.774
RUNNING TOTAL	$ (1.050)	$ (1.200)	$ (1.350)	$ (1.500)	$ (1.500)	$ (1.500)	$ (1.500)	$ (1.500)	$ (1.500)	$ (1.500)	$ 2.127	$ 2.901
RETURNED TO INVESTORS[4]	$ -	$ -	$ -	$ -	$ -	$ -	$ -	$ -	$ -	$ -	$ 2.714	$ 0.387
CUMULATIVE RETURNED	$ -	$ -	$ -	$ -	$ -	$ -	$ -	$ -	$ -	$ -	$ 2.714	$ 3.101

NOTES:

*This table reflects estimates of the timing and structure of income returned to investors and is in no manner a guarantee of the amounts or timing of such returns. Actual timing and structure depend on market conditions and contracts with involved parties (e.g., distributors, sales agent, producer's rep, etc.).

*Amounts in millions of dollars.

*Theatrical distribution is assumed to commence one year after the completion of postproduction. Actual release date will be determined by the distributor.

*A small amount of ancillary revenue is likely to occur beyond the film's 3.25-year revenue window with the agreed split between producer and investors still in effect.

*Totals may not add due to rounding.

FOOTNOTES:

1: Negative Cost - Reflects timing of the negative cost and is to take 6.5 weeks preproduction, 6.5 weeks principal photography, and 9 months postproduction.

2: Year 3, Quarters 1 & 2 subtotals are carried forward and charged against Year 3, Quarter 3 subtotal.

3: Total - Sum of 'Negative Cost,' 'Dom Subtotal,' 'Frgn Subtotal,' and 'Producer's Rep Fee.'

4: Returned to Investors - Cash from 'Total' row returned to investors. Assumes 120% of initial investment returned, then remaining cash split 50/50 with Psych Thrill LLC.

Table 3 (cont'd): Projected Cash Flow for Psych Thrill LLC (Medium)

	YEAR 4				YEAR 5				YEAR 6
	Quarter 1	Quarter 2	Quarter 3	Quarter 4	Quarter 1	Quarter 2	Quarter 3	Quarter 4	Quarter 1
Psych Thrill									
Negative Cost[1]									
Gross Film Rentals									
Home Video Revenue	$ 0.512	$ 0.512	$ 0.512	$ 0.512	$ 0.512	$ 0.410	$ 0.410	$ 0.410	$ 0.401
Pay TV Revenue		2.882							
Distribution Fee	$ (0.179)	$ (1.188)	$ (0.179)	$ (0.179)	$ (0.179)	$ (0.143)	$ (0.143)	$ (0.143)	$ (0.140)
Prints & Advertising									
Other Distributor Costs	$ (0.102)	$ (0.679)	$ (0.102)	$ (0.102)	$ (0.102)	$ (0.082)	$ (0.082)	$ (0.082)	$ (0.080)
Dom Subtotal[2]	$ 0.231	$ 1.528	$ 0.231	$ 0.231	$ 0.231	$ 0.184	$ 0.184	$ 0.184	$ 0.180
Foreign Gross	$ 0.345	$ 0.345		$ 0.230					
Sales Agent Fee & Costs	$ (0.121)	$ (0.121)		$ (0.081)					
Frgn Subtotal	$ 0.224	$ 0.224		$ 0.150					
Producer's Rep Fee	$ (0.068)	$ (0.263)	$ (0.035)	$ (0.057)	$ (0.035)	$ (0.028)	$ (0.028)	$ (0.028)	$ (0.027)
TOTAL[3]	$ 0.387	$ 1.489	$ 0.196	$ 0.323	$ 0.196	$ 0.157	$ 0.157	$ 0.157	$ 0.153
RUNNING TOTAL	$ 3.288	$ 4.777	$ 4.973	$ 5.297	$ 5.493	$ 5.649	$ 5.806	$ 5.963	$ 6.116
RETURNED TO INVESTORS[4]	$ 0.193	$ 0.745	$ 0.098	$ 0.162	$ 0.098	$ 0.078	$ 0.078	$ 0.078	$ 0.077
CUMULATIVE RETURNED	$ 3.294	$ 4.039	$ 4.137	$ 4.298	$ 4.396	$ 4.475	$ 4.553	$ 4.632	$ 4.708

Table 4: Projected Investor Returns from Psych Thrill LLC			
	Low Success	Medium Success	High Success
Total Cash Returned to Investors/Producer[1]	$1.8	$7.6	$10.5
Less Negative Cost	$1.5	$1.5	$1.5
Less Investor Priority Return[2]	$0.3	$0.3	$0.3
Adjusted Investor/Producer Profit	$0.0	$5.8	$8.7
Investor 50% Share of Adjusted	$0.0	$2.9	$4.4
Plus Investor Priority Return	$0.3	$0.3	$0.3
Plus Negative Cost	$1.5	$1.5	$1.5
TOTAL CASH RETURNED TO INVESTORS	$1.8	$4.7	$6.2
Amount Invested by Investors	$1.5	$1.5	$1.5
NET INVESTOR RETURN[3]	$0.3	$3.2	$4.7
NET RETURN PER $50,000 UNIT[4]	$ 10,000	$ 106,939	$ 155,003
NON-ANNUALIZED ROI[5]	20%	214%	310%
ANNUALIZED IRR[6]	5.9%	44.9%	56.9%

NOTES:
*This table reflects estimates of future returns to investors and is in no way a guarantee of future returns to investors.
*Totals may not add due to rounding.

FOOTNOTES:
1: Total Cash Ret. to Inv./Producer - All revenues generated by Psych Thrill LLC prior to disbursement to investors (i.e., sum of all positive 'TOTAL' amounts from cash flow).
2: Investor Priority Return - 20% of the Negative Cost that is returned to investors after repayment of the Negative Cost but before profits are split with Psych Thrill LLC.
3: Net Investor Return - The total cash returned to investors minus the amount invested by investors (i.e., minus the Negative Cost).
4: Net Return per $50,000 unit - The return earned on a single LLC unit beyond the initial investment amount, as expressed in $1 increments instead of $1,000,000 increments.
5: Non-annualized ROI - The return on investment as calculated by dividing the Net Investor Return by the Negative Cost (i.e., by the 'Amount Invested by Investors').
6: Annualized IRR (Internal Rate of Return) - The yearly rate of return on the initial investment given the timing of income in the projected cash flow. Actual timing and structure of income depend on market conditions and contracts with involved parties (e.g., distributors, sales agent, producer's rep, etc.) and will affect the annualized IRR.

APPENDIX B:
NITTY GRITTY DETAILS

(Boring but important... That's why they're in the appendix!)

GENERAL FINANCIAL
PROJECTIONS NOTES:

PROMISES

Never under any circumstances make promises. It should always be clear with your projections that they are just that, projections. If you make any promises such as, "Hey, these predictions are bound to come true," you better pray they do or you might as well sell your personal items now to raise money for your legal fund. The law does not look kindly on filmmakers who raise money through promises.

ROUNDING

The numbers in my sample plans/films were computed using Microsoft Excel. Whether you use Excel or not, you will likely be confronted with tables that have numbers that don't appear to add up due to rounding. The following table illustrates what I mean:

Table B.1: Rounding example		
Rounded	3.5 + 1.0	= 4.6
Unrounded	3.5449 + 1.0449	= 4.5898

As you can see, on the surface 3.5 + 1.0 would seem logically to compute to 4.5. However, because each figure is a rounded representation of the actual figure beneath it, the answer comes to a rounded 4.6. This type of rounding issue naturally extends to subtraction, multiplication, and division.

Rounding issues also happen when the numbers you are working with have more than just one decimal place, like 3.556 or 6.772. In those cases the issues will occur with the last digit — the "6" in the 3.556 and the "2" in the 6.772. Keep this rounding topic in mind as you examine numbers from the text and, ultimately, the numbers from your own tables. Rounding is also something to footnote in your own tables as I do in mine. Investors are familiar and forgiving with this issue, provided that you do footnote it.

TAXES

Because the entity I dealt with in the sample plans and the entity most commonly used at the moment for funding an independent film is an LLC (Limited Liability Company), taxes are not discussed in this book. In the case of an LLC, taxes are not paid by the LLC but rather by the recipients of the LLC's profits. So if I get $100 from my share of an LLC's profits, I pay taxes on this $100 in my individual tax return, and the $100 is not taxed one bit at the company level, such as when ExxonMobil pays taxes on its oil profits. There are, of course, important exceptions to this general rule, but these exceptions run beyond the scope of this book. Consult your legal counsel, and if you need to, include such exceptions in your forecasts.

STEP 1 NOTES:

SIGNIFICANTLY NAME ACTORS — When I mention "significantly name actors" I am referring to actors whose name alone is *considered* enough to draw people in to movie theaters. Academically speaking, many of these actors have no statistical impact on box office other than to possibly keep a film that bombs from bombing worse. Either way, my best advice for cheaply determining if an actor is a significant name or not is to use the same classification criteria as retired economist and complex systems authority Dr. Arthur De Vany uses. Dr. De Vany uses the term "star" instead of "significantly name actor" but nonetheless, he does so for any actor that has appeared as a lead in a film that grossed $50 million or more in domestic box office (U.S. and Canada).[1] Keep in mind with the comparable films that an actor may currently be a significant name, but at the time of release of a comparable film the actor may not have been. Also, I say "significantly name" actor instead of just "name" actor because there are many recognizable actors, especially TV stars, who do not meet the $50 million threshold.

On another note, you might be wondering how low-budget films can afford significantly name actors. If an actor wants to do a project badly enough, he or she will cut his or her rate from millions and millions to hundreds of thousands or less. Speaking in 2007, Paramount Vantage's Executive VP Jeffrey Freedman said he does not pay more than $500,000 up front for the services of an actor.[2] Industry-wide since 2007, actors' fees have only declined.

---

[1] Arthur De Vany, *Hollywood Economics: How Extreme Uncertainty Shapes the Film Industry*, 231.
[2] Carl DiOrio, "Main event: reps vs. studio execs," *Hollywood Reporter*, March 5, 2007.

While Paramount Vantage has since pretty much gone by the wayside, the point remains: top talent will work for much less if the project is right. Paramount Vantage, by the way, used to be the well-funded and powerful specialty division of Paramount Pictures, and was responsible for acquiring independent films and making movies of a similar flavor to independent films. The budgets of its in-house productions generally did not exceed $15 million.[3]

COMPARABLE FILMS FOR THE SAMPLE PICTURES — (i) *Sci-Fi Rom*: In illustrating the financial feasibility of this film I chose thought-provoking, character-driven pieces with an upbeat tone and no significantly name actors. (ii) *Mass H-Com*: Unfortunately, there were no horror or horror-comedy films on the table. Very few met the specifications of the table and the few that did were not profitable. Furthermore, collecting data on horror or horror-comedy films released straight to DVD is exceedingly expensive and difficult to do, especially since the performance of straight-to-DVD titles in non-DVD ancillary markets is not readily available, if even tracked. However, because *Mass H-Com* is of mass appeal, I chose the most profitable films that met the table's requirements because I wanted to draw a picture of what kind of revenues a large independent film audience could generate. (iii) *Psych Thrill*: I focused my search on features rated R or NC-17 and containing subject matter that was thrilling and/or handled the frailty of the human psyche. Because profitable films of this type are rare in the $5 million and under budget range, I found only five that matched. Nonetheless, the film of the group most similar to *Psych Thrill* had a box office result considered outstanding for any film in this budget range, regardless of genre.

FOREIGN VS. NON-FOREIGN — No foreign language films were included in the table of the mass appeal movie (*Mass H-Com*). Doing so would have improved results for its comparables table. However, my intuition as a business plan writer tells me that if I am an investor considering investing in an American independent film of mass appeal, I would feel more comfortable with a comparable films table comprised entirely of popular English language independents. On the other hand, I did use several foreign films in the tables of the sci-fi romance (*Sci-Fi Rom*) and thriller (*Psych Thrill*), because

[3] John Hazelton, "Niche Labels Reveal New Look," *Screen International*, May 4, 2007.

people with an interest in certain foreign language films also enjoy the intricately drawn characters and highly intelligent material of certain non-foreign films.

STEP 1A — Depending on where you look, "screen count" has different terminology. At *IMDb.com* it is called "screens," at *IMDbPro.com* it is called "sites," at *Variety* it is often called "engagements" or "theaters," and at other sources the use will shift across the spectrum from "screens" to "venues" to "engagements." On the charts and tables provided to you by Baseline StudioSystems, *IMDb*, *IMDbPro*, *Variety*, and *The Hollywood Reporter*, the term they use for screen count will refer to the number of venues (i.e., theaters) that a movie played at.

Because low-budget independent films generally do not play on more than one screen at the same venue, it is safe to say that the venue count provided by these sources can serve as a close approximation of the screen count for a particular film. And this is why, throughout this book, I take the venue count from these data sources (i.e., the number of venues a movie played at) and use it to mean my screen count (i.e., the number of actual movie screens a movie played on). Were we to analyze big studio pictures (*The Dark Knight, Monsters vs Aliens*, etc.), this assumption would break down. Pictures such as those may have played on as many as 7,000 screens in only 4,000 theaters, due to numerous multiplexes assigning two or more screens to the same movie.

STEP 1B — In the sample plans I was able to bring the opening screen count of my comparable films down to 15 screens with only one exception (26 screens). Most low-budget independents, even today, open at 15 U.S. screens or fewer and base their expansion on the success of the initial weekend. However, because of the recent glut of independent and independent-style films on the market, a rare but increasingly significant number of openings are occurring at hundreds of screens. If restricting your opening screen count omits too many high grossing films (perhaps three), then ignore the restriction. Also, if you can't find an opening screen count on IMDb, try *Variety*'s box office charts online (*www.variety.com*) or at a library such as the Margaret Herrick Library. The column showing the number of "theaters" or "engagements" (both mean the same thing) is what you want. For a reminder on my use of the term "screen count," see Step 1A's note above.

STEP 1C — The articles may mention a budget that conflicts with the budget you will later be quoted from Baseline StudioSystems ("BLSS"). Stick with the BLSS number; often times there is an ulterior motive behind the budget quoted to an entertainment reporter or to the audience in which the reporter sits (e.g., a producer wants to up the number so a potential distributor does not lowball them in negotiations).

STEP 1E —

Home Video Revenue

We are interested in all the monies producers and investors can collect in the first three years and one quarter (3 years and 3 months, or 3.25 years) after a film's theatrical release date. A distributor collects a certain amount during 3 years, and then it takes another quarter for it to return the last bits of money generated at the end of that 3 years, which is why the total time comes out to the odd 3.25 years. During this 3.25-year time span, a distributor will generally return close to 100% of a film's lifetime home video revenues. The total you get from adding the BLSS home video pieces can be used as a rough approximation of this 3.25-year total. I say "rough" because trying to nail down home video numbers is downright impossible, especially at this fine a level of detail (see page 101). The BLSS home video numbers are formulated based on first shipments of the film to home video retailers for both rental and sell-through (a.k.a. wholesale revenue), and cover the U.S. (not Canadian) market. Another thing to keep in mind is that recent films may only have a DOM_DVD_GROSS, since video is now obsolete.

Pay TV Revenue

This refers to U.S. revenue from all cable/satellite channels (TNT, TBS, etc.), premium cable/satellite channels (HBO, Showtime, etc.), pay-per-view channels, and video-on-demand. BLSS's pay TV number may or may not include revenues from airings at hotels, on airlines, and other such venues (not major sources of revenue). The data you will ultimately get from BLSS are estimates formulated by multiplying an accepted licensing percentage against box office figures.

Gross Ancillary Revenue

Merchandise revenue is an ancillary market for which revenue is not included in this model. Some low-budget films generate significant revenues from merchandising (shirts, t-shirts, action figures, etc.), but the ones that do are much more the exception than the rule. Estimating this type of revenue is unnecessary (not to mention expensive).

Less Distribution Fee (35%)

Once a distributor receives its revenue for a film, it first takes out its fee off the top before deducting any expenses. Fees vary across media (theatrical, DVD, pay TV, etc.) but generally sit in the range of 20% to 40%. A distributor handling multiple formats may charge different fees for different formats, or may merge these fees into one single percentage rate. However, for the successful films we are tracking (and the successful film for which you will be forecasting), the fee when averaged across all media should never exceed 35%, and in fact, will likely be lower. 35% is a conventional domestic fee used to perform a conservative analysis of film profits (conservative from the perspective of keeping film profits lower). Some independent films are fortunate enough to benefit from an average distribution fee below 25%. The actual average distribution fee for each film is virtually impossible to calculate because, aside from the headache of contacting every party involved, when asked, a distributor will likely give a high figure and a producer will likely give a low figure, if they each give any figure at all. A distributor will not want its next fee negotiation burdened by another producer asking why his fee isn't as low as the previous guy's, and no producer will freely admit to making less profit for their investors because of a high fee.

Less Prints and Advertising (a.k.a. P&A)

The P&A is an estimate. Each "print" of a film is the physical copy of a film that must be loaded onto a U.S. or Canadian theater's projection device.

Less Other Distributor Costs

The 20% assumed here for non-P&A expenses encompasses many items, the majority of which are DVD manufacturing, marketing, and distribution costs, with guild residuals (SAG, WGA, etc.) a distant second. DVD expenses for a popular studio title often come in around $4.00–$5.00 per DVD on a wholesale price of $15–$18, and residuals range from roughly 1%–5% (per guild/union) of distributor's gross ancillary receipts (definitions of which can vary) depending on release format and union.

Foreign Gross

For low-budget independent films not distributed internationally by a studio subdivision, foreign revenues are collected from advances paid by foreign distributors for the right to distribute a film across different media in a certain territory or territories. Once the film is released in a territory, a foreign distributor applies its distribution fee and recoups its advance and expenses before paying any leftover money (otherwise known as "overages"). Overages are extremely rare because they are particularly difficult for the owner of the film to track and collect. Imagine having to be familiar with thirty separate countries' accounting and releasing standards. The entity responsible for arranging and collecting the advances is a foreign sales agent. For the purposes of our business plan, we are making the simplifying, and more conservative, assumption that each comparable film had a foreign sales agent and not a studio subdivision using its parent company's foreign distribution arm. Then we are going further and asking, "What kind of advances would this foreign sales agent have collected in today's market?" This allows for apples-to-apples comparisons of comparable film numbers and the projections for your film.

You will notice the FRCE from Baseline StudioSystems ("BLSS") contains many foreign figures that we do not use. Under our foreign sales agent assumption, most of BLSS's foreign amounts would be retained (or I should say, would have been retained) by the local distributors rather than being returned to the sales agent. Were you to forego our assumption and use the BLSS data instead, there is no affordable manner in which to acquire foreign P&A data. On the other hand, our sales agent assumption is not foolproof either. As opposed to what we are doing now, it might be considered more complete to estimate foreign advances paid *in the past* for a comparable film. This, however, is very difficult, if not impossible. As a result, we settle on estimating each film's foreign performance based on *current* market conditions for foreign advances. It bears mentioning, in the case of studio subdivision distribution, on certain occasions, some subdivisions will augment or forego their parent company's foreign distribution capacity in favor of selling directly to territories.

As for why we multiply our total by 0.75 or leave it alone, this is to account for the fact that films often do not sell in all territories. However, if a successful film has at least one significant name, then the film may sell more territories and/or reach prices above its territories' maximums. Despite empirical evidence against the impact of significantly name actors, foreign distributors (as well as domestic) will pay more for a film with a significantly name actor.

One more thing worth keeping in mind: a film with a foreign sales agent may perform poorly at the international box office, despite having received relatively large advances from foreign distributors. This is because a film may indeed receive large advances from foreign distributors, but never live up to those advances in terms of its foreign box office performance. Also, many territories have no theatrical release, instead contributing revenue from advances in other formats.

NOTE REGARDING FOREIGN FILMS

Obviously the film for which you are proposing financing will in all likelihood open first in the U.S. or Canada, but your comparable films table may include films that first opened elsewhere. While no amount of data manipulation will turn the statistics for a foreign-released film into a domestically released film, if you follow the process for estimating "Foreign Gross," you will have a simulation of what a foreign film might have done today were its initial release domestic. The process discards such a film's past foreign performance in favor of an estimate of the foreign advances a similarly budgeted American film might garner today.

Less Sales Agent Fee and Expenses

Foreign sales agent fees are in the neighborhood of 10% to 25%. On the table I assume a fee of 20%. This is reasonable for a sales agent that did not help to finance a picture (often via a minimum guarantee). Sales agents also subtract expenses from the distribution revenue they collect. These expenses include taking a film to markets (Cannes, AFM, etc.), promoting the film to distributors, and delivering the film to distributors once the terms of a licensing agreement are reached. As with a domestic distributor, the foreign sales agent will be required by the producer to pay any residuals from advances generated, and these residuals are included among the sales agent's expenses. In the table, I assume expenses totaling 15% of Foreign Gross. Combining this with the fee of 20% arrives at the 35% total.

The Producer's Rep

Most successful low-budget independent films attract keen interest from domestic distributors before a distribution agreement is secured. The producers of these films almost universally hire a producer's representative whose job it is to generate such interest, and/or once the interest exists, to play the distributors against one another and negotiate the most favorable distribution agreement possible. Such a producer's rep is also responsible for finding a suitable foreign sales agent. In return, the producer's rep is entitled to a commission earned off of all revenues returned to a producer.

NOTE: In the movie industry, the terms "producer's rep" and "sales agent" are used interchangeably to describe the individual portrayed above. However, in this book, I only use the term "producer's rep" for the individual above and reserve use of the term "sales agent" to describe the individual responsible for engaging foreign distributors.

Less Producer's Rep Fee

This is the commission charged for the rep's services. Generally the fee runs at 15%, but for a sought-after property, such as those appearing on your comparables table, the fee comes closer to 10%. However, for the sake of erring on the more conservative side (i.e., lowering profits) we adopt the 15% figure. Regarding a producer's rep's expenses, alas, they are allowed to be deducted from revenues just like with distributors. However, because these expenses are nominal in the grand scheme of a successful film's revenues, and our 15% commission is slightly high, these expenses are not included.

Less Negative Cost

The "Negative Cost" assumes the creation of an original negative from which all other copies of the film stem (hence the term "negative") and does not include any development costs (i.e., the monies that might have been spent prior to the financing entity handing over its money for the film). You may have noticed while researching your films that some, maybe even many, were acquired at a film festival for an exorbitant amount of money called an "advance." BLSS does not account for such sales in its figures, and nor will we. When it can, the FRCE report gives you an actual figure, otherwise it provides an estimate of the negative cost (or "budget").

Net Investor/Producer Profit

This is the amount of profit left over for the producer to divvy up with the investors.

STEP 1G — Domestic free TV revenue refers to money generated from the syndicated and network television markets. Almost no independent films appear on network television, and their appearances in syndication are very infrequent with any revenues generated having a marginal impact on profits.

STEP 1K — You will notice during the research of your comparable films that many were picked up for distribution at, or after having played at, a major festival such as Cannes, Toronto, or Sundance. Some of the press' quoted acquisition prices are very close to a film's negative cost, and others are well above; the quotes for the domestic rights of foreign films are often lower. Ideally we would like to know the exact nature of each deal so then we can forecast the future of our movie (which we are already forecasting to be just as desirable). Particularly, we would like to forecast what might be paid up front for our film and how might the rest of its future deal be structured. Unfortunately, deal information for completed deals is often confidential and nearly always unattainable.

Instead, what I have done is to assume an agreement for each film where the domestic distributor takes its fee off the top, then deducts expenses, and remits 100% of the remainder to the producer and producer's rep. Also, home video revenue is treated on a net, instead of royalty, basis. A distributor courting a sought-after picture would be more than happy to accept such a deal instead of having to risk a sizeable/monstrous advance. (Of course, given the unpredictability of film performance, a producer would always favor a large advance.) Furthermore, I have assumed that each comparable film has a foreign sales agent for its foreign distribution, rather than having access to a studio subdivision that utilizes its parent company's foreign distribution arm. The goal of these assumptions is to model an investment return in the ballpark of that provided by an agreement with a large advance.

STEP 2 NOTES:

STEP 2B — If your comparable film averages are swayed by one or two very, very high numbers or one or two very, very low numbers, don't worry. What we are doing from the start, cherry picking results, is already far from statistically correct, so to impose some statistical guidelines now is ridiculous. And besides, it's not like you are taking the highest numbers to occur on your comparables table and just plugging them into your forecasts. You are letting any high numbers have an affect on their averages, as they should, and then using the averages for your forecasts. High numbers are a result, just like non-high numbers, and high numbers might occur for your film, just like non-high numbers. In fact, very high numbers in a group of lower numbers are a natural characteristic of the movie business.

While I say this, I must mention *Psych Thrill*. When you look at its comparable films box office numbers, one number sticks out like a sore thumb, *Pic N* at $25.5 million. Were *Pic N* not so similar in nature to *Psych Thrill*, I would have lowered the average box office before plugging it into my Projections Table. However, because it is the film closest in kind to *Psych Thrill*, I want its influence felt in my forecasting. As a result, I did not lower *Psych Thrill*'s comparable films box office average of $8.9 million.

STEP 2C — Do not calculate the average exhibitor share percentage by dividing the average "Exhibitor Share" by the average "Box Office Gross." The result will be a weighted average. A weighted average puts more emphasis on the percentages from the films with a higher box office gross. There is no reason to do so since the percentages for higher box office films have no more importance than the percentages for lower box office films. This warning applies also to Steps 2D and 2E where not following it will have a greater impact on your results.

STEP 2G — Deferrals are delayed payments of items in your budget and should be avoided. Often times when a deferred payment is agreed upon, the party granting the deferral agrees to take a cut in pay now for more pay later. However, the pay later is generally at a higher rate than the party granting the deferral is usually paid. For instance, a desirable editor might agree to work for your film at a rate of $2,000 now plus $18,000 in deferred pay, whereas if you had paid him up front, his pay would only have been $12,000 (these numbers are just for example). As you will see by the end of the Financial Projections chapter, deferred pay cuts down your investor returns by effectively increasing the negative cost and increasing the time before you start to receive revenues from your film. It makes more sense to make the extra effort and raise enough funds to pay all the budget items up front. Unfortunately, this is not always possible, especially with budgets in the $100,000 and $200,000 range. So if you need to, go ahead and account for any planned deferrals by adding a "Deferrals" line to your income, cash flow, and investor projections sections. By the time you are through with the Financial Projections chapter, you will be able to perform such an adjustment on your own. Since you should rarely plan to *not* raise enough money for your film (which is why a deferral would be needed), I do not explicitly illustrate their treatment in this book. For talent participations, which are different from deferrals, see Step 20.

STEP 2H — Your "Low Success" predictions will satisfy the investor priority return of 20%. To see what this is, skip ahead to Step 4D in the appendix. To establish your "Low Success" predictions, create your own version of the following table:

Domestic ratio & %	Low # suggstns		Actual Low #'s	Actual Low ratio & %
XXXXXXXX	XXXXXXXX	BO------>		XXXXXXXX
		<------HV------>		
		<-----PTV------>		
			need as 0.20000:	

BO = Box Office

HV = Domestic Home Video, PTV = Domestic Pay TV

Input your average pay TV percentage from Step 2D and your Home Video to Box Office ratio from Step 2H into the "Domestic ratio & %" column. Then choose and type in a low domestic box office figure into the "BO--->" indicated box. I am using *Sci-Fi Rom*'s numbers for the table. $0.470 million is the figure I choose and input into the box office box. The film's Home Video to Box Office ratio has been written with more decimal places ("2.005" instead of just "2.0" — the additional "05" you couldn't see before).

Domestic ratio & %	Low # suggstns		Actual Low #'s	Actual Low ratio & %
XXXXXXXX	XXXXXXXX	BO------>	$0.470	XXXXXXXX
2.005		<------HV------>		
39.0%		<-----PTV------>		
			need as 0.20000:	

Next, multiply your chosen box office number ($0.470 million in this case) by the home video ratio and pay TV percentage separately. Input the results into the "Low # suggstns" column.

Domestic ratio & %	Low # suggstns		Actual Low #'s	Actual Low ratio & %
XXXXXXXX	XXXXXXXX	BO------>	$0.470	XXXXXXXX
2.005	$0.942	<------HV------>		
39.0%	$0.184	<-----PTV------>		
			need as 0.20000:	

Then, enter the values from the "Low # suggstns" column into the "Actual Low #s" column.

Domestic ratio & %	Low # suggstns		Actual Low #'s	Actual Low ratio & %
XXXXXXXX	XXXXXXXX	BO------->	$0.470	XXXXXXXX
2.005	$0.942	<------HV------>	$0.942	
39.0%	$0.184	<-----PTV------>	$0.184000	
		need as 0.20000:		

I added some 0's to the "Actual Low #s" pay TV figure — you'll see why soon. Calculate the "Actual Low ratio & %" figures by dividing each of the "Actual Low #s" numbers by the domestic box office figure you chose ($0.470 million in our example). For the pay TV result, you will have to take your result and turn it into a percentage (e.g., 0.390 = 39.0%). The results should pretty closely match the "Domestic ratio & %" column (if they are ever-so-slightly off, that is okay).

Domestic ratio & %	Low # suggstns		Actual Low #'s	Actual Low ratio & %
XXXXXXXX	XXXXXXXX	BO------->	$0.470	XXXXXXXX
2.005	$0.942	<------HV------>	$0.942	2.004
39.0%	$0.184	<-----PTV------>	$0.184000	39.1%
		need as 0.20000:		

Next, use the numbers from the "Actual Low #s" column to calculate a "Net Investor/Producer Profit" number. You have all the numbers you need in order to do so. Remember, your "Foreign Gross" is done in the same way as the "Medium Success" "Foreign Gross" except that you use the lowest numbers in each country's range from "The Going Rate" (see Step 2F). And as for the rest of your numbers (Exhibitor Share, P&A, etc.), use the same percentages from the Medium scenario, except this time multiply them against your "Low Success" results (see Steps 2C, 2E, and 2G).

Once you get a "Net Investor/Producer Profit," take it and divide it by your film's negative cost. At this point in the process, for *Sci-Fi Rom* this comes to:

Net Investor/Producer Profit / Negative Cost = $0.103 million / $0.5 million = 0.20600

Put this number in the "need as 0.20000" box.

Domestic ratio & %	Low # suggstns			Actual Low #'s	Actual Low ratio & %
XXXXXXXX	XXXXXXXX		BO------->	$0.470	XXXXXXXX
2.005	$0.942	<------HV------>		$0.942	2.004
39.0%	$0.184	<-----PTV------>		$0.184000	39.1%
				need as 0.20000:	0.20600

If the "need as 0.20000" box is very close to 0.20000, proceed. Otherwise, choose another domestic box office figure, go back to the beginning of Step 2H in this appendix, and start over again (it's a pain in the neck, I know). If you have Excel, you can set this entire process up in such a way that the only numbers you need to adjust are those in the "Actual Low #s" column, and the remaining results simply feed off of these. Remember, we are trying to get the Net Investor/Producer Profit to be 20% of the negative cost, which is why we are focusing on this 0.20000 number.

Moving on, begin adjusting the "Actual Low #s" pay TV figure until the "need as 0.20000" box hits 0.20000. As you do so, keep checking your "Actual Low ratio & %" pay TV percentage, since it will be changing also. Don't let it get more than 5%–7% away from the one in your "Domestic ratio & %" box. If it does, start all over and pick a new box office number. In the end, you will more than likely use many, if not all, of the 0's in the pay TV figure:

Domestic ratio & %	Low # suggstns			Actual Low #'s	Actual Low ratio & %
XXXXXXXX	XXXXXXXX		BO------->	$0.470	XXXXXXXX
2.005	$0.942	<------HV------>		$0.942	2.004
39.0%	$0.184	<-----PTV------>		$0.176980	37.7%
				need as 0.20000:	0.20000

When it comes to hitting 0.20000 exactly, stick to the pay TV figure as your only means of adjustment. It is less important and a smaller percentage of the box office than home video. Feel free, as well, to adjust the pay TV figure upward if necessary; in the example it has been adjusted downward.

Once you hit the 0.20000, the numbers used to do so become your "Low Success" scenario income projections, and you can input them, if you already have not, into the Low column of your table. As stressful as this entire Step 2H may become, keep in mind that the Low projections are the least important projections of the plan.

<u>STEP 2J</u> — It may be helpful to write the income projections text after completing all other parts of the Financial Projections section. Because the income projections drive the rest of the numbers in your plan, you may want to see those other numbers first. After seeing them, you may decide to adjust your income projections. Regardless, once you do write your text, you want to discuss the overall reasoning behind your projections without getting bogged down in the methodology of your projections. A potential investor is more concerned with the clarity of your thought process than the exact technical aspects of your prediction making. Of course, be prepared to answer any questions that might come up.

Also, not every prediction needs to be discussed in the text. You will notice in the sample texts that I do not discuss the "High Success," "Medium Success," and "Low Success" Foreign Gross projections. To have done so would have overburdened the text with detail, especially since the foreign revenues are not a large percentage of the overall revenue and their methodology is already hinted at in the text of the tables themselves. I also did not discuss P&A. Instead, domestic revenue was given the focus because it more heavily drives returns; foreign revenues and P&A were left for any direct questions the potential investor might have.

On a side point, take notice with *Mass H-Com* of my use of the phrase "in the context of the comparable films table." Be careful never to say that your projections are conservative; they are not — remember how many movies fail? However, if you use this phrase in conjunction with the word "conservative," you can point to the fact that your table may not be as wildly optimistic as it could be. After all, if you follow my recommendations, you will have left the most successful independent films off of your comparables table.

STEP 3 NOTES:

CASH FLOW PROJECTIONS EXAMPLE — Pretend a rich distant relative with connections to the mob lends you a $150,000 dollars for safe keeping, and demands you earn a good return on it… or else. You decide to start a donut shop with the money — you've always loved donuts and the most frequent patrons might prove useful should things go south. Now, because you are very neurotic about how the money will be spent and about when the shop will start to earn you money (or you just value your life), you do a cash flow sheet. Before the cash flow sheet, however, you make some basic predictions. Let's say that over two years you expect to have the following revenue and expenses:

Table B.2: Donut income projections	
Donut Sales	$200,000
Dough and Sugar	-$30,000
Billboard Signs	-$50,000
Donut Building	-$70,000
Net Profit	$50,000

Then you design the following cash flow sheet anticipating when everything happens:

Table B.3a: Sample cash flow projections

	YEAR 1				YEAR 2			
	Quarter 1	Quarter 2	Quarter 3	Quarter 4	Quarter 1	Quarter 2	Quarter 3	Quarter 4
Donut Sales			$0	$5,000	$10,000	$40,000	$60,000	$85,000
Dough and Sugar			-$5,000	-$5,000	-$5,000	-$5,000	-$5,000	-$5,000
Billboard Signs				-$10,000	-$10,000	-$10,000	-$10,000	-$10,000
Donut Building	-$35,000	-$35,000						
TOTAL	-$35,000	-$35,000	-$5,000	-$10,000	-$5,000	$25,000	$45,000	$70,000

Each year is divided into four quarters with three months in each quarter. First, you expect to build your shop for $70,000 over six months: $35,000 spent to build in Qtr. 1 and $35,000 spent to build in Qtr. 2. ("Qtr." is short for "Quarter.") Now, we don't care when you start building; April, August, or January, it doesn't make a difference. We are simply making predictions starting from the moment you start building. So Qtr. 1 in Year 1 will end three months after the moment you start building.

After building you plan to start making donuts with dough and sugar supplies, and you predict these will cost $5,000 during each three-month period (i.e., every quarter). In Qtr. 3 of Year 1 (months 7 through

9) you will use your dough and sugar supplies to perfect your recipe before you sell any donuts (hence, $5,000 spent on dough and sugar in Year 1, Qtr. 3, and $0 in sales that quarter).

Then in Qtr. 4 of Year 1, you plan to buy ad space on two giant billboards across from police stations. The total quarterly charge for both billboards combined will be $10,000. In the same quarter, you decide you will officially open your shop (hence, the continued spending on dough and sugar of $5,000), and you expect people will start buying your donuts (hence $5,000 in donut sales). All of this, the billboards and the launch, will occur in months 10 through 12 of your venture (Year 1, Qtr. 4 — see "Donut Sales," "Dough and Sugar," and "Billboard Signs").

In fact, you predict that people won't be able to stop buying your donuts, and by Qtr. 4 of Year 2 you hope to end up with so many cops and people mingling together ($85,000 worth of sales) that they can't help but get together and decide to do something about all the crime in the area caused by your relative, and shebang! Your relative will get arrested and you will get to keep your community-saving donut shop. But I digress.

Let's rework the table so it's a little easier to read. For each amount of money we plan to spend, we use parentheses, and for each amount of money we expect to earn, we leave it as is. Also, let's add a running total just for peace of mind:

Table B.3b: Sample cash flow (alternate format)

	YEAR 1				YEAR 2			
	Quarter 1	Quarter 2	Quarter 3	Quarter 4	Quarter 1	Quarter 2	Quarter 3	Quarter 4
Donut Sales			$ -	$ 5,000	$ 10,000	$ 40,000	$ 60,000	$ 85,000
Dough and Sugar			$ (5,000)	$ (5,000)	$ (5,000)	$ (5,000)	$ (5,000)	$ (5,000)
Billboard Signs				$(10,000)	$(10,000)	$(10,000)	$(10,000)	$(10,000)
Donut Building	$(35,000)	$(35,000)						
Quarterly TOTAL	$(35,000)	$(35,000)	$ (5,000)	$(10,000)	$ (5,000)	$ 25,000	$ 45,000	$ 70,000
Running TOTAL	$(35,000)	$(70,000)	$(75,000)	$(85,000)	$(90,000)	$(65,000)	$(20,000)	$ 50,000

You will notice a couple of things. First, by no coincidence, the running total of $50,000 at the end matches your two-year net profit projection of $50,000. Second, when you add up the numbers across each row, such as "Dough and Sugar" at $(5,000) + $(5,000) + ... + $(5,000), the result equals the corresponding amount from the income projections, e.g., $(30,000) of dough and sugar. You can use these two facts later on to help you check your own cash flow projections.

You may also notice that all the negative amounts appearing in the table (not in the quarterly totals or running totals) add up exactly to the amount your uncle has given you. This is because you plan on investing every bit of his money into the store, quarter by quarter. Investing like this need not be the case, however. Starting in Year 2 Qtr. 1, you could start paying for stuff with donut sales money from previous quarters. Unfortunately, we're starting to discuss a topic (corporate finance) that really isn't going to help anybody understand anything right now. So let's just ignore this little fact of all the negative amounts adding up to your uncle's initial $150,000.

Moving on, what you have just examined is the sum and substance of a cash flow projection. It predicts when everything you predicted, in terms of income, occurs.

In the cash flow for your film, we take the items from your Income Projections Table and assign percentages according to how they should be spread out over time. In the donut example, these percentages would read on the cash flow table as:

Table B.3c: Sample cash flow percentage allocations

	YEAR 1				YEAR 2			
	Quarter 1	Quarter 2	Quarter 3	Quarter 4	Quarter 1	Quarter 2	Quarter 3	Quarter 4
Donut Sales			0.0%	2.5%	5.0%	20.0%	30.0%	42.5%
Dough and Sugar			16.7%	16.7%	16.7%	16.7%	16.7%	16.7%
Billboard Signs				20.0%	20.0%	20.0%	20.0%	20.0%
Donut Building	50.0%	50.0%						
Quarterly TOTAL	NA	NA	NA	NA	NA	NA	NA	NA
Running TOTAL	NA	NA	NA	NA	NA	NA	NA	NA

So 50% of the donut building money is spent in Year 1, Qtr. 1 and the other 50% in Year 1, Qtr. 2. A rounded percentage of 16.7% of the dough and sugar money is spent per quarter, every quarter, starting in Year 1, Qtr. 3. The donut sales start in Year 1, Qtr. 4 (technically the space in Year 1, Quarter 3 should be left blank, rather than 0.0%) and pick up pace as time goes on: 2.5% of the sales occur in Year 1, Qtr. 4, all the way up to 42.5% of the sales occurring in Year 2, Qtr. 4. You get the picture for the billboard signs. As you can see, across any given row, the percentages all add up to 100% because we are describing what happens to 100% of each figure from the income projections.

Take some time to understand how these percentage allocations work. Using them will be the crux of what we do with your film.

STEP 3B — Table 1.6 (and the three sample films' cash flows later on) are updated for the book. The table assumes no advances being delivered from any of the formats (except, of course, for Foreign Gross, where all you will get are advances), and takes into account the time it can take for money to go from distributors to producers to investors.

Notice that the years and quarters are generically labeled. You can never count on when the money for your film will be finally raised, so do not put dates in your cash flow. Doing so will look bad if some of your money is raised and you have to alert the investors behind this money that you are changing the dates because the rest of the money is taking a little bit of time to acquire. Investors are aware that the dates are not set, unless you set them in your plan by explicitly stating them or listing them in your cash flow.

The model begins from the point in time just after all the budget money has been raised. The theatrical release is predicted to occur in the very last moments of Year 2, Quarter 4. In reality, of course, a film may end up being released in the middle of a quarter; however, the assumed timing in the cash flow is very specific and simplified in order to allow the reader a clean calculation of the time since theatrical release — you can count it in quarters.

STEP 3C — For *Sci-Fi Rom* I assumed 1.5 years until it would be released. This is because *Sci-Fi Rom* is the type of film that, were it sought after by distributors (which our business plan assumes that it would be), would be given heavy consideration for Golden Globe and Oscar nominations. Thus, a distributor would likely release it some time between August and November to maximize its chances of attracting nominator attention. By no means am I making the prediction that the film will achieve a nomination. I am merely saying that because the film is already being predicted to be a success, and the film lends itself to such nominations, there is a good chance a distributor will release it some time between August and November.

I already know the film will have an August start and end date for production (at least that's what I'm assuming for this example). Thus, the shoot ends in August 2010; ten-and-a-half months later post ends (June 2011); then there are essentially two to five months in which to find a distributor and release the film in time for awards consideration. Two to five months is not enough time, so I forecast the release to occur the *next* awards season, 1.5 years after post ends, to be conservative (technically, in December 2012, still just in time for awards consideration). Thus, on the film's cash flow you will notice six empty quarters between the last quarter of the budget being spent and the first quarter of film rentals appearing.

This example is a bit extreme, but it shows some of the many factors you can consider in predicting when your film will be released. Don't worry, however. If you just want to keep things simple, a wholly reasonable and conservative option is to simply choose a year between the end of post and beginning of theatrical.

STEP 3G — Any Domestic Subtotal that is negative must be moved forward into a Domestic Subtotal that can absorb it. That is, if you have a *negative* Domestic Subtotal, you have to add it to the next closest *positive* Domestic Subtotal without making the new Domestic Subtotal negative.

The reason we do this is because we are assuming in our forecasts that your film picks up domestic distribution from one distributor, not at all uncommon for a successful film such as the one you are predicting. Any time that distributor comes up with a negative balance for the quarter (i.e., a negative "Domestic Subtotal"), it obviously cannot call the producers and say, "Hey, pay us some money to cover the negative balance." Instead, the distributor carries that balance forward into future quarters until that balance, and any other negative balances, are paid off with money made by the film. Incidentally, a commonly occurring reason for a negative Domestic Subtotal is that the expenses of a theatrical release push revenues into the red. Many distributors see the theatrical release as an investment in advertising that builds awareness for the project for the home video and later releases.

Now, if your Domestic Subtotals were not positive, did not look like *Mass H-Com* or *Psych Thrill*, or I sent you back here anyway, your Domestic Subtotals fall into some case covered by the two examples below. These examples are a bit difficult, but fight through them. They will give you the understanding you will need to handle your Domestic Subtotals.

Table B.4: Domestic Subtotal sample table ($ millions)

	YEAR 3				YEAR 4			
	Quarter 1	Quarter 2	Quarter 3	Quarter 4	Quarter 1	Quarter 2	Quarter 3	Quarter 4
Negative Cost		XXXX	XXXX	XXXX	XXXX	XXXX	XXXX	
Gross Film Rental		XXXX	XXXX	XXXX	XXXX	XXXX	XXXX	
Home Video Revenue		XXXX	XXXX	XXXX	XXXX	XXXX	XXXX	
Pay TV Revenue		XXXX	XXXX	XXXX	XXXX	XXXX	XXXX	
Distribution Fee		XXXX	XXXX	XXXX	XXXX	XXXX	XXXX	
Prints & Advertising		XXXX	XXXX	XXXX	XXXX	XXXX	XXXX	
Other Distributor Costs		XXXX	XXXX	XXXX	XXXX	XXXX	XXXX	
Dom Subtotal		$ (0.100)	$ 6.000	$ (0.700)	$ 0.100	$ 6.800	$ 1.600	

Here we go. Look at the monstrosity above. It is an excerpt from a cash flow table that appears nowhere else in this book. Its purpose is merely to teach and torture. I've X'd out all the portions that you need not pay attention to. Also, for each quarter I have added up the numbers that are X'd out. The sum of these numbers is called each quarter's "raw subtotal," but it is not shown on the table. Sometimes the raw subtotal matches the Domestic Subtotal, sometimes it does not. Read on.

For each quarter, add up your own raw subtotal for the quarter. That is, add together the quarter's "Negative Cost" (which should be zero), "Gross Film Rental," "Home Video Revenue," etc., all the way down to and including the quarter's "Other Distributor Costs." Then, see how I treat each of the cases from the table above:

(i) In Year 3, Quarter 2 (Y3Q2) the raw subtotal is a negative number, ($0.100). If your raw subtotal is a negative number, you enter it on your table as the Domestic Subtotal.

(ii) In Year 3, Quarter 3 (Y3Q3) you don't see it, but my raw subtotal is a positive number, $6.100. Then I check to see if there are any negative Domestic Subtotals prior to this quarter. There is a negative Domestic Subtotal in Y3Q2, ($0.100). Thus, I add it to my raw subtotal and check the result. What I get is a positive raw subtotal of $6.000 and this now becomes my Domestic Subtotal. Had my result have been a negative, I would have handled it in the fashion of example (iv).

(iii) In Y3Q4 the raw subtotal comes to a negative of ($0.700), and so I enter that as my Domestic Subtotal.

(iv) In Y4Q1 my raw subtotal comes to $0.100. Because it is positive I go back and collect all the negative Domestic Subtotals that have not yet been included as part of another quarter's Domestic Subtotal. Y3Q2's negative of ($0.100) was already included in the domestic subtotal of Y3Q3; thus the only negative subtotal I collect is ($0.700) from Y3Q4. I add the ($0.700) to my raw subtotal of $0.100, but my answer comes to another negative of ($0.600). Because of this, I simply use the original raw subtotal of $0.100 as my Domestic Subtotal.

(v) In Y4Q2 my raw subtotal, which you cannot see on the table, comes to $7.400. Now I go back in search of any non-included negative Domestic Subtotals and find ($0.700) from Y3Q4, but it occurs before my most recent positive Domestic Subtotal of $0.100 in Y4Q1. Thus, I add both the negative subtotal, ($0.700), and the most recent positive subtotal, $0.100, to my current raw subtotal of $7.400. I check the result, $6.800, and because it is positive I enter it as my Domestic Subtotal for the quarter.

(vi) The Y4Q3 raw subtotal comes to $1.600, and since there are no numbers to add to it from past quarters, the $1.600 becomes the Domestic Subtotal.

This next example serves as a rare and extreme case (a heart attack on a stick, if you will) combining examples (iv) and (v):

Table B.5: Domestic Subtotal sample table ($ millions)

	YEAR 3				YEAR 4			
	Quarter 1	Quarter 2	Quarter 3	Quarter 4	Quarter 1	Quarter 2	Quarter 3	Quarter 4
Negative Cost	XXXX	XXXX	XXXX	XXXX	XXXX	XXXX	XXXX	
Gross Film Rental	XXXX	XXXX	XXXX	XXXX	XXXX	XXXX	XXXX	
Home Video Revenue	XXXX	XXXX	XXXX	XXXX	XXXX	XXXX	XXXX	
Pay TV Revenue	XXXX	XXXX	XXXX	XXXX	XXXX	XXXX	XXXX	
Distribution Fee	XXXX	XXXX	XXXX	XXXX	XXXX	XXXX	XXXX	
Prints & Advertising	XXXX	XXXX	XXXX	XXXX	XXXX	XXXX	XXXX	
Other Distributor Costs	XXXX	XXXX	XXXX	XXXX	XXXX	XXXX	XXXX	
Dom Subtotal	$ 2.000	$ (1.500)	$ 0.500	$ (0.200)	$ (0.100)	$ 0.300	$ 4.000	

(vii) Y3Q1 is handled just like example (vi); Y3Q2 is handled just like example (i); Y3Q3 is handled just like example (iv); Y3Q4 and Y4Q1 are also handled just like example (i). For Y4Q2, the raw subtotal is $0.300, but since none of the other negatives thus far have been absorbed into a later Domestic Subtotal, I must add to the current raw subtotal all the previous quarters' negative subtotals (Y3Q2, Y3Q4, and Y4Q1) and any positive subtotals between or after them (Y3Q3). The calculation comes to ($1.500) + ($0.200) + ($0.100) + $0.500 + $0.300 and equals ($1.000). Because the total is negative, I simply record my original raw subtotal for Y4Q2 of $0.300 as that quarter's Domestic Subtotal. Then for Y4Q3, just like Y4Q2, because none of the previous negatives have been absorbed yet, I add them and the positive quarters between and after them to this quarter's raw subtotal of $5.000 (which you cannot see) and the calculation comes to ($1.500) + ($0.200) + ($0.100) + $0.500 + $0.300 + $5.000 and equals $4.000. Because the result is positive, I use it as my Domestic Subtotal for the quarter. As mentioned, this example is extreme but shows how to handle positive and negative Domestic Subtotals mixed messily together. Still alive? Just checking.

STEP 3J — If you were previously sent back to the appendix for Step 3G, you have been sent back here again for each quarter's Producer's Rep Fee.

In some cases, when a quarter shows a positive Domestic Subtotal the distributor will not return those monies. This is because of a negative balance it is still carrying forward from past quarters that cannot be paid off with monies generated in this quarter. In these cases, do not include the positive Domestic Subtotal in your calculation of the quarter's Producer's Rep Fee.

What follows are examples of when to use the Domestic Subtotal in calculating a quarter's Producer's Rep Fee. The examples draw on the examples already painfully covered in Step 3G's entry above in this appendix. The appendix entries of Steps 3G and 3J are difficult, and for this I apologize. But unfortunately there is no easy way around them.

Table B.4: Domestic Subtotal sample table ($ millions)

	YEAR 3				YEAR 4			
	Quarter 1	Quarter 2	Quarter 3	Quarter 4	Quarter 1	Quarter 2	Quarter 3	Quarter 4
Negative Cost		XXXX	XXXX	XXXX	XXXX	XXXX	XXXX	
Gross Film Rental		XXXX	XXXX	XXXX	XXXX	XXXX	XXXX	
Home Video Revenue		XXXX	XXXX	XXXX	XXXX	XXXX	XXXX	
Pay TV Revenue		XXXX	XXXX	XXXX	XXXX	XXXX	XXXX	
Distribution Fee		XXXX	XXXX	XXXX	XXXX	XXXX	XXXX	
Prints & Advertising		XXXX	XXXX	XXXX	XXXX	XXXX	XXXX	
Other Distributor Costs		XXXX	XXXX	XXXX	XXXX	XXXX	XXXX	
Dom Subtotal		$ (0.100)	$ 6.000	$ (0.700)	$ 0.100	$ 6.800	$ 1.600	

(i) Year 3, Quarter 2 (Y3Q2) — Because the Domestic Subtotal here is negative, ($0.100), do not use it in calculating the Producer's Rep Fee.

(ii) Year 3, Quarter 3 (Y3Q3) — This Domestic Subtotal has successfully included Y3Q2's Domestic Subtotal. Therefore, use it in determining the quarter's Producer's Rep Fee.

(iii) Y3Q4 — Just like with example (i), do not use it in calculating a fee.

(iv) Y4Q1 — This positive Domestic Subtotal is unable to include Y3Q4's negative. As a result, do not use it in calculating a Producer's Rep Fee.

(v) Y4Q2 — This positive subtotal includes all the appropriate negative and positive subtotals from the past. Thus, use it in making your fee.

(vi) Y4Q3 — This positive Domestic Subtotal has no interference from past Subtotals. Again, it is cool to use in determining the Producer's Rep Fee.

Table B.5: Domestic Subtotal sample table ($ millions)								
	YEAR 3				YEAR 4			
	Quarter 1	Quarter 2	Quarter 3	Quarter 4	Quarter 1	Quarter 2	Quarter 3	Quarter 4
Negative Cost	XXXX	XXXX	XXXX	XXXX	XXXX	XXXX	XXXX	
Gross Film Rental	XXXX	XXXX	XXXX	XXXX	XXXX	XXXX	XXXX	
Home Video Revenue	XXXX	XXXX	XXXX	XXXX	XXXX	XXXX	XXXX	
Pay TV Revenue	XXXX	XXXX	XXXX	XXXX	XXXX	XXXX	XXXX	
Distribution Fee	XXXX	XXXX	XXXX	XXXX	XXXX	XXXX	XXXX	
Prints & Advertising	XXXX	XXXX	XXXX	XXXX	XXXX	XXXX	XXXX	
Other Distributor Costs	XXXX	XXXX	XXXX	XXXX	XXXX	XXXX	XXXX	
Dom Subtotal	$ 2.000	$ (1.500)	$ 0.500	$ (0.200)	$ (0.100)	$ 0.300	$ 4.000	

(vii) Y4Q2 & Y4Q3 — Y4Q2's Domestic Subtotal is unable to include the appropriate past Subtotals, and thus, should not be used to calculate a Producer's Rep Fee. However, Y4Q3's subtotal is able to include the appropriate past Subtotals, so include Y4Q3's in the calculation of the Y4Q3 Producer's Rep Fee.

As a general note for this step, the only times you are not calculating a Producer's Rep Fee are when both the domestic distributor and the foreign sales agent representing your film have no money to return to the producer. In some cases only the foreign sales agent may have revenue to return, and in others only the domestic distributor may have revenue to return; in both cases the producer's rep will charge his or her fee against whatever is returned.

STEPS 3N–3R — In words, what we are doing in these steps is returning to the investors any cash received from the domestic distributor and foreign sales agent (after the producer's rep fee, of course), until the investor priority return is met (20% or 1.2 x the budget), then splitting the remainder of any monies 50/50 between the producer and investors.

Here's a more detailed, quarter-by-quarter breakdown of the table that is provided as an example for these steps:

Table 1.7: *Sci-Fi Rom* cash returned to investors ($ millions)								
	YEAR 3			YEAR 4				YEAR 5
	Quarter 2	Quarter 3	Quarter 4	Quarter 1	Quarter 2	Quarter 3	Quarter 4	Quarter 1
TOTAL	$ -	$ 0.057	$ 0.068	$ 1.485	$ 0.178	$ 0.089	$ 0.471	$ 0.054
RUNNING TOTAL	$ (0.500)	$ (0.443)	$ (0.375)	$ 1.110	$ 1.289	$ 1.378	$ 1.849	$ 1.903
RPT	$ 0.600	$ 0.600	$ 0.543	$ 0.475	$ -	$ -	$ -	$ -
RETURNED TO INV.	$ -	$ 0.057	$ 0.068	$ 0.980	$ 0.089	$ 0.045	$ 0.236	$ 0.027
CUMULATIVE RET.	$ -	$ 0.057	$ 0.125	$ 1.105	$ 1.194	$ 1.239	$ 1.474	$ 1.501

YEAR 3, QUARTER 2 (Y3Q2) — Thus far only the budget of the film has been spent with no revenues returned. This is reflected in the crossed-out Running Total of $(0.500) million.

Y3Q3 — A total of $0.057 million is returned to the producer. I subtract the TOTAL of $0.057 million from the Running Priority Total (RPT) of $0.600 million and get a positive result of $0.543 million. My new RPT becomes $0.543 million, and I enter the "TOTAL" amount of $0.057 million into the RETURNED TO INVESTORS row. What has happened here is that money has been returned to the investors, but not yet enough to meet their priority return of 20% (or 1.2 x the budget). Now we are only $0.543 million away from meeting this priority return, after which all cash is split evenly between producer and investors.

Y3Q4 — A total of $0.068 million is returned to the producer. I subtract the TOTAL of $0.068 million from the RPT of $0.543 million and get a positive result of $0.475 million. Then my new RPT becomes $0.475 million, and I proceed to enter the "TOTAL" amount of $0.068 million into the RETURNED TO INVESTORS row. Y3Q4 matches what happened in Y3Q3 except with different numbers.

Y4Q1 — A total of $1.485 million is returned to the producer. I subtract the "TOTAL" of $1.485 million from the RPT of $0.475 million and get a negative result. Because of this, I run the calculation: Amount Returned = RPT + 0.5 x (TOTAL − RPT). Substituting the quarter's numbers the equation comes to: Amount Returned = $0.475 million + 0.5 x ($1.485 million − $0.475 million). The result is $0.980 million, and I enter it in "RETURNED TO INVESTORS." Then, the remaining quarters' TOTALs are split 50/50. What has happened during this quarter (Y4Q1) is that the investors have finally been returned their 20% priority return (we know this because of the negative result at the beginning of this paragraph), and money received by the producer beyond this point no longer flows directly to investors, but is split 50/50 between producer and investors. Looking at it from the point of view of breaking down the Amount Returned equation, first we give the investor the remainder of the Running Priority Total (RPT), then we split (multiply by 0.5) the remaining cash for the quarter (signified by "TOTAL – RPT") with the investor.

Y4Q2 — We multiply the total of $0.178 million by 0.5 for a result of $0.089 million and enter the result in "RETURNED TO INVESTORS." In other words, the producer splits the cash for the quarter 50/50 with the investor. This continues for the rest of the quarters in the cash flow.

STEP 4 NOTES:

STEP 4D — There are many different ways to split the money between the investors and producer of a project. For the sample films of this plan I have chosen one that closely resembles the breakdown used by independent film producers close to me. It goes as follows: any monies returned to the producer by the domestic distributor and foreign sales agent, after the producer's rep has received his or her fee, are first returned to the investors until the budget has been repaid. Then, any further monies are still returned straight to the investors until an amount equal to 20% of the budget has been returned. This 20% is called the "investor priority return." After the 20% level has been met, any additional monies are split 50/50 between the producer and investors.

As an example, the budget of *Psych Thrill* is set at $1.500 million. The first $1.500 million received by the producer will be returned to the investors. Then another 20% (the investor priority return), or $0.300 million, will be further returned to the investors. So in effect, $1.800 million is returned to the investors (120%) before the producer receives a cent. Any monies after this $1.8 million will be split 50/50 between the producer and investors.

If you choose a different producer/investor allocation, don't forget to readjust your Low Success projections in addition to making any cash flow adjustments (Steps 2H, 3N).

The producer/investor allocation of monies laid out here treats investors more favorably than is common. Typically, investors recoup closer to the neighborhood of 110% of their investment before the 50/50 split occurs. However, the independent producers with whom I deal feel, as do I, that the investors deserve better than the typical treatment. They make the project possible and bear the brunt of the risk. They are last in line, apart from the producer, in making money off of the project. In fact, the producer can be seen as almost being first in line because of the producing fee he or she receives from the budget, though many independent producers will tell you this is the first item scaled back in trying to make an affordable film.

STEP 4J — For each sample film in this book, I have described the formation a Limited Liability Company (LLC). The LLC's purpose in each case is to raise money for, create, and make money off of the film for which it was created. An LLC is currently the most popular business entity for raising money for and creating an independent film, and each independent film with which I have worked has been overseen by an LLC. The type of LLC most beneficial to filmmakers is a so-called "manager-managed LLC," meaning the principal filmmakers (usually the producers), manage the money supplied to the LLC by the investors and do so without being required to run most decisions past them. Of course the managers of the LLC's money have to make decisions in line with how they represented themselves to investors; they can't, for instance, take the money and build a supermarket or fly to Aruba for some R&R.

Each state has its own regulations regarding LLCs, but generally, in the case of a film, investors purchase investment units (a.k.a. "membership units") from an LLC. For instance, an LLC worth $1,000,000 might offer 20 units valued at $50,000 each or 1,000,000 units valued at $1 each. An investor might purchase two units for a total investment in the LLC worth $100,000 in the first case or $2 in the second case (though, when the units are in very small dollar amounts, there is typically a minimum number of units, far beyond two, that must be purchased). The total value of an LLC can match the budget of a movie, and membership units can be sold off to different investors until that budget is met.

Investors can generally invest in as many LLC units as they wish. Where investors are based determines which state's or states' LLC laws will be followed. In the case of the sample films, the table below lists the number of units available for investment in each film's LLC, the size of each unit, and the budget of each film:

Table B.6: LLC units per sample film			
	Units	Per Unit Size	Budget ($ millions)
Sci-Fi Rom	20	$ 25,000	$0.500
Psych Thrill	30	$ 50,000	$1.500
Mass H-Com	24	$ 50,000	$1.200

There are numerous ways to set up an LLC, but one alternative to table B.6 is to make the units $1,000 each in size, and require a minimum investment of $25,000 in the case of *Sci-Fi Rom* and $50,000 in the case of the other two pictures. That allows more flexibility in the amount of investment that can be made.

If you are interested in researching other company types to serve as the business entity for your film, or for more LLC details, see entertainment attorney Mark Litwak's website, *www.marklitwak.com* (also see an article by him at *www.independentfilms.org/film-financing/* for a taste of LLC regulations). Another great source is *Nolo's Quick LLC* (4th Edition) by attorney Anthony Mancuso, copyright 2007. It tells you everything about LLCs from a non-film perspective. Regardless of the entity you choose, in the end you will need the services of an entertainment attorney with expertise in independent film financing to ensure that the entity is properly created.

STEP 4L — Internal rate of return (IRR) is basically a way of answering the following: If your investors could magically construct a savings account that would earn as much money as this project might earn, what would be the interest rate on that account? The internal rate of return (IRR) is that rate. Let's examine the following table for some help:

Table B.7: *Psych Thrill* Medium investor returns (quarterly IRR of 9.7145%; $ millions)													
	YEAR 3			YEAR 4				YEAR 5				YEAR 6	
	Quarter 2	Quarter 3	Quarter 4	Quarter 1	Quarter 2	Quarter 3	Quarter 4	Quarter 1	Quarter 2	Quarter 3	Quarter 4	Quarter 1	
$ 0.979		$ 2.714											
$ 0.127			$ 0.387										
$ 0.058				$ 0.193									
$ 0.203					$ 0.745								
$ 0.024						$ 0.098							
$ 0.037							$ 0.162						
$ 0.020								$ 0.098					
$ 0.015									0.078				
$ 0.013										0.078			
$ 0.012											0.078		
$ 0.011												$ 0.077	
$ 1.500	TOTAL												

Yes, it looks confusing as anything, but let's start by ignoring the far left column for now. This table shows the quarterly amounts returned to investors in *Psych Thrill*'s "Medium Success" cash flow scenario. So in Year 3, Quarter 3 ("Y3Q3" for short), the investors will receive back $2.714 million (or "$2.714m" for short), in Y3Q4 $0.387m will be returned, and so on and so forth until the final quarter where $0.077m will be returned.

The quarterly IRR for *Psych Thrill*'s Medium cash flow scenario was calculated at 9.7145%. That is, the magical savings account would be offering the investors an interest rate of 9.7145% every three months (i.e, every quarter) were the investors able to place their money into the account, instead of placing their money into, and earning money back from, the film. For example, if I put $100 dollars into the account on January 1st, then three months later at the beginning of April my account would hold $109.71 (rounded).

Now, what do the numbers on the far left of the table represent? Well, those are the amounts the investors would have to stick into the fairy tale savings account in order to earn the amounts forecasted in each quarter. For instance, if the investors place $0.979m into the account at the very beginning of the investment and withdraw it at the end of Y3Q3, the $0.979m will have turned into $2.714m because of the 11 quarters of interest it will have earned. Were the investors to place $0.127m into the bank and withdraw it 12 quarters later at the end of Y3Q4, the $0.127m will have turned into $0.387m because of the interest earned over each of those quarters. Notice what the total of these initial deposits into the magical savings account comes to... $1.500m, the budget of the film.

So the IRR can also be thought of like this: break your budget (a.k.a. investment) into many pieces and the IRR is the rate of return (or "interest") each of those pieces has earned once it is returned back to the investor. For example, piece number one is $0.979m, and when it is returned to the investors under this "Medium Success" scenario, it will have turned into $2.714m, which translates into a quarterly rate of return of 9.7145%. Piece number eleven, $0.011m, when it is returned in Y6Q1, will have become $0.077m, a quarterly interest rate again of 9.7145%.

As an important side note, generally when people discuss IRR it is discussed in terms of yearly IRR instead of the quarterly IRR we have been discussing thus far. You will see in the steps how to convert from quarterly to yearly. Nonetheless, when being discussed in a yearly fashion, the IRR means the exact same thing we have established above, except that the quarterly rate has been turned into a yearly rate. It's the same thing as discussing how much your savings account earned over one year as opposed to three months: the concept of amount earned hasn't changed, just the time frame. Incidentally, *Psych Thrill*'s Medium scenario IRR comes to an annual rate of 44.9%. That is the rate I quote for it in the sample text.

STEP 40. NOTE ON IRR VS ROI — The IRR gives us a sense of the timing of the return of cash from an investment. Two identical size investments can have the same ROI but different IRRs. Let me illustrate using an extremely oversimplified movie example. Suppose that you invest $100 in a movie (Movie 1) and that movie, miracle of all miracles, returns you $150 one year later, and that's it. At the same time, you invest $100 in a movie (Movie 2) that returns $25 at the very end of Quarter 2 (a half-year later) and $125 at the very end of the year, and that's it. Your ROI for both investments would be 50% because you made $50 over-and-above the initial $100 that you invested. However, the IRR for each investment would differ, as the table below demonstrates:

Table B.8: IRR comparison

		YEAR 1		
	Quarter 1	Quarter 2	Quarter 3	Quarter 4
Movie 1 with $100 initial investment.				
Cash Returned	$0	$0	$0	$150
Annual IRR: 50.0%				
Movie 2 with $100 initial investment.				
Cash Returned	$0	$25	$0	$125
Annual IRR: 56.2%				

Your IRR goes up for Movie 2 because you received some of the money sooner than with Movie 1. In the case of Movie 2 you can think of it like having $25 to earn interest on while you wait for the rest of the investment to be returned (i.e., the $125). With Movie 1, on the other hand, you don't have access to that $25 until two quarters later when it is returned to you along with the other $125. In any case, the key point to remember is that between two choices, getting X amount of money back from an investment sooner or getting X amount of money (the same amount) back from an investment later, the earlier your receive the money back, the higher the IRR.

STEP 4P — If you think your returns fall too far out of the 30%–50% range, you can seek to include higher or lower grossing films on your Comparable Films Table by altering your screen count limits. For instance, to increase your return percentages, eliminate a restriction on the opening weekend screen count or raise your maximum screen count (e.g., from 600 to 800). Do the opposite to lower your returns. You can also affect returns by increasing or decreasing your budget, but only do so in conjunction with the producer of your project, and in the case of lowering it, only do so if the project can still legitimately be completed through postproduction. If you are unable to change the level of your predictions, be they too high or too low, you may want to explain the reasons for their levels in the text of your income projections. Even though *Mass H-Com*'s returns were not too far out of range, notice how I focused on the low budget and large target audience of the film to explain its high returns. This same strategy could have been used were the returns too far out of range.

STEP 4Q — An ROI multiple conveys how much total money an investment returns, whereas an ROI conveys how much money an investment returns net of the initial investment. For example, an ROI multiple of 1.5x means that an investment of $100 returned $150 total cash. The ROI on the same investment would be 50%. This is because my profit, after subtracting out the initial investment, is $50. Then dividing $50 by $100 leaves me with 50% for my ROI.

STEP 5 NOTES:

EXHIBITION MARKET — If you are in Los Angeles, information on exhibitors can be found chiefly in the "Exhibition" and "Admissions" clipping files at the Margaret Herrick Library. Some but not nearly as much info can be found in the "Independent Exhibition" and "Theaters – Art Houses" clipping files, with the latter containing the least number of useful articles out of the group.

In the exhibition text of *Mass H-Com* you will notice the line "While specialty theaters generally cater to niche audiences, they do carry independent films, and sometimes studio films, of mass appeal." The line is inserted to make clear that independent films of mass appeal are played in specialty theaters. I have been asked by investors why studios don't just adopt the independent film model and pump out films of mass appeal for dirt cheap. Therein lies the problem — dirt cheap; studios cannot make films for dirt cheap. Overhead costs, the general inefficiency of a large company, and the fact that people working on a studio picture tend to request more money knowing a studio is footing the bill make the words "dirt cheap" mean a figure well north of $10 million.

You or your investors might then wonder why studios don't just buy low-budget independent films of mass appeal after they have already been made — they do. That is one of the purposes of their specialty divisions (e.g., Fox Searchlight, Focus Features, Sony Pictures Classics, etc.). Even in such a case, however, the purchased film will hardly ever be released in the same manner as a mainstay studio picture because when placed side-by-side, the mainstay studio picture will have a certain slickness in its production quality, and in all likelihood, a higher number of significantly name actors, than the low-budget independent could have afforded. This slickness and presence of name actors are seen by the studio as a way to keep the audience from hating the film, which they often end up doing anyway; in other words, the reasoning goes that at least the movie's audiences will come for the actors, good songs, nice camera shots, locations, and maybe even some special effects. Unfortunately for studios, the presence of significantly name actors has not been statistically shown to increase the predictability of a film's financial success, and I can only imagine that the other factors (a.k.a. "slickness"), despite being impossible to measure, lead to the same result.[4] In all fairness to the studios, the success of independent films is no easier to predict.

STEP 8 NOTES:

__CALCULATING A PERCENTAGE CHANGE__ — Let's say I have a total of $10 billion of sales in 2004 and $15 billion in 2009. To calculate the percentage change, do the following:

$$\text{Percentage Change} = \$15 \text{ billion} / \$10 \text{ billion} - 1$$
$$= 1.5 - 1$$
$$= 0.5$$
$$= 50\%$$

---

[4] For a more in-depth discussion of an actor's effects on film performance see *Hollywood Economics* by Arthur De Vany, and *Entertainment Industry Economics* (7th Edition) by Harold L. Vogel, 157-158, footnotes 68 and 71.

So, sales grew a total of 50% over these five years. This calculation also works with percentages themselves. Let's say that the Drama genre was 10% of the box office in 2004 and 15% in 2009. Doing the same calculation:

Percentage Change = 15% / 10% - 1
            = 1.5 - 1
            = 0.5
            = 50 %

Meaning that the genre grew a total of 50% in box office share from 2004 to 2009. These calculations work for any time frame, one month, one year, two years, three years, etc., and can be used to calculate declines in value as well. For example, a genre might have fallen in box office share by 25% from 2004 to 2009.

MASS H-COM TEXT — In the second paragraph of the text for this step I provided a brief recent history of trends in the horror genre to show how the film would appeal to horror fans even more. The trend covering zombies was done by examining all recent horror films that had grossed $2.0 million or above. I used *Weekly Variety*'s "Top 250" lists and asked friends of mine in the industry who were horror buffs to help me spot all the horror films. For films released post–December 31st and obviously not on the latest "Top 250" list, I used IMDb and consulted those same friends to make sure I hadn't missed any of the latest horror releases. The other, more qualitative horror trend described in the text was discovered by pouring through the Margaret Herrick Library's "Horror" clipping files. Can you believe it? The staff at Margaret Herrick have actually collected every article they could find covering aspects of the horror genre — what a godsend! If you're not in L.A., do an Internet search of "horror movies" and "trends" and you should be able to find plenty of material.

STEP 24 NOTES:

DESCRIBING AN OFF YEAR — Below is what I would have written for this step of an early 2006 business plan, commenting on the abysmal year of 2005 (box office stats are from the MPAA, which is the source I would have used at the time as opposed to Nielsen EDI):

2005 U.S. box office receipts fell 5.7% from 2004's all-time record high of $9.54 billion to $8.99 billion, but when removing the effects of 2004's extreme exception, *The Passion of the Christ*, this drop shrinks to 2.0%. *The Passion* became the highest grossing independent film of all time ($370 million domestic) in large part due to Christian churchgoers, who were targeted as a group by the picture's promoters, despite hardly, if ever, being targeted as such in the past. Even with the fall in box office, 2005 recorded a record-tying seven films grossing over $200 million versus five in 2004, showing that good movies were still rewarded with large revenues. This result, coupled with the fact that 2005 saw major volatility and significant increases in retail gas prices, indicates that 2005 box office performance may have actually been quite robust. Another reason for the decline was competition from 81% of American households with DVD devices, 61% with Internet access, 40% with broadband access, and 24% with video-on-demand (VOD).[5] Although these percentages represent competition to box office figures, they also serve as a boon to ancillary receipts. Ancillary receipts are revenue generated from non-box office sources such as DVD/home video and pay TV. Regardless of a decline in the overall DVD/home video market, which includes elements such as television, music, and children's non-feature titles, the top 20 home video movie titles actually held steady and generated slightly more revenue than the top 20 titles of 2004 (up 0.4%).[6] It also bears mentioning that pictures often generate more gross revenue in home video release than in the box office. Looking to the future, competition from other entertainment media will keep box office growth at a modest 5.6% through 2009, and while independent films similar to *Sci-Fi Rom/Mass H-Com/Psych Thrill* generate the vast majority of their revenue from domestic sources, international revenue streams for movies in general (studios included) are expected to boom over the next eight years, easily surpassing their North American counterparts.[7]

---

[5] "U.S. Entertainment Industry: 2006 Market Statistics" by Motion Picture Association Worldwide Market Research.

[6] Comparisons based on calculations using data from Video Business's online site: *www.videobusiness.com/info/CA6301486.html*.

[7] Box office growth calculation based on "DVD sales forecast at four times B.O." by Jill Goldsmith, *Daily Variety*, August 15, 2005; international revenue comments based on "It's a New World Order for Film" by Staff reporting data from Kagan Research, *Screen International*, December 9, 2005.

I am assuming here that I wrote the plan in March of 2006, but without any of the running box office or home video totals for 2006 that normally would have been available by the time — imperfect, I know, but for the point I'm making, having that data available would have only made the writing easier. In the Market Analysis & Marketing Strategy section, where you discuss the health of independent films, you also want to place events in a positive light. Even if things are going poorly, emphasize how good independent films are still in great demand, and then highlight some of the most recent, best performing ones.

STEP 27 NOTES:

STATISTICS UNDERLYING MOVIE RISK — According to the sample risk statement, somewhere in the neighborhood of 20%–30% of major theatrical films are profitable; not surprisingly then, it is also true that just under 20% of theatrically released films account for 80% of the industry's total domestic gross.[8] This leads to the common, paradoxical, but correct observation that the average film makes money, and to the incorrect assumption that the average film is the most commonly occurring film. Were you to take all the films from any size time period (days, weeks, months, or years) and compute the average box office, the number would be quite high in relation to most of the films in the group (there are far more films in release at any one time than just the top 10). However, if you were to take that same group and calculate what was the most commonly occurring box office number, the figure would be quite low in relation to the average. The successful films are often really successful and greatly raise the average of a group consisting chiefly of not-so-successful films. Thus, using the average revenues that movies have earned as a predictor of what a future movie might earn can be quite misleading, especially when one considers what the most likely event is: earning very low revenues.

In fact, using averages to predict movie performance can be downright foolhardy when considering the fact that the underlying probability distribution for a movie's revenue is not the friendly Normal distribution we were all taught in school. (Remember that funny-looking bell curve

80/20

---

[8] Harold L. Vogel, *Entertainment Industry Economics: A Guide for Financial Analysis*, 7th ed., 65, 133; Arthur De Vany, *Hollywood Economics: How Extreme Uncertainty Shapes the Film Industry*, 261.

that had a nice mean coupled with a variance, often measured using standard deviation, to describe how far results might stray from the mean?) In fact, the variance for movie revenues is infinite, a characteristic of the underlying distribution, the so-called stable Paretian distribution. So trying to take an average revenue of past films and using it as an approximation of what a future film might earn is useless. All you end up with is an estimate of future revenues plus or minus infinity. How would you feel if I told you your investment might return $1.0 million plus or minus infinity — not so great, huh? Some very rich people have actually attempted to get around this problem by investing in a portfolio of films with the mindset that one or more hits will pay for the many misses. While they are correct in thinking that they have increased their chances of a hit, they have also increased the variance, or wide variety, of different portfolio returns they could face, as opposed to what generally happens with a diversified stock portfolio where the variance decreases; the increased variance is another odd property of the underlying stable Paretian distribution. You might wonder, how could a variance be any greater than infinity? Well, for any group of movies you analyze in a certain time period, the variance will indeed compute to a finite number, but this number is a very large finite number. The number gets larger and larger the greater the number of movies in your group. The infinite variance of which I have spoken is the theoretical variance and in practice it is demonstrated by the huge variance you see in movie revenues for a group of movies across time. Lost? That's okay. Just know that most portfolios of films don't help you earn high movie returns either, unless they get lucky.[9]

What does all this mean for your business plan? The predictions for your film's performance are meaningless because the numbers they are based on are meaningless. While accurate conveyers of what happened in the past, the numbers that drive the predictions serve no predictive value. Statistically speaking, the predictive numbers are driven by the stable Paretian distribution which suffers from an ever-changing average

---

[9] Arthur De Vany, comment on "Movie Investors," Arthur De Vany blog, posted November 16, 2006, www.arthurdevany.com/the_movie_business/; comment on "Moving the Stakes: Changing Risk Bearing and Reward in Film Finance," posted September 12, 2006, Ibid.; comment on "Trimming Hedges," posted July 16, 2006, Ibid.

and infinite variance.[10] As a result, the numbers in any film business plan (or studio forecasting model for that matter) that compute an average and use that average to predict the result for one film or a group of films are meaningless. Anyone trying to tell you otherwise is misinformed, at best.

Why not just make predictions based on the stable Paretian distribution and any empirical data out there on movie revenues? Unfortunately, for one film there is no statistic or analysis that has been shown to meaningfully help you trim your risk (i.e., make a reliable prediction about the film). Therefore it falls on intangible factors such as story quality and passion of the filmmakers to curtail risk. It bears mentioning, the only reason movie studios manage to exist is because of the licensing fees they derive from their vast libraries of movies and television shows. Were it not for these fees, the studios would sink.[11]

INTERESTING NEED TO UNDERSTAND THAT MORE

---

[10] Arthur De Vany, comment on "Trimming Hedges," Arthur De Vany blog, posted July 16, 2006, Ibid.

[11] For discussions of the core businesses critical to studio survival see "Movies, Money and Madness" by Peter J. Dekom in *The Movie Business Book* (3rd Edition), edited by Jason E. Squire, 101-103; and *Entertainment Industry Economics* (7th Edition) by Harold L. Vogel, 135.

APPENDIX C: RECOMMENDED READING

(C'mon! At least read some of these.)

BOOKS

Your best bet for accessing some of these materials is through specialized libraries like a film, law, or business school library. Some of these sources (including the periodicals) are just way too expensive to buy on your own.

43 Ways to Finance Your Feature Film: A Comprehensive Analysis of Film Finance (updated 3rd Edition) by John W. Cones
(Carbondale: Southern Illinois University Press, 2008)

The Art of Film Funding: Alternative Financing Concepts by Carole Lee Dean
(Los Angeles: Michael Wiese Productions, 2007)

The Biz: The Basic Business, Legal and Financial Aspects of the Film Industry (3rd Edition) by Schuyler M. Moore
(Los Angeles: Silman-James Press, 2007)

Business Plans Handbook: A Compilation of Actual Business Plans Developed by Businesses Throughout North America, Volume 13 by Lynn M. Pearce (Editor)
(Detroit: Gale Cengage, 2007)

Dealmaking in the Film & Television Industry: From Negotiations To Final Contracts (2nd Edition) by Mark Litwak
(Los Angeles: Silman-James Press, 2002)

Entertainment Industry Contracts: Negotiating and Drafting Guide by Jay S. Kenoff and Richard K. Rosenberg, edited by Donald C. Farber
(Miamisburg: LexisNexis, 2008)
– Excellent resource with sample movie contracts for all stages of distribution and beyond (see volumes 1 & 2), in addition to running commentary on those contracts.

Entertainment Industry Economics: A Guide for Financial Analysis (7th Edition) by Harold L. Vogel
(Cambridge and New York: Cambridge University Press, 2007)

Entertainment Law Third Edition: Legal Concepts and Business Practices, by
Thomas D. Selz, Melvin Simensky, Patricia Acton, and Robert Lind
(Eagan: Thomson Reuters/West, 2008)
– Detailed commentary on legal aspects of the entertainment industry
(stick to volumes 1 & 2, chapters 1, 2, 3, 4, and 9).

The Ernst & Young Business Plan Guide (3rd Edition) by Brian R. Ford, Jay
M. Bornstein, Patrick T. Pruitt
(Hoboken: John Wiley & Sons, 2007)

The Feature Film Distribution Deal: A Critical Analysis by John W. Cones
(Carbondale: Southern Illinois University Press, 1997)

Hollywood Economics: How Extreme Uncertainty Shapes the Film Industry by
Arthur De Vany
(London and New York: Routledge, 2004)

*Independent Feature Film Production: A Complete Guide from Concept Through
Distribution* by Gregory Goodell
(New York: St. Martin's Griffin, 1998)
– No need to buy the 2003 version, which is a reissue of the 1982 version.

The Independent Film Producer's Survival Guide: A Business and Legal Sourcebook
by J. Gunnar Erickson, Harris Tulchin, and Mark Halloran
(New York: Music Sales Corporation, 2005)

Film Industry Contracts by John W. Cones
(West Los Angeles: self-published, 1993)
– Mentioned because it has a sample of a PPM (technically, it contains a
Regulation D feature film limited partnership offering memorandum).

The Insider's Guide to Independent Film Distribution by Stacey Parks
(Amsterdam and Boston: Elsevier, 2007)

*A Killer Life: How an Independent Film Producer Survives Deals and Disasters in
Hollywood and Beyond* by Christine Vachon
(New York: Simon & Schuster, 2006)

Lindey on Entertainment, Publishing and the Arts: Agreements and the Law
(3rd Edition) by Alexander Lindey and Michael Landau
(Eagan: Thomson Reuters/West, 2008)
– Sample contracts and legal commentary (stick to volume 3, chapter 6).

The Movie Business: The Definitive Guide to the Legal and Financial Secrets of Getting Your Movie Made by Kelly Charles Crabb
(New York: Simon & Schuster, 2005)

The Movie Business Book (3rd edition), edited by Jason E. Squire
(New York: Simon & Schuster, 2004)

Movie Money: Understanding Hollywood's (Creative) Accounting Practices
(2nd Edition) by Bill Daniels, David Leedy, and Steven D. Sills
(Los Angeles: Silman-James Press, 2006)

Nolo's Quick LLC: All You Need to Know About Limited Liability Companies
by Anthony Mancuso
(Berkeley: Nolo, 2007)

The Pocket Lawyer for Filmmakers: A Legal Toolkit for Independent Producers by
Thomas A. Crowell
(Amsterdam and Boston: Elsevier, 2007)

The Producer's Business Handbook by John J. Lee Jr. and Rob Holt
(Amsterdam and Boston: Elsevier, 2005)

Producing, Financing and Distributing Film: A Comprehensive Legal and Business Guide (2nd Edition) by Paul A. Baumgarten, Donald C. Farber, and Mark Fleischer
(New York: Limelight Editions, 1992)

Raising Capital: Get the Money You Need to Grow Your Business (2nd Edition)
by Andrew J. Sherman
(New York: AMACOM Books, American Management Association, 2005)

Risky Business: Financing and Distributing Independent Films by Mark Litwak
(Los Angeles: Silman-James Press, 2004)

Shooting to Kill: How an Independent Producer Blasts Through the Barriers to Make Movies That Matter by Christine Vachon
(New York: Avon Books, 1998)

Film Production Management 101: The Ultimate Guide for Film and Television Production Management and Coordination by Deborah S. Patz
(Los Angeles: Michael Wiese Productions, 2002)

Writing a Convincing Business Plan (3rd Edition) by Arthur DeThomas, Ph.D. and Stephanie Derammelaere, M.B.A.
(Hauppauge: Barron's Educational Series, 2008)

PERIODICALS

The Hollywood Reporter
(*www.hollywoodreporter.com*)

Screen Digest
(*www.screendigest.com*)
– Great facts and figures for all markets (theatrical and ancillary).

Screen International
(*www.screendaily.com*)

Variety
(*www.variety.com*)
– Amazing weekly box office figures online.

INDEX

accounting statements, 95, 98

actors, *see* "significantly name actors," "letters of intent"

advances, 31, 78-79, 176

advances (foreign), 173-174

angel investors:

    definition, xii

    desired returns, 29

assumption agreement, 98

attorneys, use/necessity of, xiv-xv, xvi, 126

awards season, 51

Baseline StudioSystems, 50:

    contact info, 2

    data and Comparable Films Table, 5-6, 6-7, 171-175

    FRCE reports, 2, 4

    price, xiii

BLSS, *see* "Baseline StudioSystems"

blue sky laws, 119

box office:

    data sources, 100-101

    lack of predictability, 31

budgets:

    conflicting sources, 171

    forecasting range, 2

    low budget, definition, xii

Buena Vista (a.k.a. Disney), 3

business plans:
     confidentiality, 120
     cover page, 120, 128
     definition, xi
     legality of, xiv
     multi-film, xii
     order of, 125
     strategy for use, xiv-xv
     underlying assumption, xvi, 72
Calhoun, Dave, 57
cash flow:
     lack of certainty, 14, 24
     timing/schedule, 14-17, 185-186
Cash Flow Projections Table, 14-24, 182-192:
     amount returned to investors, 21-23, 190-192
     basic assumptions, 17, 185-186, 186
     checking for errors, 23-24
     definition/demonstration, 182-184
     Domestic Subtotal examples, 186-189
     Producer's Rep Fee examples, 189-190
     samples, 37-38, 46-47, 161-162
casting, 82
comedy films, lack of foreign appeal, 72, 80
Comparable Films Table, 1-8, 168-176:
     distribution assumptions, 176, 186
     how to fill in, 5-7, 171-175
     samples, 34-35, 43-44, 158-159
Company Description, 81-85
Crabb, Kelly Charles, 67, 99
d-cinema, 69
data, see "statistics, locating them," "Baseline StudioSystems"
deferrals, 12, 177
Dempsey, John, 63
describing an off year, 199-201
De Vany, Arthur, 121, 123, 168, 198, 202, 203
Dekom, Peter J., 203
digital intermediate, 100

digital projectors, *see* "d-cinema"

DiOrio, Carl, 106, 168

distribution, *see also* "Motion Picture Distribution":

    deals, structure of, 14, 31, 176, 186

    expenses, *see also* "Other Distributor Costs," 68-69, 75, 186, 189

    fees, 68-69, 75, 172

    forecasting timing of, 17, 185-186

    fractionalization of rights, 68

    Internet distribution, 68

    overview, 73-74

    strategy for attaining, 72, 78-80

    timing of, 74

distributors:

    control, 69, 75

    criteria for film selection, 71

    returning money, 186, 189, 190

Domestic Subtotal, 18-19, 186-189

DreamWorks, 3

DVDs, *see also* "home video market," "home video statistics":

    expenses, 69, 172

    maturing market, 102

equity, definition, xii

Executive Summary, 109-116

exhibition market, where to find information on, 197

Exhibitor Share percentage, 10

exhibitors, 55

expenses, *see also* "Other Distributor Costs":

    distribution, 68-69, 75, 186, 189

    DVDs, 69, 172

    foreign sales agent, 174

    producer's rep, 175

    theatrical, 186, *see also* "prints and advertising"

fees:

    distribution, 68-69, 75, 172

    foreign sales agent, 174

    producer's rep, 175

festivals, where to find descriptions of, 72

films, unsuccessful, xvi
Financial Projections, 1–48, 167–197:
        sample, 31–48, 155–163
Financing (section), 93–98
Fitzgerald, Chad, 95
Focus Features, 3, 198
forecasting, fruitlessness of, xv, 31, 201–203
foreign distribution rights, 73–74
foreign films, 169–170, 174
Foreign Gross, *see also* "foreign revenue," 6, 11–12, 13, 173–174, 185:
        and significantly name actors, 173–174
foreign revenue, 32
foreign sales agent, 76, 78–79, 173–174, 174–175, 190
Fox 2000, 3
Fox Atomic, 3
Fox Searchlight, 3, 198
FRCE reports, 2, 4
free TV, 7, 175
Freedman, Jeffrey, 168
Fritz, Ben, 57, 59
Galloway, Stephen, 57, 65
genres, year-to-year comparisons, 53–54
Goldsmith, Jill, 200
Goldstein, Patrick, 63
Gore, Chris, 72
growth rates, 101
Hazelton, John, 169
Holland, Chris, 72
Hollywood Pictures, 3
Hollywood Reporter, The:
        "The Going Rate" article, 6, 11, 12, 13, 179
        indie supplements, 71
        online price xii
        online searching xii
Holt, Rob, 69
home video market, 102
home video numbers, 171

home video statistics sources, 101-102

horror films, foreign appeal, 80

horror trends, cataloguing, 199

How to Complete the Plan, 125-126

IMDb.com, 3, 4:

    price, xii

    shooting format, 88

IMDbPro.com, xii

Income Projections Table, 9-14, 176-181:

    "High Success" projections, 13

    "Low Success" projections, 12-13, 178-180

    "Medium Success" defined, 9

    samples, 36, 45, 160

    text, 14, 181, 225

independent film:

    checking status of, 3-4

    data, difficulty in collecting, 49

    definition, xi-xii

    describing the market, 49-51

    difficulty achieving success, 72

    mass appeal, 197-198

    versus studio, 105-106, 197-198

Industry Overview, 99-107, 199-201:

    portraying news positively, 102-103, 199-201

Information and Risk Statement, 117-124, 201-203

internal rate of return, 27-28, 194-196:

    investor expectations for, 29, 197

    versus return on investment, 196

international TV, 7

investor priority return, 24-25, 178, 192-193

Investor Projections Table, 24-30, 192-197:

    samples, 39, 48, 163

investor return expectations, 29, 197

investors, *see* "angel investors"

IRR, *see* "internal rate of return"

Iser, Larry, 95

King, Susan, 64

lawyers, *see* "attorneys"

Lee Jr., John J., 69

letters of intent, 82

limited liability company, 26, 193-194

Litwak, Mark, 67, 72, 194

LLC, *see* "limited liability company"

logline, 87

low budget, definition, xii

"Low Success" recommended method, 178-180

Mancuso, Anthony, 194

Margaret Herrick Library:

    about, xiii

    clipping files, xiii, 4, 52, 67, 99, 100, 197, 199

    current stats binder, 54, 99, 100

Market Analysis & Marketing Strategy, 49-65:

    Internet marketing, 52

    marketing strategy, general, 52, 56-57

    word-of-mouth, 51, 56

mass appeal, 169, 197-198

McDonald, Kathy A., 57

McIntyre, Gina, 64

merchandise revenue, 171-172

MGM, 3, 103

Microsoft Excel and rounding, 18, 167

Miramax, 3

Mohr, Ian, 76

Motion Picture Association of America, 54, 100:

    Movie Attendance Survey, 54

    U. S. Entertainment Industry Market Statistics, 100

Motion Picture Distribution, 67-80

movie profitability, 9, 122, 201

movies, process described, 104

movies, unsuccessful, *see* "films, unsuccessful"

MPAA, *see* "Motion Picture Association of America"

MTV Films, 3

Munoz, Lorenza, 55, 63

name actors, *see* "significantly name actors"

negative, cut, 100

New Line, 3

news, finding the positive, 51

Nickelodeon Movies, 3

Oscar nominees, 50

Other Distributor Costs, 12, 69, 74, 172

overages, 173

P&A, *see* "prints and advertising"

Paramount, 3

Paramount Classics, 70

Paramount Vantage, 3, 70, 168-169

Parks, Stacey, 67, 72

pay TV, 7, 171

pay TV licensing percentage, 10

percentage change, calculating, 198-199

Picturehouse, 3

Pinsker, Beth, 57

portfolios of films, xii, 202

PPM, *see* "Private Placement Memorandum"

prints and advertising, 69, 74-75:

      foreign, 173

      P&A percentage, 11

private placement memorandum:

      definition, xv, 94

      price, xv

private placement offering, xv, 118-119

producer's rep, 78, 174-175, 190

Product Description, 87-92

profit participations, 94-95

promises, 9, 167

registering securities, 118-119

Regulation D, 118

residuals, 95-96, 98, 172

return on investment, 26-27, 196

return on investment multiple, 29, 197

return on investment versus return on investment multiple, 197

returning money to investors, 190-193

returns, investor expectations for, 29

risk, 201–203

ROI, *see* "return on investment"

Ross, Matthew M., 64

Rogue, 3

sales agent, *see* "foreign sales agent"

Sample Plan in Its Entirety, 128–163

sample tables:

    Cash Flow Projections Table, 37–38, 46–47, 161–162

    Comparable Films Table, 34–35, 43–44, 158–159

    Income Projections Table, 36, 45, 160

    Investor Projections Table, 39, 48, 163

screen counts, 2, 3, 9, 50, 51–52, 70, 170, 197:

    defined, 170

Screen Gems, 3

Securities and Exchange Commission, 117, 118–119

shooting:

    formats, locating, 88

    mentioning time of year, 88–89

ShoWest, 103

Sherman, Andrew J., 119

significantly name actors:

    affordability of, 168–169

    and Foreign Gross, 173–174

    box office impact, 198

    definition, 168

Sony, 3

Sony Pictures Classics, 3, 198

specialty films, 50

specialty theaters, 83

Sperling, Nicole, 55

Squire, Jason E., 99, 203

stable Paretian distribution, 202

statistics, locating them, *see also* "Baseline StudioSystems":

    box office, 100–101

    budget, 171

    home video, 101–102

    independent film, 49-51

    movie industry, 100-101

    moviegoers, 54

story synopsis, 87-88

straight-to-DVD titles, 169

studio versus independent films, 105-106, 197-198

studios:

    cost of doing business, 106, 198

    mass appeal movies, 197-198

    key to survival, 203

Swart, Sharon, 96

Szalai, Georg, 107

taxes, 168

theatrical release, expenses, 186

theatrical release, importance of, 73, 75

timing:

    cash flow, 14-17, 185-186

    distribution, 17, 74, 185-186

Touchstone, 3

TriStar, 3

Twentieth Century-Fox, 3

Universal, 3

Variety:

    indie supplements, 71

    limited release list, 50, 71

    online price, xii

    online searching, iii

    Top 250 list, 53, 199

Vogel, Harold L., 9, 67, 69, 99, 102, 122, 198, 203, 232

Walt Disney Pictures, 3

Warner Brothers, 3, 70

Warner Independent, 3, 70

weighted averages, warning against, 177

ABOUT THE AUTHOR

JEREMY JUUSO graduated *cum laude* in economics from Harvard College. Upon graduation he accepted a Harvard fellowship and taught economics at a British boarding school to students applying to Oxford and Cambridge. Since England, he has worked at MGM's treasury and investor relations departments, the financial markets research firm Bigdough.com (now part of Ipreo Holdings), and the production company Fly High Films, where he currently serves as financial advisor and writes business plans for the company. Jeremy is also the founder of Jeremy Juuso Consulting, a firm specializing in the writing of film business proposals, publication of film data, and education of investors on the basics of the movie business (*www. jeremyjuuso.com*).

Don't forget! Visit *mwp.com* for some free spreadsheets that will save you time, and perhaps even some money, when you use them for your business plans.

JEREMY JUUSO CONSULTING

www.jeremyjuuso.com
consulting@jeremyjuuso.com

WRITING A BUSINESS PLAN FOR AN INDEPENDENT FILM?

Whether your business plan stands alone or complements a private placement memorandum (PPM), it needs to answer the same basic question:

Why should you be trusted with lots of money?

By putting together a thorough and well-thought-out business plan, you eliminate yourself as the source of uncertainty in a film investment.

Films are among the riskiest investments a person can make, and a poorly put-together business plan only adds to that risk. Would you give your money to someone with a shoddy proposal?

From cash flow projections to overviews of the industry, I can point you in the right direction, lay out a detailed step-by-step approach, or work with you to get it all done.

ARE YOU AN INVESTOR?

Are you familiar with the basics of the film industry?

There are many pitfalls to watch for in the realm of film financing. Avoid becoming yet another victim. Get to know the process, from financing to production to the collection of revenues.

Whether it's digital distribution or profit participations, I can help you understand the movie business. It is unlike any other.

See *www.jeremyjuuso.com* for the latest data on independent films.

MICHAEL WIESE PRODUCTIONS

Our books are all about helping you create memorable films that will move audiences for generations to come.

Since 1981, we've published over 100 books on all aspects of filmmaking which are used in more than 600 film schools around the world. Many of today's most productive filmmakers and writers got started with our books.

According to a recent Nielsen BookScan analysis, as a publisher we've had more best-selling books in our subject category than our closest competitor – and they are backed by a multi-billion dollar corporation! This is evidence that as an independent – filmmaker or publisher – you can create the projects you have always dreamed of and earn a livelihood.

To help you accomplish your goals, we've expanded our information to the web. Here you can receive a 25% discount on all our books, buy the newest releases before they hit the bookstores, and sign up for a newsletter which provides all kinds of new information, tips, seminars, and more. You'll also find a Virtual Film School loaded with articles and websites from our top authors, teacher's guides, video streamed content, free budget formats, and a ton of free valuable information.

We encourage you to visit www.mwp.com. Sign up and become part of a wider creative community.

Onward and upward,
Michael Wiese
Publisher, Filmmaker

If you'd like to receive a free MWP Newsletter,
click on www.mwp.com to register.

FILM & VIDEO BOOKS

TO RECEIVE A FREE MWP NEWSLETTER, CLICK ON WWW.MWP.COM TO REGISTER

SCREENWRITING | WRITING

And the Best Screenplay Goes to... | Dr. Linda Seger | $26.95

Archetypes for Writers | Jennifer Van Bergen | $22.95

Cinematic Storytelling | Jennifer Van Sijll | $24.95

Could It Be a Movie? | Christina Hamlett | $26.95

Creating Characters | Marisa D'Vari | $26.95

Crime Writer's Reference Guide, The | Martin Roth | $20.95

Deep Cinema | Mary Trainor-Brigham | $19.95

Elephant Bucks | Sheldon Bull | $24.95

Fast, Cheap & Written That Way | John Gaspard | $26.95

Hollywood Standard, The | Christopher Riley | $18.95

I Could've Written a Better Movie than That! | Derek Rydall | $26.95

Inner Drives | Pamela Jaye Smith | $26.95

Joe Leydon's Guide to Essential Movies You Must See | Joe Leydon | $24.95

Moral Premise, The | Stanley D. Williams, Ph.D. | $24.95

Myth and the Movies | Stuart Voytilla | $26.95

Power of the Dark Side, The | Pamela Jaye Smith | $22.95

Psychology for Screenwriters | William Indick, Ph.D. | $26.95

Rewrite | Paul Chitlik | $16.95

Romancing the A-List | Christopher Keane | $18.95

Save the Cat! | Blake Snyder | $19.95

Save the Cat! Goes to the Movies | Blake Snyder | $24.95

Screenwriting 101 | Neill D. Hicks | $16.95

Screenwriting for Teens | Christina Hamlett | $18.95

Script-Selling Game, The | Kathie Fong Yoneda | $16.95

Stealing Fire From the Gods, 2nd Edition | James Bonnet | $26.95

Way of Story, The | Catherine Ann Jones | $22.95

What Are You Laughing At? | Brad Schreiber | $19.95

Writer's Journey, – 3rd Edition, The | Christopher Vogler | $26.95

Writer's Partner, The | Martin Roth | $24.95

Writing the Action Adventure Film | Neill D. Hicks | $14.95

Writing the Comedy Film | Stuart Voytilla & Scott Petri | $14.95

Writing the Killer Treatment | Michael Halperin | $14.95

Writing the Second Act | Michael Halperin | $19.95

Writing the Thriller Film | Neill D. Hicks | $14.95

Writing the TV Drama Series – 2nd Edition | Pamela Douglas | $26.95

Your Screenplay Sucks! | William M. Akers | $19.95

FILMMAKING

Film School | Richard D. Pepperman | $24.95

Power of Film, The | Howard Suber | $27.95

PITCHING

Perfect Pitch – 2nd Edition, The | Ken Rotcop | $19.95

Selling Your Story in 60 Seconds | Michael Hauge | $12.95

SHORTS

Filmmaking for Teens | Troy Lanier & Clay Nichols | $18.95

Ultimate Filmmaker's Guide to Short Films, The | Kim Adelman | $16.95

BUDGET | PRODUCTION MGMT

Film & Video Budgets, 4th Updated Edition | Deke Simon & Michael Wiese | $26.95

Film Production Management 101 | Deborah S. Patz | $39.95

DIRECTING | VISUALIZATION

Animation Unleashed | Ellen Besen | $26.95

Citizen Kane Crash Course in Cinematography | David Worth | $19.95

Directing Actors | Judith Weston | $26.95

Directing Feature Films | Mark Travis | $26.95

Fast, Cheap & Under Control | John Gaspard | $26.95

Film Directing: Cinematic Motion, 2nd Edition | Steven D. Katz | $27.95

Film Directing: Shot by Shot | Steven D. Katz | $27.95

Film Director's Intuition, The | Judith Weston | $26.95

First Time Director | Gil Bettman | $27.95

From Word to Image | Marcie Begleiter | $26.95

I'll Be in My Trailer! | John Badham & Craig Modderno | $26.95

Master Shots | Christopher Kenworthy | $24.95

Setting Up Your Scenes | Richard D. Pepperman | $24.95

Setting Up Your Shots, 2nd Edition | Jeremy Vineyard | $22.95

Working Director, The | Charles Wilkinson | $22.95

DIGITAL | DOCUMENTARY | SPECIAL

Digital Filmmaking 101, 2nd Edition | Dale Newton & John Gaspard | $26.95

Digital Moviemaking 3.0 | Scott Billups | $24.95

Digital Video Secrets | Tony Levelle | $26.95

Greenscreen Made Easy | Jeremy Hanke & Michele Yamazaki | $19.95

Producing with Passion | Dorothy Fadiman & Tony Levelle | $22.95

Special Effects | Michael Slone | $31.95

EDITING

Cut by Cut | Gael Chandler | $35.95

Cut to the Chase | Bobbie O'Steen | $24.95

Eye is Quicker, The | Richard D. Pepperman | $27.95

Invisible Cut, The | Bobbie O'Steen | $28.95

SOUND | DVD | CAREER

Complete DVD Book, The | Chris Gore & Paul J. Salamoff | $26.95

Costume Design 101 | Richard La Motte | $19.95

Hitting Your Mark – 2nd Edition | Steve Carlson | $22.95

Sound Design | David Sonnenschein | $19.95

Sound Effects Bible, The | Ric Viers | $26.95

Storyboarding 101 | James Fraioli | $19.95

There's No Business Like Soul Business | Derek Rydall | $22.95

FINANCE | MARKETING | FUNDING

Art of Film Funding, The | Carole Lee Dean | $26.95

Complete Independent Movie Marketing Handbook, The | Mark Steven Bosko | $39.95

Independent Film and Videomakers Guide – 2nd Edition, The | Michael Wiese | $29.95

Independent Film Distribution | Phil Hall | $26.95

Shaking the Money Tree, 2nd Edition | Morrie Warshawski | $26.95

OUR FILMS

Dolphin Adventures: DVD | Michael Wiese and Hardy Jones | $24.95

On the Edge of a Dream | Michael Wiese | $16.95

Sacred Sites of the Dalai Lamas– DVD, The | Documentary by Michael Wiese | $24.95

Hardware Wars: DVD | Written and Directed by Ernie Fosselius | $14.95

ALCOHOLISM TREATMENT

The Nelson-Hall Series in Social Work

Consulting Editor: Charles Zastrow
University of Wisconsin–Whitewater